What Can I Do Now?

Engineering

Second Edition

Books in the
What Can I Do Now? Series

Art
Computers
Engineering, Second Edition
Fashion
Health Care
Music
Nursing, Second Edition
Radio and Television, Second Edition
Safety and Security, Second Edition
Sports, Second Edition

What Can I Do Now?

Engineering

Second Edition

Ferguson

An imprint of Infobase Publishing

What Can I Do Now? Engineering

Ferguson
An imprint of Infobase Publishing
132 West 31st Street
New York NY 10001

ISBN-10: 0-8160-6026-6
ISBN-13: 978-0-8160-6026-9

Library of Congress Cataloging-in-Publication Data

Engineering. — 2nd ed.
    p. cm. — (What can I do now?)
  Includes index.
  ISBN 0-8160-6026-6 (hc : alk. paper)
  1. Engineering—Vocational guidance—Juvenile literature.
  TA157.E537 2007
  620.0023—dc22   2006028877

Ferguson books are available at special discounts when purchased in bulk quantities for businesses, associations, institutions, or sales promotions. Please call our Special Sales Department in New York at (212) 967-8800 or (800) 322-8755.

You can find Ferguson on the World Wide Web at http://www.fergpubco.com

Text design by Kerry Casey
Cover design by Takeshi Takahashi

Printed in the United States of America

VB Hermitage 10 9 8 7 6 5 4 3 2 1

This book is printed on acid-free paper.

All links and Web addresses were checked and verified to be correct at the time of publication. Because of the dynamic nature of the Web, some addresses and links may have changed since publication and may no longer be valid.

Contents

Introduction

If you're considering a career in engineering—which presumably you are since you're reading this book—you must realize that the better informed you are from the start, the better your chances of having a successful, satisfying career.

There is absolutely no reason to wait until you get out of high school to "get serious" about a career. That doesn't mean you have to make a firm commitment right now. Indeed, one of the biggest fears most people face at some point (sometimes more than once) is choosing the right career. Frankly, many people don't "choose" at all. They take a job because they need one, and all of a sudden 10 years have gone by and they wonder why they're stuck doing something they hate. Don't be one of those people! You have the opportunity right now—while you're still in school and relatively free of major adult responsibilities—to explore, to experience, to try out a work path or two. Wouldn't you really rather find out sooner than later that you're not as interested in chemical engineering as you thought? That maybe you'd prefer to be a materials engineer, or a civil engineer, or a biomedical engineer?

There are many ways to explore the engineering industry. This book gives you an idea of some of your options. Section 1, "What Do I Need to Know About Engineering?" will give you an overview of the field—a little history, where it is today, and promises of the future; as well as a breakdown of its structure (how it's organized) and a glimpse of some of its many career options.

Section 2, "Careers," includes 10 chapters, each describing in detail a specific engineering or technician specialty—aerospace, biomedical, chemical, civil, electrical and electronics, environmental, industrial, materials, and mechanical. The educational requirements for these specialties range from bachelor's degree to Ph.D. These chapters rely heavily on first-hand accounts from real people on the job. They'll tell you what skills you need, what personal qualities you have to have, and what the ups and downs of the jobs are. You'll also find out about educational requirements—including specific high school and college classes—advancement possibilities, related jobs, salary ranges, and the future outlook.

Section 3, "Do It Yourself," urges you to take charge and start your own programs and activities where none exist—school, community, or the nation.

The real meat of the book is in Section 4, "What Can I Do Right Now?" This is where you get busy and do something. The chapter "Get Involved" will clue you in on the obvious volunteer and intern

1

positions and the not-so-obvious summer camps and summer college study, high school engineering programs, and student engineering organizations.

While the best way to explore engineering is to jump right in and start doing it, there are plenty of other ways to get into the engineering mind-set. The "Surf the Web" chapter offers you a short annotated list of engineering Web sites where you can explore everything from job listings (start getting an idea of what employers are looking for now) to educational and certification requirements to on-the-job accounts to practical engineering problems.

"Read a Book" is an annotated bibliography of books (some new, some old) and periodicals. If you're even remotely considering a career in engineering, reading a few books and checking out a few magazines is the easiest thing you can do. Don't stop with this list. Ask your librarian to suggest more engineering materials.

"Ask for Money" is a sampling of engineering scholarships. Since most people need money for school, you should become familiar with these. You have to actively pursue scholarships; no one is going to come up to you in the hall one day and present you with a check because you're such a wonderful student. Applying for scholarships is work. It takes effort. And it must be done right and often a year in advance of when you need the money.

"Look to the Pros" is the final chapter. It's a list of professional organizations that you can turn to for more information about accredited schools, education requirements, career descriptions, salary information, job listings, scholarships, and much more. Once you become an engineering student, you'll be able to join many of these. Time after time, professionals say that membership and active participation in a professional organization is one of the best ways to network (make valuable contacts) and gain recognition in your field.

High school can be a lot of fun. There are dances and football games and lots of activities and clubs to join. Maybe you're in band or play a sport. Whoever you are, take a minute and try to imagine your life 5 or 10 years from now. Where will you be? What will you be doing? Whether you realize it or not, how you choose to spend your time now—studying, playing, watching TV, working at a fast food restaurant, or hanging out—will have an impact on your future. Take a look at how you're spending your time now and ask yourself, "Where is this getting me?" If you can't come up with an answer, it's probably "nowhere." The choice is yours. No one is going to take you by the hand and lead you in the "right" direction. It's up to you. It's your life and your future career. You can do something about it right now!

SECTION 1

What Do I Need to Know About Engineering?

Earth spaceship lands on Mars?

Yes, thanks to our earthling engineers, *we* are now the aliens. NASA's *Odyssey* and *Pathfinder* missions to Mars, as well as the *Viking* missions in the 1970s, number among this century's most challenging, creative, and awesome engineering feats. Just think of it: we have the ability to envision, create, and launch a spacecraft a mind-boggling 100 million miles through space to land on a different planet in a predetermined location. From that craft we can deploy rovers to navigate the rugged terrain via remote control and analyze rocks and soil, take scenic photographs, monitor the weather, and then send back to Earth all the information they have gathered. Wow!

The number of engineering branches that directly and indirectly contributed to these recent Mars missions is impressive: aerospace engineers devised the way to get to and then land on Mars; mechanical engineers designed the spacecraft and the rovers; optical engineers were responsible for the amazing images we see of the planet; electrical and computer engineers worked on the complex computer circuitry and electronics involved with space travel; and the list could go on and on. Some of these engineers may work individually, but for the most part, they all work together as a team. The aerospace engineers may have a great idea, but the mechanical and electrical engineers may tell them whether or not the idea is feasible. And then the light bulbs go on above their heads and the fun of creating something from nothing begins.

Engineers make things work. Their creative ingenuity impacts our lives and our societies in many ways people never even notice. Not only are they involved in the breathtaking excitement of space travel, but they also have their hands in more down-to-earth, behind-the-scenes projects like designing safe and lasting bridges, designing the hottest new theme park rides, making sure drinking water is clean and safe, and even figuring out ways to make heavy-traffic areas safer and less congested. In almost every area of the modern world you can look around and see the results of the brainpower and vision of engineers.

GENERAL INFORMATION
A lot of knowledge, creativity, thoughtfulness, and pure hard work go into engineering. Humankind has been "engineering," so to speak, since the invention of tools. From that point on we began our ceaseless quest to create tools and systems that helped us live our lives better. There have been a lot of mistakes along the way, but we learned from them and built a foundation of engineering laws and principles.

We can trace the development of civilization to the present day through engineering hallmarks like Stonehenge, the Egyptian pyramids, the ancient cities of Greece, the extensive system of roadways and aqueducts built by the early Romans, Europe's fascination with fortresses and cathedrals, the invention of dams, electricity, the automobile, the airplane, the building of canals and cross-continental railways, nuclear energy, putting a man on the moon, sending the first private craft into space—and that's just skimming the surface of the many things engineers are responsible for that built our civilizations and defined how we think of ourselves and our societies.

The rise of the first cities in 3000 B.C. in Mesopotamia (modern-day Iraq) created a need for engineers, though there was certainly no concept of what an engineer was then. These early engineers did not apply scientific principles to their work, but rather they learned by example, from mistakes, and from the urgency of pure need. People relied on these early engineers to address their everyday needs and survival. To protect against enemy attacks, engineers learned to heighten and strengthen building walls through the use of brick (a building material most likely invented by accident). To bring food and water into the city, engineers constructed a system of levees, small canals, and reservoirs.

The first engineer of prominence whose architectural legacy has survived millennia was the ancient Egyptian builder, Imhotep. He designed and built what is commonly believed to be the first pyramid, the Step Pyramid, around 2650 B.C. just outside of present-day Cairo. Modern engineers marvel at the skills the ancient Egyptians demonstrated in the building of the pyramids. To build a structure as massive and architecturally perfect as a pyramid at a time of very limited building resources (the invention of the wheel was in its infancy—they had nothing like cranes, levels, or any sort of machinery to move the large heavy stones)

was a task of incredible ingenuity. The ancient Egyptians used sledges to transport the stones from the distant quarries where they were mined. The main method they used to move the huge stones (some weighing up to 55 tons) up the pyramid was a method called *jacking,* which used wedges and levers to slowly but surely move the stones higher and higher.

The engineers of ancient Greece studied more complex principles of geometry and put them to use in advanced architectural designs. These engineers used five basic machines to help them in their building: the wheel, the pulley, the lever, the wedge, and the screw. More complex building methods and different building materials began to appear with the Greeks. They developed a variety of joints, made use of the column as a load reliever, commonly used post-and-beam construction, and they used the arch, although rarely. The Greek engineers found use for iron, lead, limestone, and marble. Other Greek contributions to engineering include studies on the lever, gearing, the screw, the siphon, and the concepts of buoyancy, and the invention of force pumps, hydraulic pipe organs, and the metal spring.

Whereas the Greeks were the theorists of early engineering, the Romans were the projectors and administrators. They busily set out to construct many great public works, like building roads, bridges, tunnels, aqueducts, and even plumbing for each city home. Rome's major concern for establishing a system of civil engineering was to aid its war machine. Military engineers were responsible for building roads and bridges (to better access future conquests and protect their empire), and baths (to relax the warriors after battle), and of course, for developing a variety of weaponry. The Roman military engineer's greatest responsibility, however, was the fortification of army camps. They built all kinds of fortifications, which included walls of varying thickness, height, and shape to better repel would-be attackers.

Modern engineering's true beginnings are mostly rooted in the 17th and 18th centuries, where mathematical principles and laws of physics began to be understood and developed. Isaac Newton's groundbreaking research in mathematics and physics was quickly picked up by engineers and put to practical use. Aside from enlightening the world about gravity, Newton's work in mechanics produced the generalization of the concept of force, the formulation of the concept of mass (his first law), and the principle of effect and counter-effect (his third law). Other mathematicians and engineers of the time, enlightened by Newton's findings, went on to make mathematical discoveries that paved the way for the work of future engineers.

It wasn't until the 18th century that the first schools of engineering were established. Previously, most young engineers learned their skills by apprenticeships, if they were lucky enough to get one. A French military engineer, Sébas-

Connecting Two Oceans

The building of the Panama Canal was a feat of epic proportions. It was the largest and most expensive engineering project ever undertaken. Costing an estimated $3.6 billion, the canal took 33 years to complete from the first shovel in the ground in 1881, to the first boat passing through in 1914.

There were constant setbacks as numerous engineers attempted its completion. The French engineer Ferdinand de Lesseps, builder of the Suez Canal, was the first to have at this giant task. Almost as soon as work began many of his crew began to die of tropical diseases. Malaria and yellow fever killed thousands. Working conditions in the jungles of Panama were miserable and morale was low. Eight years, $287 million, and 20,000 lives later, the whole affair became a scandal and the French called it quits.

This was good news for U.S. President Theodore Roosevelt. He saw the Panama Canal as the key to the United States' rise to that of superpower. He paid the newly created Panama government 10 million dollars to resume work and hired engineer John Frank Stevens to oversee the project. Stevens changed the French plan to include a series of locks to carry ships up and down through the canal. In 1907, George Washington Goethals, an army engineer, took over construction of the canal. He overcame endless setbacks and worked on improving labor relations, while still staying true to Stevens' vision. The canal finally opened for business on January 7, 1914, with the unceremonious passing of the *Alexandre la Valley*.

tien le Prestre de Vauban, recognized the need to have an actual corps of engineers in the military to study and improve the building of fortifications, bridges, and roads. Shortly thereafter, engineering schools began to appear throughout France, and then the rest of Europe, and finally in the United States. In 1775, the U.S. Continental Congress stated, "That there be one Chief Engineer at the Grand Army . . . [and] that two assistants be employed under him . . . ," and thus began the United States Corps of Engineers. This new need for engineers prompted the beginning of scientific schools at Harvard (1847), Yale (1861), Massachusetts Institute of Technology (1865), and other engineering schools.

Vauban's plan to educate engineers was largely for military purposes. Armies needed easy ways to get from point A to point B, so roads and bridges had to be built (the Romans, we have seen, did this very well). It was around this time too, that the civil engineer came on to the scene as a separate discipline. When military engineers built roads, bridges, canals, and other public works, they tended to build them only when it served a very specific military purpose. Cities needed better water supply and sanitation facilities, and local roads that could link smaller communities. As cities grew, they tended to do so in a not-too-orderly fashion, so civil engineers were needed to plan the cities. In 1771, John Smeaton, the first self-proclaimed civil engineer, founded the Society of Civil Engineers with the objective of bringing together like-minded engineers and other men of

> There can be little doubt that in many ways the story of bridge building is the story of civilization. By it we can readily measure an important part of people's progress.
> —Franklin D. Roosevelt, October 18, 1931

(financial) power to design and build public works.

With the advent of steam power and the industrial revolution at the end of the 18th century, great engineering accomplishments seemed to happen every day: from the steam engine and the large-scale mining of coal, to the cotton gin and new agricultural technology, the world was changing quickly. New processes for manufacturing iron and steel made their use more common in all branches of engineering, which was evidenced by the first suspension bridge, erected by J. Finley in the United States in 1801. This invention made possible the building of bridges in locations where a standard mid-span support bridge could not feasibly be built, and greatly improved transportation. A suspension bridge is suspended by cable attached to and extending between supports or towers—a modern-day example is the Golden Gate Bridge in San Francisco. Over the years suspension bridge technology was improved and they became a common sight throughout the world.

The 19th century marked the dawn of electrical engineering. Many scientists at the time, excited over this new, and most likely profitable, phenomenon, electricity, dove headfirst into all its mysteries and intricacies, making many valuable discoveries. Once these scientists laid down the principles of the field, engineers, inventors, and scientists put these principles to practical applications, like Samuel Morse's invention of the telegraph in 1837, Alexander Graham Bell's telephone in 1876, Thomas Edison's light bulb in 1878, Nikola Tesla's electric motor in 1888, and many others. By the early 20th century, much of the infrastructure of modern society as we know it was coming to light.

The first major engineering feat of the 20th century was Orville and Wilbur Wright's first controlled flight of a powered airplane. Aeronautical engineering, as it came to be known, was a dangerous endeavor at its outset, and early engineers labored for a long period of time without significant success. Gliders were the first airplane design to test the skies and provided engineers with valuable information on aerodynamics. The Wright brothers came up with the idea of fixing a motor to their plane for long-distance flight and made several failed (though educational) attempts to take off. Finally, in 1903 they succeeded in flying an engine-powered biplane for 59 seconds. Over the next two years they made more adjustments and tests and eventually ended up selling planes to the U.S. military.

As with previous centuries, it was the military and war that fueled most of our major engineering advancements. The 20th century has been no different. The U.S. and European militaries recognized

> Engineers . . . are not mere technicians and should not approve or lend their name to any project that does not promise to be beneficent to man and the advancement of civilization.
> —John Fowler,
> English civil engineer (1817–98)

immediate potential in airplanes and put its engineers to work on making them safer, more maneuverable, faster, and rugged. By 1914, just in time for World War I, militaries fitted their planes with radios, navigational equipment, and guns. Planes were also designed to haul and drop bombs. European navies invested heavily into submarine research. The German navy, although a latecomer to the submarine, was the early leader in this technology, and during World War I its U-boats (*untersee boots*) were greatly feared by Allied ships at sea.

Fighter plane and submarine design advanced even further by World War II. Military engineers increased the plane's and sub's speed, range, and general mechanical abilities to make them easier to operate. By 1942 the German air force flew the first real jet plane, which reached speeds of more than 500 miles per hour.

One of this century's most profound engineering innovations came in the 1930s with nuclear power. In the race to develop the atomic bomb, the U.S. government spearheaded the Manhattan Project to study, develop, and learn about nuclear power. As nuclear engineers began to realize the awesome peaceful potential of nuclear power, schools were established to study this extremely dangerous new technology and a new branch of engineering—nuclear engineering—was born.

In the 1950s, the Cold War brought about fierce technological and military competition between the United States and Russia, necessitating the services of all types of engineers. The exploration of space became another area where engineers sought to demonstrate their country's technological dominance. In 1957, the Soviets launched *Sputnik,* the world's first orbiting satellite. The United States countered with its own satellite, *Explorer I,* in early 1958. In the early 1960s, Russia and America set their sights on the moon and engineers from both countries worked feverishly to be the first to land a man on the moon. And in 1969, the world was awestruck when U.S. astronaut Neil Armstrong stepped from his spacecraft onto the rocky surface of the moon.

Even today engineering marvels still abound, from the skyscrapers in our cities, to the artificial heart, to the tiny computer processors in many of the electronics we buy. In one of the most exciting recent breakthroughs, test pilot Mike Melvill piloted *SpaceShipOne* to an altitude of more than 62.5 miles in 2004—the internationally recognized boundary of space—becoming the first person to pilot a privately built craft into space.

Additionally, the rapid speed at which computer technology is progressing is unprecedented. Big news one month in the computer industry is almost ancient history two or three months down the road. Modern society is becoming increasingly automated, as the use of robotics becomes increasingly commonplace.

According to the 1828 charter of the British Institution of Civil Engineers, engineering is "the art of directing the great sources of power in nature for the use and convenience of man." Most engineers will hold true to this as an accurate definition of their field, with perhaps a few additions. Not much of the philosophy has changed since 1828. What has changed is the scope and method of engineering, which began as an empirical art and has gradually developed into a highly specialized science.

Fast Facts

There are approximately 340 U.S. colleges and universities offering bachelor degree programs in engineering that are accredited by the Accreditation Board for Engineering and Technology.

STRUCTURE OF THE INDUSTRY

The engineering industry comprises many fields of study, all employing unique and sometimes similar methods of science to reach practical solutions to problems and questions in all industries. There are five basic areas of study in which engineers in all branches of the industry can specialize: research, development, application, management, and maintenance. While an engineer may work exclusively in one of these areas, it is more common for their knowledge and duties to overlap. For example, research and development are commonly linked and called R&D. Those working in the application side of a project may often find themselves working on maintenance calls.

All engineering projects begin with research. The type and scope of research will be different in each branch of engineering, but generally, once a goal has been set by an industry or institution and brought to the engineers, they set out to find possible ways to solve it. This could entail visiting a manufacturing plant to get a firsthand understanding of an industrial problem. It could entail testing different materials for a specific space application. It could also require the engineer to struggle over mathematical or computer applications, as well as spend long hours in a laboratory mixing chemicals. The scope of research is limitless. Some research engineers work independently, seeking to find new principles

and processes for a specific branch of engineering.

Closely tied to research is development. Development entails applying the results of a research project to a specific function. Since there may be more than one way of doing this, a development team must perform tests and studies to find the best way. A research engineer may have to come up with several useable materials for a part on an airplane, but it is up to the development team to figure out which of those materials works best in the big picture. For example, a certain material might be chosen for an exterior part on a plane. It may work fine and be durable and weather resistant, however a development team might discover the material reacts negatively to the exhaust of the engines, or that at certain altitudes and speeds it reacts differently than when on the ground. Given these observations, the development team will reject the material and look for one that's more stable under these types of stresses.

With the research and development complete, the real fun begins—project application. Engineers use the data from the R&D studies and apply them to the design and production of materials, machines, methods, or to whatever the ultimate goal is. For example, a team of civil engineers, after finding the best materials and location for building a bridge in Alaska, will then set out to design and build the bridge. A team of industrial engineers, having studied an outdated method of production at a manufacturing plant and having researched newer methods specific to that type of manufacturing, will

> From the point of view of modern science, design is nothing, but from the point of view of engineering, design is everything. It represents the purposive adaptation of means to reach a preconceived end, the very essence of engineering.
>
> —Edwin T. Layton Jr., Author

begin implementing the new method and train plant employees.

A *management engineer,* who earlier may have been part of the R&D or application team, will be responsible for keeping the developed idea working. They study their work as it was intended to function—whether that be machinery, a drawbridge, or a carving knife—and look for ways to improve on it in the future. If a team of electrical engineers designs a new system of electronic circuits for a home entertainment system, they may find that once everything is in place and the system has been manufactured that there are certain minor aspects that can be improved. While the development team is supposed to have found these possible flaws before production, it is almost impossible to catch every possible little glitch. Engineers consider this learning from experience and will improve the design in the future.

Maintenance, the final stage in an engineering project, is concerned with the project's upkeep. A team of mechanical engineers, for example, may have designed a machine to package coffee in tin containers. The engineers visit the plant, set it up, and go home with everyone satisfied. Two months later, a maintenance engineer, who was likely involved in the application process, is called back to the plant to fix a problem in the system—the coffee keeps overflowing, causing waste. These sorts of maintenance calls are fairly common, as it takes a while with any new project to work out the bugs. Again they learn from experience, and similar systems in the future will probably not have the same problem.

Fast Facts

Young engineers just entering the field with a bachelor's degree can earn as much as 75 to 100 percent more per year than those in nonengineering fields with a bachelor's degree.

Engineers in a particular industry, say in nuclear engineering, will of course be trained in nuclear engineering, but they will also have to understand many principles from other branches of engineering. Depending on their specific studies, the nuclear engineers may need understanding of environmental, chemical, aerospace, mechanical, electrical, industrial, materials, naval, or computer engineering.

Professional Engineer, or PE, is a licensure that indicates that the engineer has completed education and experience requirements and passed tough exams. PEs are under legal responsibility for their engineering work and are bound by an ethics code to protect the public health and safety. PEs have graduated from an accredited engineering program, have had at least four years' experience under a licensed PE, and have passed the Principles and Practice of Engineering (PPE) exam.

CAREERS

If you want a career in engineering, you'll have to specialize. However, the engineer specializing in any field is usually required to have basic knowledge of other engineering fields, since most problems engineers face are complex and interrelated. There are more than 25 engineering specialties recognized by professional societies, and depending on your particular aptitude and interests—whether you're a nuts-and-bolts type person or a computer jock—the doors to a career in engineering are open. The following paragraphs describe some of the most prominent engineering careers.

- *Aeronautical and aerospace engineers* deal with the development, manufacturing, maintenance, and testing of all types of aircraft. Aeronautical engineers must have thorough knowledge of aerodynamics as well as navigation systems and structural design. As an aerospace engineer you may study celestial mechanics (how objects act in space), or you may be concerned with fluid mechanics or structural design. Whatever your specialty, you will have to be an ace math student, as complex mathematics are the norm in this field.
- *Biomedical engineers* are highly trained scientists who apply engineering and life science principles to problems in medical research and health care. They design health care instruments and devices or apply engineering principles to the study of human systems.
- *Ceramic engineers* are specialized materials engineers who work with nonmetallic elements such as clay and inorganic elements such as zirconia. They perform research; design processing methods, machinery, and equipment; and create new ceramic materials and products.
- *Chemical engineers* use their skills and understanding of chemistry, physics, mathematics, and other engineering principles in the design of equipment and manufacturing processes for the production of chemicals and other goods made from chemical processes. They help develop products such as plastic, metal, gasoline, detergents, pharmaceuticals, and foodstuffs. They develop or improve safe, environmentally sound processes while determining the least costly production method for the product.
- Civil engineering is one of the broadest fields in the industry. *Civil engineers* are responsible for the lay of the land. They design roads (including highways, skyways, and small farm roads), bridges, tunnels, harbors, railroads, airports, water supply systems, and many other construction projects in your community. Wherever there is a large construction project under way, a civil engineer is usually in charge or behind the scenes planning and troubleshooting. When the work is done, the civil engineer is responsible for maintenance and upkeep strategies to ensure public safety.
- *Electrical and electronics engineers* are concerned with developing practical applications of electricity in all its forms. Electrical engineers work with "heavy current" electricity in developing equipment and processes

Employment of Engineers by Specialty

Specialty	Number Employed	Percentage
Electrical and electronics	292,000	19.8
Civil	228,000	15.4
Mechanical	215,000	14.5
Industrial, including health and safety	194,000	13.1
Aerospace	78,000	5.3
Computer hardware	74,000	5.0
Environmental	47,000	3.2
Chemical	33,000	2.2
Materials	24,000	1.6
Nuclear	16,000	1.1
Petroleum	14,000	0.9
Biomedical	7,600	0.5
Mining and geological, including mining safety	5,200	0.4
Marine engineering (includes naval architecture)	4,900	0.3
Agricultural	2,900	0.2
All other engineers	243,000	16.4

Source: U.S. Department of Labor, 2002

that produce and distribute electricity, such as systems that generate high-power electricity. Electronics engineers work with "light current" electricity in developing virtually anything that uses electricity, from a computer to a camera to a satellite.

- *Computer hardware engineers* design, build, and test computer hardware (such as computer chips and circuit boards) and computer systems. They also work with peripheral devices such as printers, scanners, modems, and monitors, among others. Hardware engineers are employed by a variety of companies, some of which specialize in business, accounting, science, or engineering.

- *Industrial engineers* plan and implement strategies for the most efficient means of industrial production. They study how the balance of machinery, labor, and raw materials is most effectively and safely put to use in a production process. They work at large industrial manufacturing plants, medical centers, and other large complexes. As an industrial engineer you will have to have a keen sense of economics, as saving money is often a primary objective.

- Everything has to be built with something, and that's where the *materials engineer* comes in. Materials engineers develop and test different materials for specific products, from the skin of the space shuttle to the soles of your shoes. They may develop more environmentally safe materials or work on methods of disposing hazardous materials safely. A materials engineer studies a product's design, and based on the various functions of the product, suggests the most appropriate materials, whether they be metals, alloys, plastics, composites, fibers, or other materials.

- *Mechanical engineers* design, test, build, and maintain all kinds of mechanical devices, components, engines, and systems. One of their chief concerns is the production, transmission, and use of power.

- *Metallurgical engineers* are specialized materials engineers who develop new kinds of metal alloys and adapt existing materials to new uses. They are sometimes called *metallurgists*.

- *Mining engineers* deal with the exploration, location, and planning for removal of minerals and mineral deposits from the earth. These include metals (iron, copper), nonmetallic minerals (limestone, gypsum), and coal. Mining engineers conduct preliminary surveys of mineral deposits and examine them to ascertain whether they can be extracted efficiently and economically, using either underground or surface mining methods. They plan and design the development of mine shafts and tunnels, devise means of extracting minerals, and select the methods to be used in transporting the minerals to the surface. They supervise all mining operations and are responsible for mine safety.

- *Nuclear engineers* are concerned with the design, construction, and safety of nuclear reactors, radioactive waste sites, and devices using nuclear energy. They study ways to apply radiation in the diagnosis and treatment of diseases. In addition to power production and health applications, nuclear engineers find work in space exploration, agriculture, environmental concerns, and transportation.

- *Optical engineers* apply the concepts of optics to research, design, and develop applications in a broad range of areas. Optics, which involves the properties of light and how it interacts with matter, is a branch of physics and engineering. Optical engineers study the way light is produced, transmitted, detected, and measured to determine ways it can be used and to build devices using optical technology.

- *Packaging engineers* design the packaging for consumer goods such as food, electronics, medical products, toys, appliances, clothing, and other items. Packages are designed to protect products, provide benefit to consumers, conserve natural resources, and minimize waste through recycling.
- *Petroleum engineers* seek the best location and method of tapping (drilling) an oil or natural gas reservoir to extract as much from the reservoir as possible. They are also responsible for finding the most economic means of developing oil or gas sites. Some petroleum engineers may specialize in geological engineering, which is concerned with finding accessible oil and gas reservoirs. Petroleum engineers are skilled in geology, physics, and the engineering sciences.
- *Plastics engineers* are specialized materials engineers who create, design, and test polymeric materials to manufacture useful end products, from plastic automobile parts to biodegradable polymers for a packaging company to plastic fibers for clothing.
- *Quality control engineers* plan and direct activities involved in the processing and production of materials in order to ensure specified standards of quality. They select the best techniques for a specific process or method, determine the level of quality needed, and take the necessary action to maintain or improve quality performance.

- *Robotics engineers* design, develop, build, and program robots and robotic devices, including peripheral equipment and computer software used to control robots. This job title may be used to refer to any engineer who works primarily with robots. In many cases, these engineers may have been trained as mechanical, electronic, computer, or manufacturing engineers. A small, but growing, number of engineers trained specially in robotics are graduating from colleges and universities with robotics engineering or closely related degrees.
- *Safety engineers* are concerned with preventing accidents. They work in many different branches of engineering, from mechanical to transportation engineering. As a safety engineer you may study ergonomics to develop human-friendly machines that reduce repetitive motion disorders, or you may prepare fire evacuation plans for a large factory or office complex. Safety engineers are found at construction sites, environmental hazard spots, insurance companies, transportation offices, and similar workplaces.
- *Software engineers* are responsible for customizing existing software programs to meet the needs and desires of a particular business or industry. First, they spend considerable time researching, defining, and analyzing the problem at hand. Then, they develop software programs to resolve the problem on the computer.
- *Transportation engineers* are civil engineering specialists who plan,

design, and operate all methods, structures, and systems that transport people and goods in a safe, convenient, rapid, and environmentally responsible manner. Typical projects they work on are streets, highways, tollways, airports, transit systems, railroads, and harbors.

Engineers are assisted by *engineering technicians and technologists.* These workers are employed in all engineering disciplines, and are differentiated most commonly by the type of education they receive. Engineering technicians typically have an associate degree in engineering technology, although some learn their skills via a combination of postsecondary training and on-the-job training. Engineering technologists typically have a bachelor's degree in engineering technology. Some engineering technicians and technologists pursue advanced education and become engineers.

EMPLOYMENT OPPORTUNITIES

According to the U.S. Department of Labor, there are nearly 1.5 million engineers employed in the United States—with many millions more employed throughout the world. Since engineering is such a broad field, there are literally thousands of different places you can find employment, depending on your specialty. Engineers are needed in virtually every field. Whether you want to work for a small company or a large firm, indoors or outdoors, nine to five or the graveyard shift, there are engineering careers available for you. You can find your engineering career at a desk behind a computer with regular hours not far from your home; or you may find your engineering career in the workshop with a socket set in one hand, a computer-aided calibrator in the other, and a little grease under your nails; or you may find your engineering career in the dank sewers of a major city as you plan a more effective method of waste management.

As a mechanical, automobile, chemical, industrial, plastics, or robotics engineer you may find employment with one of the Big Three U.S. automobile makers (Ford, Chrysler, and General Motors), as well as any of the thousands of private manufacturing companies. As an aeronautical or aerospace engineer you will almost certainly try to land a job at NASA or a major commercial firm like Boeing. Civil engineers can find jobs with local and city governments, with construction firms, with the military or federal government, and even large corporations. The petroleum and chemical engineer can seek jobs, naturally, with petroleum and gas companies like BP, Texaco, and Exxon, or they can look for jobs with major chemical companies like Dow Chemical, Eastman Chemical Company, or E. I. DuPont. Environmental and biological engineers will have no problem finding employers at the Environmental Protection Agency, industry, or consulting firms. Companies producing high-tech equipment for commercial and industrial use look for skilled electrical engineers, as well as software, mechanical, materials, and plastics engineers.

Engineers are also employed by local, state, and the federal government—194,000 in 2004, according to the U.S. Department of Labor. Some federal employers of engineers include the National Aeronautics and Space Administration, and the Departments of Agriculture, Defense, Energy, Interior, and Transportation.

Other possibilities for engineers can be found in academia as instructors or researchers.

INDUSTRY OUTLOOK

We live in a rapidly changing, high-tech world, where the major riddles of one year are solved the next year. Who's behind this? Well, largely it's engineers. Engineers wield tremendous influence on our lives, cultures, and societies. As the world changes with the latest technologies and as we grow accustomed to the luxuries they offer, there will be an increased demand for highly skilled, innovative professionals to continue the trend. These advancing technologies will put pressure on industry to improve and update their current systems—whether they be for production facilities or corporate offices—if they are to stay competitive. Some branches of engineering are certain to remain strong for the long term, like biomedical, civil, environmental, mechanical, electrical, computer, and safety.

In the past two decades the computer industry has grown at an unprecedented rate. While its volatility scares some people away, the field has a great need for skilled engineers to continue its growth, so job prospects and outlook are strong for the long term. The computer industry is fiercely competitive. Cutbacks and lay-offs are common, but those engineers who stay up-to-date with the current high-tech trends will have little trouble locating another job.

Cities and neighborhoods are always changing. Roads and bridges wear out and need to be repaired or rebuilt. For this reason alone civil engineers will always be in demand. Traffic in our cities and suburbs continues to be a problem and will require the attention of transportation engineers. As the atmosphere becomes more polluted and begins to negatively affect our lives, measures will be taken to find alternative energy sources. While this may be somewhat bad news to the petroleum engineer, any effect on the industry will be offset by the efforts required of other engineers to find a solution.

As we continue to damage the environment, environmental and biological engineers will find themselves busily trying to rectify this. Many governmental agencies and big businesses are becoming more sensitive to environmental concerns, especially as complex regulations pass through Congress. Despite this, there is sometimes less governmental money for major projects such as the Superfund cleanup.

Due to recent increases in defense spending due to the war on terror, prospects for aerospace engineers have improved somewhat. But stiff competition among nongovernmental employers has meant that companies work from a tight budget and may not expand production. While aerospace jobs in research and development remain stable, few new jobs will be added.

SECTION 2

Careers

Aerospace Engineers

SUMMARY

Definition
Aerospace engineers work in teams to design, build, and test machines that fly within the earth's atmosphere and beyond.

Alternative Job Titles
None

Salary Range
$50,993 to $84,090 to $117,680+

Educational Requirements
Minimum of a bachelor's degree. Advanced degree recommended.

Certification or Licensing
Required for certain positions

Employment Outlook
Decline

High School Subjects
Computer science
Mathematics
Physics

Personal Interests
Building things
Computers
Figuring out how things work

Look up into the bright, blue yonder at a Boeing 777, and you'll see Jeanne Yu's work. The Boeing engineer designed the flight deck air distribution system for this popular jetliner.

Although many of us take a safe airplane ride for granted, it takes countless hours and many highly trained workers, such as Jeanne, to develop and test the critical systems contained in any aircraft. The Boeing 777 flight deck air distribution system was no different.

"Early in the program," Jeanne recalls, "a problem was identified with hot air entering the flight deck during flight-test take-offs. So, they asked me to assemble a team of engineers and they piled us on an airplane and flew us to Phoenix, where it was over 100 degrees, to fix it."

Jeanne and her team worked late into many evenings to develop tests to try to isolate the problem, so that they could confirm or invalidate these theories during test flights the next day.

"Phew! Talk about being on the hot seat," she remembers. "It meant trying to squeeze two to three theories and testing them out as rapidly as possible and as much on the ground as possible."

All of Jeanne's hard work paid off. She and her team identified an unexpected problem with an unrelated system that forced hot air into the flight deck just on take-off and fixed the problem.

"It was a turning point for me," she says, "as I gained confidence to come up with solutions and to deal with all the people-related issues simultaneously."

Jeanne's work didn't stop with the 777. She is currently leading a team that is responsible for the cabin environment of Boeing's newest aircraft, the 7E7 Dreamliner, which is scheduled to come into service in 2008.

WHAT DOES AN AEROSPACE ENGINEER DO?

Aerospace engineering encompasses the fields of aeronautical (aircraft) and astronautical (spacecraft) engineering. Although aerospace science is a very specialized discipline, it is also considered one of the most diverse. This field of engineering draws from such subjects as physics, mathematics, earth science, aerodynamics, and biology. Some aerospace engineers specialize in designing one complete machine, perhaps a commercial aircraft, whereas others focus on separate components such as for missile guidance systems.

Although the creation of aircraft and spacecraft involve professionals from many branches of engineering (e.g., materials, electrical, and mechanical), aerospace engineers in particular are responsible for the total design of the craft, including its shape, performance, propulsion, and guidance control system. In the field of aerospace engineering, professional responsibilities vary widely depending on the specific job description. *Aeronautical engineers* work specifically with aircraft systems, and *astronautical engineers* specialize in spacecraft systems.

Throughout their education and training, aerospace engineers thoroughly learn the complexities involved in how materials and structures perform under tremendous stress. In general, they are called upon to apply their knowledge of the following subjects: propulsion, aerodynamics, thermodynamics, fluid mechanics, flight mechanics, and structural analysis. Less technically scientific issues must also often be dealt with, such as cost analysis, reliability studies, maintainability, operations research, marketing, and management.

There are many professional titles given to certain aerospace engineers. *Analytical engineers* use engineering and mathematical theory to solve questions that arise during the design phase. *Stress analysts* determine how the weight and loads of structures behave under a variety of conditions. This analysis is performed with computers and complex formulas.

Computational fluid dynamic (CFD) engineers use sophisticated high-speed computers to develop models used in the study of fluid dynamics. Using simulated systems, they determine how elements flow around objects; simulation saves time and money and eliminates risks involved with actual testing. As computers become more complex, so do the tasks of the CFD engineer.

Design aerospace engineers draw from the expertise of many other specialists.

They devise the overall structure of components and entire crafts, meeting the specifications developed by those more specialized in aerodynamics, astrodynamics, and structural engineering. Design engineers use computer-aided design programs for many of their tasks. *Manufacturing aerospace engineers* develop the plans for producing the complex components that make up aircraft and spacecraft. They work with the designers to ensure that the plans are economically feasible and will produce efficient, effective components.

Materials aerospace engineers determine the suitability of the various materials that are used to produce aerospace vehicles. Aircraft and spacecraft require the appropriate tensile strength, density, and rigidity for the particular environments they are subjected to. Determining how materials such as steel, glass, and even chemical compounds react to temperature and stress is an important part of the materials engineer's responsibilities.

Quality control is a task that aerospace engineers perform throughout the development, design, and manufacturing processes. The finished product must be evaluated for its reliability, vulnerability, and how it is to be maintained and supported.

Marketing and sales aerospace engineers work with customers, usually industrial corporations and the government, informing them of product performance. They act as a liaison between the technical engineers and the clients to help ensure that the products delivered are performing as planned. Sales engineers also need to anticipate the needs of the customer, as far ahead as possible, to inform their companies of potential marketing opportunities. They also keep

Lingo to Learn

aerodynamics The study of gases in motion, principally applied in the design of airplanes.

aeronautics The design and construction of aircraft.

aerospace The science and technology of flight; also the atmosphere and the regions of space around it.

airplane A winged vehicle capable of flight, generally heavier than air and driven by jet engines or propellers; the six main parts of an airplane are the fuselage, wings, stabilizer, rudder, engines, and landing gear.

astronautics The science and technology of space flight.

gravity Natural force that pulls objects on or near Earth toward Earth.

NASA National Aeronautics and Space Administration. NASA oversees the United States space exploration program.

satellite A free-flying object that orbits Earth, another planet, or the Sun.

space Begins where Earth's atmosphere is too thin to affect objects moving through it, about 100 miles above Earth.

thrust The push given by a rocket to its engines; thrust is required for an object to escape the pull of gravity.

trajectory Flight path.

abreast of their competitors and need to understand how to structure contracts effectively.

WHAT IS IT LIKE TO BE AN AEROSPACE ENGINEER?

Jeanne Yu has been a cabin environment strategy and technology leader at Boeing Commercial Airplanes for 15 years. Before working at Boeing, she was employed as a thermal analyst at Sandia Laboratories for five years. Asked what she likes about being an aerospace engineer, Jeanne responds, "It's fun! I have had so many different experiences and every day and every year is different. I find that exciting."

Multitasking is probably a good word that describes Jeanne's daily activities. "As an engineer," she explains, "I've found that I juggle many balls or projects simultaneously. . . . At the beginning of a project, we work to develop a good plan, but often find along the way that plans need to be adjusted because of surprises and unexpected constraints."

As a cabin environment strategy and technology leader, Jeanne is responsible for a wide variety of tasks. "I spend approximately 25 percent of a typical day talking to people all over the country to move projects forward or to discuss approaches for new projects; 20 percent in strategic planning—developing plans for projects; 20 percent in meetings to discuss and share data; 20 percent analyzing, documenting, or reading papers to assess a situation; and 15 percent of my day using e-mail to support the afore-

mentioned activities, continue communication, and address new issues."

Aerospace engineers work in various settings depending on their job description. Those involved in research and design usually work in a traditional office setting. They spend considerable time at computers and drawing boards. Engineers involved with the testing of components and structures often work outside at test sites or in laboratories where controlled testing conditions can be created.

In the manufacturing area of the aerospace industry, engineers often work on the factory floor itself, assembling components and making sure that they conform to design specifications. This job requires much walking around large production facilities, such as aircraft factories or spacecraft assembly plants.

Jeanne works indoors in a cubicle office environment, but adds that, "I travel frequently between buildings, giving me time to think and walk outdoors. In the last 20 years, though, I have worked in laboratories, in the airplane factory, at airports, and most fun, on airplanes—flying in the cargo compartment is quite an experience."

Engineers are sometimes required to travel to different cities, states, and countries to consult with companies that make materials and other needed components. Others travel to remote test sites to observe and participate in flight testing or for seminars or other types of professional education. Jeanne often has the opportunity to travel for business, both domestically and internationally. She says her favorite trips have been to Singapore,

Japan, and Washington, D.C. Alberto Arteaga, an XM radio platform integrated product team leader at Boeing Satellite Systems, also travels for his job. "I have been to Malaysia, Canada, French Guiana, and various cities in the United States," he says. "My most memorable travel for work has been to support launch campaigns where my team configures the satellites, which are mounted on top of the launch vehicle. My team monitors the spacecraft's health and declares its readiness for flight. It's a tremendous feeling and satisfaction when our mission group acquires the satellite after launch and we retrieve signals from the satellite from outer space."

HAVE I GOT WHAT IT TAKES TO BE AN AEROSPACE ENGINEER?

Aerospace engineers need a diverse group of skills to be successful in their careers. According to Jeanne Yu, the most important personal quality for aerospace engineers is emotional resilience. "Things often don't go the way you expected and you need to be able to dust yourself off and pick yourself up and start again with another approach," she says. "At Boeing, this is a key attribute, as we need to replan and often change direction midstream after a lot of investment in one direction. But resilience allows you to be flexible and come up with smarter solutions long term."

Since so many aerospace-related tasks require the skills of a wide variety of professionals, aerospace engineers need to be able to work together as a team. "The ability to successfully work together with people is a skill I value as a manager," Jeanne says. "Teams need to be responsible for the overall success. Collaboration inevitably ends up with elegant solutions to complex problems that individuals could not have come up with on their own."

Alberto Arteaga feels that the most important personal and professional qualities for engineers are "resilience, persistence, and a dedication to accomplishing your task and/or projects in the most timely and efficient manner. An engineer," he adds, "needs to put quality above all other aspects of the job to ensure first-pass success. An engineer must also have strong communication skills to coordinate and flow out requirements with other disciplines and peers to completing a project."

To Be a Successful Aerospace Engineer, You Should . . .

- enjoy detail-oriented, exacting work
- be good at problem solving
- like working with others as a member of a team
- have strong mathematical, science, and computer skills
- be a good communicator
- be curious and inventive

Other important skills for aerospace engineers include mathematical, science, and computer acumen; the ability to visualize the forms and functions of structures; and a well-developed curiosity about the world around them.

HOW DO I BECOME AN AEROSPACE ENGINEER?

Education

High School

While in high school, follow a college preparatory program. Doing well in mathematics and science classes is vital if you want to pursue a career in any type of engineering field. The American Society for Engineering Education advises students to take calculus and trigonometry in high school, as well as laboratory science classes. Such courses provide the skills you'll need for the problem solving that is essential in any type of engineering.

Postsecondary Training

Aerospace engineers need a bachelor's degree to enter the field. More advanced degrees are necessary for those interested in teaching or research and development positions.

While a major in aerospace engineering is the norm, other majors are acceptable. For example, NASA recommends a degree in any of a variety of disciplines, including biomedical engineering, ceramics engineering, chemistry, industrial engineering, materials science, mechanical engineering, metallurgy, optical engineering, and oceanography.

Jeanne Yu earned a master's degree in mechanical engineering with an emphasis on thermosciences, thermal analysis, and fluid mechanics. "This was rigorous training to develop the foundational knowledge for solid understanding of the physics," she says, "but, additionally, this education formulated and evolved my approach for problem solving, which is critically used every day."

You should make sure the college you choose has an accredited engineering program. The Accreditation Board for Engineering and Technology (ABET) sets minimum education standards for programs in these fields. Graduation from an ABET-accredited school is a requirement for becoming licensed in many states, so it is important to select an accredited school. Currently, approximately 250 colleges and universities offer ABET-accredited engineering programs. Visit ABET's Web site, http://www.abet.org, for a listing of accredited schools.

Some aerospace engineers complete master's degrees and even doctoral work before entering this field. Advanced degrees can significantly increase an engineer's earnings. Students continuing on to graduate school will study research and development, with a thesis required for a master's degree and a dissertation for a doctorate. About one-third of all aerospace engineers go on to graduate school to get a master's degree.

Certification or Licensing

All states require engineers to be licensed. There are two levels of licensing for engineers. Professional engineers (PEs) have graduated from an accredited engineering curriculum, have four years of engineering experience, and have passed a written exam. Engineering graduates need not wait until they have four years experience, however, to start the licensure process. Those who pass the Fundamentals of Engineering examination after graduating are called engineers in training (EITs) or engineer interns or intern engineers. The EIT certification usually is valid for 10 years. After acquiring suitable work experience, EITs can take the second examination, the Principles and Practice of Engineering exam, to gain full PE licensure. Jeanne feels the examination was challenging. She notes that studying for the examination "is a lot of work and the timing is never good, but it is worthwhile to gain perspective on the value of your skills and helps you build a reference for where to get information when you need it to fulfill a consultation request. I don't really use the license, but there still is general respect in our field to have PE on your badge."

In order to ensure that aerospace engineers are kept up-to-date on their quickly changing field, many states have imposed continuing education requirements for relicensure.

INTERNSHIPS AND VOLUNTEERSHIPS

Engineering programs that require an internship usually either have an established internship program set up in partnership with local companies, or the program's placement department works with the student to locate a suitable internship that will fulfill the requirements. Required internships generally last between one and two semesters and offer no pay; instead, the experience counts for a stipulated number of credit hours, in accordance with the degree program's requirements.

One of the reasons why many degree programs are so involved in the internship aspect of the program is that they want to guarantee that each of their students is in a positive learning environment, taking full advantage of the practical, on-the-job experience to augment their classroom studies. Students should always check with their program administrators if they want to obtain credit for their intern experiences, as some programs are extremely finicky about extending credit for internships. Usually, the company offering the internship must prove to the school that the student is actually learning valuable skills and gaining on-the-job experience, instead of just working for the company for free. Internships solicited by the student (and which are not required by the degree program) may, in fact, offer some form of stipend in addition to, or in the place of, counting toward credit hours at a university. Students can work in these internships during the summer.

WHO WILL HIRE ME?

The U.S. Department of Labor reports that approximately 78,000 aerospace engineers are employed in the United States. Many aircraft-related engineering jobs are found in Texas, Washington, Florida, and California, where large aerospace companies are located. Almost half of all aerospace engineers work in the aircraft and parts, guided missile, and space vehicle industries. Government agencies, such as the Department of Defense and NASA, employ approximately 10 percent of aerospace engineers. Other employers include engineering services, research and testing services, and electronics manufacturers.

Many students begin their careers while completing their studies through work-study arrangements that sometimes turn into full-time jobs. Most aerospace manufacturers actively recruit engineering students, conducting on-campus interviews and other activities to locate the best candidates. Students preparing to graduate can also send out resumes to companies active in the aerospace industry and arrange interviews. Many colleges and universities also staff job placement centers, which are often good places to find leads for new job openings.

Students can also apply directly to agencies of the federal government concerned with aerospace development and implementation. Applications can be made through the Office of Personnel Management or through an agency's own hiring department.

Professional associations, such as the National Society of Professional Engineers (http://www.nspe.org) and the American Institute of Aeronautics and Astronautics (http://www.aiaa.org), offer job placement services, including career advice, job listings, and training.

Related Jobs

- aerodynamicists
- aeronautical and aerospace technicians
- aeronautical products sales engineers
- aerospace engineering educators
- astronauts
- astronomers
- astrophysicists
- electrical and electronics engineers
- industrial engineers
- mechanical engineers
- physicists
- robotics engineers and technicians
- stress analysts

WHERE CAN I GO FROM HERE?

As in most engineering fields, there tends to be a hierarchy of workers in the various divisions of aerospace engineering. This is true in research, design and development, production, and teaching. In an entry-level job, one is considered simply an engineer, perhaps a junior engineer. After a certain amount of experience is gained, depending on the position, one moves on to work as a project engineer, supervising others. Then, as a managing engineer, one has further responsibilities over a number of project engineers and their teams. At the top of the hierarchy is the position of *chief engineer*, which involves authority over managing engineers and additional decision-making responsibilities.

As engineers move up the career ladder, the type of responsibilities they have tend to change. Junior engineers are highly involved in technical matters and scientific problem solving. As managers and chiefs, engineers have the responsibilities of supervising, cost analyzing, and relating with clients.

All engineers must continue to learn and study technological progress throughout their careers. It is important to keep abreast of engineering advancements and trends by reading industry journals and taking courses. Such courses are offered by professional associations or colleges. In aerospace engineering especially, changes occur rapidly, and those who seek promotions must be prepared. Those who are employed by colleges and universities must continue teaching and conducting research if they want to have tenured faculty positions.

WHAT ARE THE SALARY RANGES?

In 2005, the median salary for all aerospace engineers was approximately $84,090 per year, according to the U.S. Department of Labor. The lowest paid 10 percent earned $57,250 or less, while the highest 10 percent earned more than $117,680 annually. Experienced engineers employed by the federal government earned a mean salary of $93,050 in 2005. Federal employees often enjoy greater job security and often more generous vacation and retirement benefits.

Aerospace engineers with bachelor's degrees earned average starting salaries of $50,993 per year, according to a 2005 salary survey conducted by the National Association of Colleges and Employers. With a master's degree, candidates were offered $62,930, and with a Ph.D., $72,529.

All engineers can expect to receive vacation and sick pay, paid holidays, health insurance, life insurance, and retirement programs.

WHAT IS THE JOB OUTLOOK?

Overall, employment in this field is expected to decline through 2014, according to the U.S. Department of Labor. The aerospace industry has gone through difficult times since the late 1980s, and more job losses are predicted for the immediate future. Reduced or stagnant space program budgets and the continuing wave of corporate downsizing have all combined to cut severely into the aerospace industry.

A slowdown in airline traffic and a decrease in orders for new commercial aircraft will limit job opportunities for aerospace engineers employed in the private sector. Job opportunities for aerospace engineers employed by the government will be better. As a result of the September 2001 terrorist attacks, the federal government has increased defense-spending budgets in order to build up the armed forces. More aerospace engineers will be needed to repair and add to the current air fleet, as well as to improve defense technology. Engineers are also needed to help make commercial aircraft safer, designing and installing reinforced cockpit doors and onboard security screening equipment to protect pilots, crew, and commercial passengers.

Despite cutbacks in the space program, the development of new space technology and increasing commercial uses for that technology will continue to require qualified engineers. Facing reduced demand in the United States, aerospace companies are increasing their sales overseas, and depending on the world economy and foreign demand, this new market could create a demand for new workers in the industry.

Although the number of actual aerospace engineering jobs is expected to decline through 2014, opportunities for new aerospace engineers should be good as a result of declining enrollments in aerospace engineering programs and a large number of expected retirements during this time period. These openings are expected to account for most of the new jobs in the industry, but job satisfaction and longevity are high, so turnover is usually low.

Alberto Arteaga feels that the future employment for aerospace engineering is endless. "As a society," he says, "we are continuously probing for more information on Earth and in outer space. Aerospace engineering is the key to many of the daily services that society has become accustomed to, such as cell phones, pagers, television, radio, and videoconferencing."

Biomedical Engineers

SUMMARY

Definition
Biomedical engineers apply engineering principles to problems in medical research and health care.

Alternative Job Titles
None

Salary Range
$44,060 to $71,840 to $113,590+

Educational Requirements
Minimum of a bachelor's degree. Advanced degree recommended.

Certification or Licensing
Voluntary

Employment Outlook
Faster than the average

High School Subjects
Biology
Chemistry
Mathematics
Physics

Personal Interests
Building things
Computers
Figuring out how things work
Science

One of Gabriele Niederauer's biggest challenges as the director of research and development at osteoBiologics, Inc. is to help develop an implant that will aid in repairing articular cartilage, which will allow orthopedic surgeons to consider an off-the-shelf resorbable scaffold to help treat damaged joint surfaces.

"If we can move development forward at a pretty rapid pace, we may be the very first company in the United States to get such a product approved," she says, her voice brimming with pride.

Gabriele and her team of biomedical engineers are proving that you don't have to be a Johnson & Johnson or another huge company to get things done and make a difference.

"It's not always the big companies with the huge budgets," she says, "it can also be the little companies that are very lean, mean, and focused and act quickly. One of my team's favorite comments is that we work in dog years—one of our years is the equivalent to seven years at a major company. We have to be very efficient to get things done, but if you have a good team and the necessary funding to support your programs, you can achieve just as much."

WHAT DOES A BIOMEDICAL ENGINEER DO?

Biomedical engineers bridge the gap between the mechanical world and the world of flesh and blood. They use their understanding of engineering to help solve problems in health care. They work in cooperation with doctors, technicians, and engineers from a variety of fields to develop and test machines, materials, and techniques that give patients hope for longer, fuller lives.

On the surface, the fields of engineering and medicine seem far apart. Engineers work with steel, fluids, and mathematical principles to create new and better things. Doctors work with the most amazing machine—the human body. Ever since the first artificial limb was used to replace a missing leg, however, engineering and medicine have worked together. Engineers use their knowledge of physical laws to study the operations of the natural world. Better understanding of how systems within the body work can lead to new treatments and tools for doctors. The wonders of modern medicine, from the simplest artificial limbs to artificial hearts, are due in part to the work of biomedical engineers.

There are a number of subfields within biomedical engineering. Some people in these fields work in basic research, exploring theories and broad concepts. Others use that knowledge to build, test, and eventually market products or equipment—such as implants like titanium hip joints or diagnostic machines like the ultrasound machine used to examine organs and tissues without surgery. Engineers also work in adapting these new devices to the medical environment by customizing software and training personnel.

Whatever their role, biomedical engineers work closely with people from many different fields. They need the input and cooperation of doctors and medical scientists, but they also work with marketing and sales departments, foundations that issue grants, and machine shops that build prototypes of new devices. Specialists to some extent, biomedical engineers are also generalists who know something about a variety of disciplines.

Biomedical engineers can work in a number of different environments, depending on their specialty. For example, clinical engineers work mostly in hospitals, while engineers who have moved into sales or marketing may spend more time traveling. Other biomedical engineers teach at colleges and universities. Tejal Desai is an associate professor of biomedical engineering at Boston University. She has been an educator since 1998. She was recently featured in *Popular Science* magazine's "Brilliant 10" list, which profiles extremely promising young scientists. "I started as an assistant professor right after graduate school," she says. "Since then, I have taught both graduate and undergraduate students in biomedical engineering. The pros of working as a

---

Some Products of the Biomedical Industry

- artificial hearts and kidneys
- artificial joints
- automated medicine delivery systems
- blood oxygenators
- cardiac pacemakers
- defibrillators
- laser systems used in surgery
- medical imaging systems (MRIs, ultrasound)
- sensors that analyze blood chemistry

---

teacher are being in a constantly changing and dynamic field where I can make a difference in terms of teaching and research. It is rewarding seeing students learn and go on to impact the field. The cons are the many different aspects of the job that one has to juggle and the lack of time! But, it is well worth it!"

WHAT IS IT LIKE TO BE A BIOMEDICAL ENGINEER?

Gabriele Niederauer is the director of research and development at OsteoBiologics, Inc., a medical device manufacturer in San Antonio, Texas. She has been a biomedical engineer for 12 years. "As a college senior," Gabriele says, "I did a project on the use of ceramics in medicine. It really intrigued me, and I think that the prospect of taking materials and designing them to help people is really what attracted me to becoming a biomedical engineer."

As the director of research and development, Gabriele is responsible for a variety of tasks that are critical to her company's growth. "Depending on what stage of product development we're in," she says, "it can vary anywhere from traveling with our president/CEO to different investors, to serving as the technical resource for our technology, to managing our intellectual property portfolio (if anyone in the company has a new invention that could be patentable, we work with our attorneys to prepare that disclosure and get it filed)."

Gabriele also oversees her company's regulatory applications and works with the Food and Drug Administration (FDA) to get clearance for products. "All medical products are categorized either into devices (standard implants), drugs/pharmaceuticals, or biologics," she says. "We mostly focus on devices. The FDA classifies these devices based on the time they spend in the body and the risks associated with them. So, if you have a drill bit that you use in orthopedics to drill out a piece of bone, that doesn't even require FDA clearance as long as you meet certain medical device manufacturing guidelines. An instrument like an arthroscope that goes into the body for about half an hour is a Class 1 device. A Class 2 device would be something like a synthetic material that is implanted in the body. The most stringently regulated products are those that have never been used for specific indications or use. An example of this type of device is one that we are currently developing that can be used for the repair of cartilage. This type of product has to undergo very rigorous clinical testing to get clearance by the FDA. The application tends to be more cumbersome and involved based on its level of classification. Each product has certain indications and requirements from a performance standpoint and guidelines that you have to follow. It's a pretty intricate process."

Biomedical engineers work in a wide variety of settings. Gabriele has an office, but other biomedical engineers at her facility work in clean rooms and research and development, histology, and quality control testing laboratories. "I spend some time in the lab," she says, "but not

To Be a Successful Biomedical Engineer, You Should . . .

- have good problem-solving skills
- be a good communicator
- be able to get along with many types of people
- be a compassionate person
- have an aptitude for math and science
- have an inquisitive mind

nearly as much as I used to. The other development engineers in my group spend about 25 percent of their time in the lab. They spend the rest of their time creating drawings, writing reports, and designing experiments."

Some biomedical engineers travel to off-site laboratories, conferences, factories, and to medical offices as a part of their job duties. "I travel," Gabriele says, "to a lot of the medical meetings that are in our specialty—for example, the Arthroscopy Association of North America, which meets twice a year. We display product and talk to our consulting physicians to get feedback. I also travel to meet one-on-one with doctors to explain our technology, try to convince them to use our products, and receive feedback on what type of products they need to help treat their patients."

DO I HAVE WHAT IT TAKES TO BE A BIOMEDICAL ENGINEER?

Engineering and medicine are among the most demanding fields of study, attracting students of the highest caliber. Those interested in biomedical engineering must be good students prepared to study hard. Interests in math and science are important. You must have good problem-solving skills and an inquisitive mind. Problem solving often requires a new approach, so the ability to think creatively is critical.

Biomedical engineers are often links between very different areas of expertise. For this reason, it is necessary to learn about other fields, such as electrical, material, and chemical engineering. Because they spend so much time talking with other professionals, they need to be excellent communicators.

In addition to technical skills, Gabriele Niederauer believes that intuition and common sense about the design of devices and systems are key to being successful in the field. "You have to study chemistry, math, and science," she says, "but when it gets right down to it, you have to have a gut feeling on something and take the knowledge that you learned and critically put it together with your common sense to make a wise decision and think 'outside the box.' You also need to be well rounded. Getting straight A's in college is not everything. You need to be able to work as a team player, be confident, know when to ask others for help, know when to keep pushing for solutions to problems, and really be able to work together for a com-

mon goal. These are the traits that I look for as a manager."

As with any job, there are difficulties. Working with a number of different fields means there is always more to learn. Biomedical engineers face challenges other engineers do not. Instead of dealing strictly with materials that have known properties, they must grapple with biological systems that are never the same.

HOW DO I BECOME A BIOMEDICAL ENGINEER?

Education

Gabriele Niederauer has a B.S. in ceramic engineering from Clemson University, an M.S. with a co-major in materials science engineering and biomedical engineering from Iowa State University, a Ph.D. in biomedical engineering (with an emphasis on biomaterials) from Iowa State University, and a postdoctoral fellowship in orthopedic biomechanics from the University of Texas Health Science Center. "The training was lengthy and challenging," Gabriele says, "but it provided me with a diverse base knowledge for my current endeavors."

High School

The course of study for biomedical engineering is very demanding. High school students should take as much math and science as possible, including trigonometry, calculus, biology, physics, and chemistry. Communications classes are good, as are problem-solving classes (like logic). Those living near a facility that does biomedical work may wish to arrange a tour or talk to professionals to see if biomedical engineering is of interest.

"The brightest high school students are entering the field of biomedical engineering because of the intellectual challenge and the excitements of new technological advances," Tejal Desai explains. "This major is often quite competitive to gain admission at the undergraduate level. The best preparation is doing well academically, having a strong quantitative and science background, and being able to manage time and activities well. This is an interdisciplinary field, so it is helpful to be well versed in multiple areas."

Postsecondary Training

The minimum degree required for working in biomedical engineering is a bachelor's degree, but usually an advanced degree is required. "A bachelor's will prepare you to be an engineer/technician," Tejal says, "but for more advanced research and work in biomedical device companies or biotech, one needs a master's or Ph.D. Biomedical engineering is such a broad field that the undergraduate degree just begins to scratch the surface, and the graduate degree helps one develop more depth."

Undergraduate study is roughly divided into halves. The first two years are devoted to theoretical subjects like abstract physics and differential equations in addition to the core curriculum most undergraduates take. The third and fourth years are spent with more applied science.

The Accreditation Board for Engineering and Technology (ABET) sets minimum education standards for programs in these fields. Graduation from an ABET-accredited school is a requirement for becoming licensed in many states, so it is important to select an accredited school. Visit ABET's Web site, http://www.abet.org, for a listing of accredited schools.

There are a number of excellent graduate-level programs. During graduate programs, students work on research or product development projects headed by faculty.

Certification or Licensing

Engineers whose work may affect the life, health, or safety of the public must be registered, or licensed, according to regulations in all 50 states and the District of Columbia. Applicants for registration must have received a degree from an ABET-accredited engineering program and have four years of experience. They must also pass a written examination administered by the state they wish to work in.

Internships and Volunteerships

It stands to reason that the more "real world" research experience people have, the better their chances of finding a job after school. Internships are one way of getting that type of marketable experience, as well as a way to network with possible employers. Gabriele Niederauer spent four months of her junior year of undergraduate college in an internship at a ceramic processing plant in Germany (where she was born). "The internship was very useful," she says. "The existing manufacturing process was causing a high number of defective parts to be produced.

My assignment was to determine which step in the production process was causing the part failures."

WHO WILL HIRE ME?

When looking for a job, Tejal Desai believes that it is important for graduates to "be both a strong engineer and a strong biologist and to be able to communicate to others what skills you are uniquely suited to bring. Employers may advertise for an electrical or mechanical engineer to work on biomedical devices, but what they really need is a biomedical engineer, so be patient and persistent and sell your ability to integrate knowledge and work across disciplines."

Approximately 7,600 biomedical engineers are employed in the United States, according to the U.S. Department of Labor. Biomedical engineers work at universities, hospitals, in government, and in private industry (mainly in the pharmaceutical and medicine manufacturing and medical instruments and supplies industries). A great deal depends on what type of engineering a person does. Rehabilitative and clinical engineers may find more opportunities in hospitals, for example. Research and product development are done at private companies like Boston Scientific, Johnson and Johnson, and Baxter. Universities hire professional engineers to work in their labs alongside professors and graduate students. Government funding that in the past could be counted on to support basic research at universities has been one of the victims of budget cuts in recent years. Some of this loss has been replaced by private industry through cooperative partnerships. Federal and state regulatory agencies must approve new devices and procedures before they can be marketed. On the federal level, the Food and Drug Administration is the primary employer of biomedical engineers.

WHERE CAN I GO FROM HERE?

There are a number of career paths for biomedical engineers. Biomedical engineers can continue researching, move into management, or get into government service. The interdisciplinary nature of biomedical engineering means that those in the field often have the background and experience to move easily into other dimensions of business like marketing and sales. Established professionals can become consultants. As new technologies are developed, there are opportunities for entrepreneurs to go into business for themselves. Gabriele Niederauer plans to continue in the research and development arena and possibly become a vice-president of research and development. "I really enjoy working for small companies," she says, "and I think that as I get more well-rounded experience, my ultimate goal would be to become president/CEO of a company."

WHAT ARE THE SALARY RANGES?

Salaries vary greatly depending on education, experience, and place of employment. According to the U.S. Department of Labor, biomedical engineers had a median yearly income of $71,840 in 2005. At the low end of the pay scale, 10 percent earned less than $44,060 per year, and at the high end, 10 percent earned more than $113,590 annually.

According to a 2005 survey by the National Association of Colleges and Employers, the average beginning salary for those with bachelor's degrees in biomedical engineering was $48,503. Those with master's degrees had beginning salaries that averaged $59,667 per year.

Related Jobs

- anatomists
- animal breeders
- biomedical engineering educators
- biomedical equipment technicians
- ergonomists
- geneticists
- instrumentation technicians
- orthotic and prosthetic technicians
- pathologists
- pharmacologists
- physicians
- physiologists
- surgeons
- veterinarians

College professors and Ph.D.'s in private industry can earn $65,000 per year and more, depending on the number of years of experience they have. Those with established research credentials can earn substantially more as consultants to business and government.

WHAT IS THE JOB OUTLOOK?

Job growth is expected to be stronger than average as the population ages and the health care industry continues to grow. Generally, older people require more tests and procedures than younger people do. And while the industry is changing rapidly as managed care assumes a more dominant role, the search for better (and less expensive) ways of treating patients will continue to drive bioengineering research and development. MRI, ultrasound, CAT scans, PET scans, artificial hearts, kidney dialysis, tissue replacement technology, artificial joints and limbs, and dozens of other advances in medicine are the products of bioengineering. Biomedical engineers and the professors to train them will be needed to produce the tools for the next generation of treatments.

Tejal Desai predicts that "the job market will continuously expand as more and more people realize the strengths of biomedical engineers. Opportunities range from biotech/pharma, medical devices, medical imaging, bioinformatics, and micro/nanotechnology companies."

Chemical Engineers

SUMMARY

Definition
Chemical engineers use their knowledge of mathematics, chemistry, and other natural sciences gained by study, experience, and practice to develop economic ways of using materials and energy for the benefit of humanity.

Alternative Job Titles
None

Salary Range
$39,690 to $77,140 to $124,600+

Education Requirements
Minimum of a bachelor's degree. Advanced degree recommended.

Certification or Licensing
Required for certain positions

Employment Outlook
Little change

High School Subjects
Biology
Chemistry
Computer science
Mathematics

Personal Interests
Computers
Figuring out how things work
Reading/books
Science

It was the worst case of stage fright Professor Michael Matthews had ever encountered.

Students in his unit operations lab were preparing to make oral presentations, but one young lady was absolutely terrified—her eyes filled with fear.

"She was truly petrified," Michael recalls, "so much that I had to dismiss all of the class except her two teammates before she was able to stammer through her presentation. I saw little chance of her passing or becoming an engineer because verbal communications and public speaking are essential to success in the field."

Helping a student master her fear of public speaking was a little outside his area of expertise, but Michael had an idea. He remembered that a chapter of Toastmasters met weekly in the engineering building. He called the local chapter organizer to ask if Toastmasters could help.

"I accompanied her to the first meeting," he remembers, "made introductions, and assured that she would not faint in terror.

"One month later, before the lab presentations, she came to me in excitement and claimed that she was going to dazzle the class with her presentation. And she did! She was confident, poised, well organized, had a strong command of the facts, and had no trouble answering questions. My jaw dropped, as did the other students'. I have never seen such a complete turnaround. She went on to do just fine in the course."

WHAT DOES A CHEMICAL ENGINEER DO?

In the most simple of terms, *chemical engineers* study ways to convert raw materials into finished products. Specifically, chemical engineers invent new types of materials, synthesize new or existing materials, transform combinations of elements of matter, and then develop the process by which these same chemical changes can occur safely, efficiently, and on a large scale.

Whether they work for a plastics manufacturer, a processed-foods corporation, or a drug development company, chemical engineers are concerned with applying their scientific and technical knowledge in innovative ways to solve problems. The end result is always the creation of a useful material; be it a garbage bag that rapidly decomposes, a fat-free dessert, or a cure for the common cold.

Finding the solution isn't valuable if that solution can't be applied in practical situations. For example, Dr. Selman Waksman discovered in the late 1930s that certain chemical combinations were successful at destroying harmful bacteria. Calling his chemical warriors "anti-biotics," he envisioned saving millions of lives.

Unfortunately, the chemical compounds Dr. Waksman had discovered could only be produced in small quantities in his laboratory. Of what use were they to the average man if they were too expensive to mass-produce and distribute? Thankfully, Dr. Waksman enlisted the help of chemical engineers who first designed a method of reproducing the chemicals en masse by mutating their structure, and then developed special methods for "brewing" the chemicals in huge, oversized tanks. Their efforts allowed these new wonder drugs to be produced in a cost-effective manner, guaranteeing their impact on human lives around the globe.

Today, chemical engineers work on the large-scale preparation of substances in production plants. Their goal is to find safe, environmentally sound processes; to make the product in a commercial quantity; to determine the least costly method of production; and to formulate the material for easy use and safe, economic transport.

For most chemical engineers, the steps outlined above translate into what is known as *process engineering.* Process engineering involves creating new processes to meet the specific needs of a given product, including selecting or designing the proper equipment, supervising the construction of a plant and/or the production system, and overseeing tests, or "pilot runs." In addition, the chemical engineer is often called upon to monitor the day-to-day operations of the production plant itself, or one of the areas within the plant. The chemical engineer's work isn't finished once the system or plant is in place; on the contrary, the chemical engineer constantly tries to improve the product, the system, the production, or any combination of these aspects of the process, working to make them safer, more efficient, more cost-effective, or more friendly to the environment.

Among the typical industries in which chemical engineers work are chemical, fuel, environment, aerospace, plastics, pharmaceutical, and food. In the most common field of these industries, manufacturing, chemical engineers are busy finding out ways to convert raw materials into products. These products can be as specialized as a liquid coating for a part on a rocket engine, or as common as a new longer-lasting sole for your shoes.

Depending on what industry they work in, chemical engineers' duties vary. Chemical engineers working in *environmental control,* for example, develop strategies to reduce or alleviate pollution at the source, as well as treat those wastes produced by their plant which cannot be eradicated. *Safety officers* are responsible for designing and maintaining plants and processes that are safer for both workers and the community. Chemical engineers working in the specialty of *biomedicine* may work with physicians to develop new methods of tracking the chemical processes taking place within the human body, or they may develop artificial organs that temporarily replace real organs until donor organs are found. In general, chemical engineers are employed in the research and design, development, production, and management areas of companies, but many of

---

Lingo to Learn

first law In all processes energy is simply converted from one form to another, or transferred from one system to another.

heat exchanger A device that allows the heat from a hot fluid to be transferred to a cooler fluid without the two fluids coming into contact.

lixiviation The process of separating soluble components from a mixture by washing them out with water.

second law Heat cannot pass from a cooler to a hotter body without some other process occurring.

thermochemistry The study of how heat affects chemical substances, especially after a chemical reaction.

thermodynamics The study of heat and other forms of energy.

transmutation The transformation of one element into another by radioactive decay or by the bombardment of the nuclei with particles.

---

their duties may require that they work in more than one, or all, of these areas. In fact, engineers frequently work closely with others to solve problems unique to their area of expertise.

No matter where a student's interests lie, he or she can find a rewarding career in chemical engineering. Even within a specific area, there are many applications, and, therefore, careers. For example, chemical engineers work in food production to design better ways of producing particular types of food *and* they work to develop environmentally safe pesticides and fertilizers. Some chemical engineers teach at the high school and college level. Others work as consultants to the government, executives and managers at chemical engineering professional associations, computer systems designers, environmental lawyers, patent lawyers, and even brewers of specialty beers. In short, the field is only as limited as the imaginations of those who work in it.

WHAT IS IT LIKE TO BE A CHEMICAL ENGINEER?

Michael Matthews has been a chemistry educator since 1987, when he began his teaching career at the University of Wyoming. He is currently a professor in the Department of Chemical Engineering at the University of South Carolina. What's a typical day like for Michael? "A professor's job balances teaching, research, and service. During a regular semester," Michael says, "I usually spend a half hour to an hour getting mentally prepared and organized to teach a class. Prior to this mental preparation I will have spent one to three hours on the details of the class period, such as reading and making notes, solving or finding example problems, grading, and looking up information in other texts or on the Web. Actually teaching the class and answering questions usually takes an hour and a half. Around this, I will work in committee and faculty meetings with my university colleagues. Research activities take up a good deal of time. Typically I am reading and discussing reports with my students, and I spend a good deal of time coordinating with

other research specialists within and outside of my university. With a research group of about 10 people [which focuses on understanding thermodynamic, transport, and kinetic behavior of solvents and materials that may promote more green and sustainable methods of chemical and material manufacturing], as well as a number of outside collaborators, I require a couple of project meetings a week, and then individual half-hour meetings with the graduate students. There is usually some writing and calling, as well as extensive reading to do associated with research, teaching, or service work."

In addition to these tasks, Professor Matthews must respond to unscheduled activities such as drop-in visits from students or colleagues, phone calls, and e-mails. "These days, everyone inside and outside the university communicates by e-mail," he says, "and it takes a good hour or even two daily to read, respond, file, and/or delete messages. It is helpful to be a fast reader and to have good typing skills."

Michael considers the chance to work with students as one of the best aspects of his job. "It is a pleasure to see students grow and mature in four or five years, and there are always new and talented people coming into a university," he says. "I also enjoy associations with very energetic, intelligent, and interesting faculty. I feel fortunate in that academia is an open profession; that is, I can travel to meetings and associate freely with people from other schools, as well as industry and government. Another important aspect is intellectual freedom; that is, the opportunity to work on new and exciting research projects of your own creation and imagination. Chemical engineers have an opportunity to work on problems that are of vital importance to individuals and to society, problems such as developing clean and sustainable energy, integrating biology with chemical engineering, and manufacturing chemicals with no pollution. On a more personal level, university professors are usually regarded with respect by society, and there is security once one attains tenure in a university."

DO I HAVE WHAT IT TAKES TO BE A CHEMICAL ENGINEER?

Albert Einstein once said, "No amount of experimentation can ever prove me right; a single experiment can prove me wrong." Like all scientists, chemical engineers are trained to pay attention to every aspect of their work, from the largest, most obvious elements, to the most minute details of individual experiments. In addition to the technical importance of recognizing how small, seemingly minor aspects can have drastic effects on the overall success of a project, there is also a compelling, practical reason for paying close attention to details; chemical engineers often work with very dangerous chemical processes, so any error leading to a malfunction can quite possibly represent life-threatening consequences.

It should go without saying that chemical engineers must practice scientific methods, and among the personal qualities intrinsic to exercising those methods

are an inquisitive nature and excellent analytical and problem-solving skills.

In order to solve problems, chemical engineers must first identify and then prioritize problems (as problems often come in batches), determining how each fits into the larger picture that is their project. Every project has a host of issues that threaten a successful resolution. Chemical engineers, like other scientists, must learn how to differentiate and rank these issues in order of importance.

Not to be underestimated are the verbal and written skills which are necessary in any field, but especially in a field dependent on communicating complicated data, experiments, and systems.

Joe Cramer, a chemical engineer who is currently the director of technical programming for the American Institute of Chemical Engineers, considers integrity and reliability as perhaps the two most important personal characteristics for chemical engineers. "I think that it's essential," he says, "in the performance of my duties that everyone I deal with knows that my word means something and that I can be relied on to do what I promise (to the best of my ability and, of course, subject to things not always under my control). I also think that chemical engineers need common sense and an ability to break down complex problems into manageable segments. Additionally, math and science are, of course, very useful tools, but just tools."

Finally, travel can be a large part of the chemical engineer's job. While not all engineers go to sites, laboratories, pilot plants, and conferences, many of them do. This may mean traveling down the

To Be a Successful Chemical Engineer, You Should . . .

- be a stickler for detail and have strong problem-solving skills
- have good communication skills, both written and verbal
- be inquisitive
- have an aptitude for math and science
- have patience in order to solve problems that seem unsolvable
- be willing to travel

street, to a neighboring suburb, out of state, or perhaps even out of the country. Joe travels approximately 30 to 40 days a year; 20 of these days are spent attending conferences. When he worked in project management at another company, he spent as many as 120 days annually traveling.

HOW DO I BECOME A CHEMICAL ENGINEER?

Education

High School

Potential chemical engineers should consider taking as many science, mathematics, and computer science courses as possible. Typical classes that will help provide a solid base for further, advanced work in this field are chemistry, math (including algebra, geometry, calculus, and trigonometry), physics, and computer sciences. Courses in English and the humanities are also crucial in helping to develop strong communication and interpersonal skills. Joe Cramer recommends that aspiring engineers take some writing courses. "Communications," he says, "is an important component of working in the real world and excelling there can really boost your career."

Foreign languages are another wise investment; in today's global marketplace, the knowledge and familiarity with another culture's customs and language can not only mean the difference between success and failure, but it can also help to set you apart from the crowd when it's time for promotions or to search for a new job.

What else can you do to prepare for college? Michael Matthews recommends that you learn how to become a good reader, listener, and questioner. "Classes that require interaction and discussion are important," he says. "Jobs or extra-curricular activities that require talking and listening, dealing with customers, answering questions, and that require independent thinking and personal responsibility are good ways to prepare for college."

Postsecondary Training

Students dreaming of a career in chemical engineering should be aware that the minimum requirement for entry-level positions as chemical engineers is a bachelor's degree in chemical engineering. Before you spend the time and money applying to various schools, you should make certain that the college or university you plan to attend has been approved by the Accreditation Board for Engineering and Technology (http://www.abet.org) and the American Institute of Chemical Engineers (http://www.aiche.org); there's no sense working toward a degree in an unaccredited program. Approximately 150 colleges and universities offer accredited programs. Most programs last four years, although some may last longer and require a commitment to graduate study.

In the first two years of typical chemical engineering programs, students study chemistry, physics, mathematics, computers, and some basic engineering courses like materials science and fluid mechanics. Similar material is covered in high school, but these college courses present students with a much more advanced view.

In the third and fourth years students take classes in advanced chemistry, heat balance, materials balance, reactor design, mass transfer, heat transfer, thermodynamics, and chemical process economics, to name but a few.

Most programs require students to take some classes in the humanities, as well as a technical writing course, since communications and writing are an important part of the job.

Are most students prepared for the demands of a chemical engineering education? According to Professor Michael Matthews, most students are generally well prepared academically. "When there is a weakness," he explains, "it is usually a lack of rigorous math courses and problem solving skills. Even when the math courses appear on the high school transcript, there is sometimes a more subtle weakness, and that is in having true problem solving skills. Problem solving can be a variety of things. Sometimes students are weak at reading word problems and converting those to the language of equations. Some students have problems with time management, study habits, and balancing classes, study time, recreation, and sleeping and eating. Other students have problems relating to college faculty; the students may lack confidence or the ability to ask meaningful questions and to persist until they get good answers. Some students are just too shy and retiring when it comes to dealing with their teachers. All of these are important aspects of student success."

Although bachelor's degree graduates face a wide variety of career options, those who obtain higher degrees undeniably enter their careers at a higher, more specialized level than do their colleagues with only bachelor's degrees. Many positions in research and teaching are open only to M.S. and Ph.D. candidates and, of course, the salaries for those with advanced degrees are considerably higher.

Certification or Licensing

Certification in chemical engineering is called licensing. A licensed engineer is called a professional engineer (PE). Chemical engineers must be licensed as professional engineers if their work involves providing services directly to the public. Employers want to be able to advertise their companies as containing only professional engineers. Not only does it reflect well upon them, but it also means they know they've hired quality engineers, or that they will soon have quality engineers. Licensing also assures employers that they meet state legal regulations.

Requirements vary from state to state but generally it takes about four to five years to become a licensed PE. Students can begin the process while still in college by taking the Fundamentals of Engineering (FE) exam. The exam lasts eight hours and covers everything from chemistry, physics, and mathematics to more advanced knowledge of engineering sciences.

The next step to acquiring the designation of Professional Engineer is obtaining four years of progressive engineering experience. Some states require you to obtain your experience under the supervision of a PE. Once your four years are up you can take the Principles and Practice of Engineering (PPE) exam specific to chemical engineers (there's one for many other branches of engineering, too). If you pass the rigorous exam you can officially call yourself a PE.

Joe Cramer has extensive knowledge of the licensing process. He is a PE and serves on the chemical engineering committee of the National Council for the Examination of Engineers and Surveyors, which oversees the process of preparing PE exams. "The process is very detailed," he explains, "and the exam, while not easy, is quite fair. It is designed so that a minimally competent engineer with four years experience should be able to pass and get his or her professional engineering license."

Internships and Volunteerships

Many schools require that their degree students fulfill an internship. Intended to provide students with hands-on work experience, the internship experience also grants students the opportunity to network and gain a deeper insight into how the industry works. If an internship is required, it usually lasts from 4 to 12 months, or roughly somewhere between one and two semesters. Schools are usually instrumental in locating internships, but placing cold calls or writing query letters to companies you have already carefully researched can also be an effective way of locating a quality internship. Internships required by the school are usually unpaid; students are often compensated in the form of credit toward semester hours.

In addition to landing an internship via your school, you might also choose to find an internship on your own by contacting companies directly. The American Institute of Chemical Engineers offers links to companies that offer internships to students at its Web site, http://www.aiche.org/careerservices/studentempl.

"Our university has an active co-op program," Michael says, "and some companies also hire summer interns. One strong feature of our department is undergraduate research; many of our students earn money and valuable experience by working 5 to 15 hours a week in the lab. Through this they get experience in reading, writing, and independent thinking. Research also gives students an opportunity to attend professional meetings, speak in public, and get published. All of these programs are voluntary, but are highly encouraged."

WHO WILL HIRE ME?

Joe Cramer really made the extra effort to land his first job. He explains: "I got my first job right out of my Ph.D. program by sending out more than 100 applications. I was offered one position in R&D with the Naval Research Lab in Washington, D.C., and one more applied position (in the Environmental Engineering Department) with Stone & Webster Engineering Corporation, a large engineering contractor located in Boston. I took the Stone & Webster position and worked first on environmental studies and analyses, and then moved into the management of projects and technical programs. Initially most of my work dealt with performing environmental analyses and impact assessments for proposed engineering/construction projects (mostly for electric generating plants) and then later I moved into the management of these projects and later yet into the management of Stone & Webster's process plant safety services program. All told I was with Stone & Webster for nearly 20 years."

Approximately 33,000 chemical engineers are employed in the United States, according to the U.S. Department of Labor. Fifty-five percent of all chemical engineers are employed by manufacturing industries. Many are employed by the chemical, petroleum, pharmaceutical, food, electronic, pulp and paper, plastic, rubber, textile, metal, cement, and aerospace industries, as well as at government agencies such as the Department of Energy and the Environmental Protection Agency. Others, such as Michael Matthews, are employed in academia.

Most colleges and universities with accredited programs are visited yearly by recruiters who are eager to hand qualified graduates an appealing employment package. At first, of course, you will have to participate in on-campus interviews during the end of your last semester. Those who do not receive offers from recruiters can still expect to move into their profession relatively quickly. Many smaller companies don't send out recruiters but instead advertise at the university placement center, as well as in trade journals, in professional association newsletters, and on the Internet. A small percentage of entry-level jobs in chemical engineering are found in newspapers.

If your chemical engineering program in college requires you to take an internship, this can be an excellent opportunity leading to full-time employment after you graduate.

You can apply directly to specific companies or government agencies by sending them your resume along with a cover letter detailing your skills and qualifications, and why you would like to work for them.

In addition to academic preparation, Michael Matthews advises chemical engineering students to take full advantage of their school's resources that will offer

Chemical Engineering's Greatest Hits

1. *Air.* Chemical engineers designed ways to process and use the main components of the air we breathe—oxygen and nitrogen—in numerous important applications, such as steel making, welding, the production of semiconductors, and deep freezing food.

2. *Atoms.* The world became a different place after chemical engineers split the atom and isolated its isotopes. Medicine, power generation, biology, and metallurgy have all advanced considerably since this discovery.

3. *Crude oil.* Crude oil (unrefined petroleum) is used in more ways than you might think. It is the building block for such things as synthetic fibers and plastics, and can be used in the making of soaps, cosmetics, shower curtains, and shampoos.

4. *Drugs.* Antibiotics were rare and extremely expensive in the early part of this century. Chemical engineers did not invent antibiotics, but they did invent ways to make their production larger and cheaper so that the general public could afford them.

5. *Environment.* While they may not have been as responsible in the past, today's chemical engineer works hard to clean up past problems as well as develop new manufacturing processes that are environmentally friendly.

6. *Food.* World crop production is much higher than it was 50 years ago, thanks to the work of chemical engineers. They have produced fertilizers and pesticides that made crops healthier and more resistant to disease.

7. *Plastics.* Plastics are everywhere. Try to imagine life without them. Chemical engineers have played a large role in the creation of plastics, from the nylon used in clothing to the polystyrene commonly used today in things like milk cartons.

them an advantage when it comes to landing a job. "Enroll in your school's career services center as a freshman," he suggests. "Seek out co-operative education opportunities, which are the surest way to finding the job you want. If not co-op, then get a summer internship in engineering. Go to all the job fairs and interview opportunities. Learn to talk, listen, answer questions, and represent yourself with confidence. Get acquainted with the companies that you interview. Be flexible, and be prepared to move around. Get to know your professors, and be sure to ask for letters of reference from the faculty and employers for whom you have performed well."

WHERE CAN I GO FROM HERE?

In the private and government sectors, chemical engineers advance based on their qualifications, although to different employers one aspect or area of expertise may weigh more heavily come promotion time. Engineers with only a bachelor's degree execute the experiments, plans, or systems as designed or created by senior chemical engineers. While it is certainly not impossible to advance without more education, it is much more difficult.

Chemical engineers with advanced degrees, on the other hand, are much more likely to direct research projects and quickly advance into managerial and supervisory positions. Generally, the larger the company the greater the degree of specialization required or expected of the engineer (i.e., the more advanced education and hands-on experience) but, as a result, larger companies offer greater opportunities in terms of career growth.

Other chemical engineers teach and/or do research studies at universities and colleges. Depending on the size of the school and the amount of funding devoted to the research project, these positions can be competitive in terms of salaries and benefits.

A small percentage of chemical engineers decide to teach in high schools. While the pay will not be as good, many find it highly rewarding to teach others about the field.

WHAT ARE THE SALARY RANGES?

The average starting salary for chemical engineers varies depending on what field you are working in. Petroleum tends to pay among the highest salaries, and environmental services tends to pay among the lowest salaries to its young recruits. The U.S. Department of Labor reports that the median annual salary for chem-ical engineers was $77,140 in 2005. The lowest paid 10 percent earned less than $49,350; the highest paid 10 percent earned more than $113,950 annually.

Salaries in engineering often reflect your level of education as well as your years of experience. According to a 2005 salary survey by the National Association of Colleges and Employers, starting annual salaries for those with bachelor's degrees in chemical engineering averaged $53,813; those with master's degrees, $57,260; those with doctorates, $79,591.

According to the U.S. Department of Labor, teachers of chemical engineering at the postsecondary level earned salaries that ranged from less than $39,690 to more than $124,600, with a median of $74,540 in 2003. Chemistry teachers at the junior college level earned mean annual salaries of $61,040.

Chemical engineers with a bachelor's degree who have become PEs can climb the salary ladder and over time earn more

Related Jobs

- chemical engineering educators
- chemical engineering technicians
- chemical equipment sales engineers
- chemical test engineers
- chemical-design engineers
- chemists
- industrial chemicals workers
- laboratory testing technicians
- technical directors of chemical plants

than $100,000 a year. Salary increases for chemical engineers have consistently stayed ahead of inflation.

WHAT IS THE JOB OUTLOOK?

Because chemical engineers are employed in so many industries, the future is partially dependent on how well each industry performs. Michael Matthews feels that the current job market is okay, with the most promising opportunities in energy (fuels and energy conversion), environmental (pollution prevention and regulatory work), and in biological or biomolecular engineering. "A number of chemical engineers also go to professional schools like medicine or law or business," he says. "One area that has been declining is textiles."

Joe Cramer feels that the employment outlook for chemical engineers is good, but that the field is changing rapidly. "Chemical engineers are working less and less in traditional plant settings or on traditional process design activities," he says. "Today's chemical engineers are more

likely to work on bio-related areas or on doing things on the nano or molecular scale. Information technology and its applications to chemical process control and design is another growth area."

In general, chemical engineers can expect little overall change in employment growth through 2014, according to the U.S. Department of Labor. Other strong bets for chemical engineers in the coming years are microelectronics, specialty chemicals, and plastics. Petroleum and mining have limited futures, as these resources become depleted and new technologies or materials replace them. However, there are fewer students entering college to study these fields, which could create a demand in the near future for qualified people to fill replacement positions.

Additionally, more chemical engineers will be taking jobs in service industries, and will find work as consultants, in environmental services, in law, medicine, and academics. There will still be plenty of positions opening in manufacturing for entry-level workers and those with more experience.

Civil Engineers

SUMMARY

Definition
Civil engineers are involved in the design and construction of the physical structures that make up our surroundings, such as roads, bridges, buildings, and harbors.

Alternative Job Titles
Construction engineers
Design engineers
Research engineers
Structural engineers
Surveying and mapping engineers

Traffic engineers
Transportation planners

Salary Range
$44,410 to $66,190 to $100,000+

Educational Requirements
Minimum of a bachelor's degree. Advanced degree recommended.

Certification or Licensing
Required for certain positions (licensing)

Employment Outlook
Average growth

High School Subjects
Mathematics
Physics
Personal interests
Building things
Figuring out how things work
Science

Lovers of California wine should raise a toast to Joshua Marrow, a California-based civil engineer, the next time they savor their favorite vintage.

Until 1997, according to Marrow, "there had been virtually no testing data on the performance of the wine barrel storage system in California wineries during earthquakes (with respect to the collapse and damage to wine barrels or injury to people in the facilities)."

When he was asked to write an engineering report about the expected performance of the wine barrels stored in just one facility (which was worth nearly $250 million), he could have—due to time and budgetary constraints—reported his findings and offered recommendations on how to protect this pricey wine supply simply based on his good engineering judgment.

"Instead," he explains, "I chose to take the 'longer' road and actually answer the wine industry with hard science. Our project was funded by the wine industry as a whole, took nearly seven years to complete, and now serves as the basis for assessing risk in wine barrel storage facilities. Considering that nearly all of the barrels used in the California wine industry are stored on this system (an estimated $15 billion in wine in California alone), the research was very important in understanding the true financial loss."

In 2003, Joshua's work was validated when an earthquake hit the central California wine-growing region. "The earthquake damaged numerous wineries," he explains, "and proved to be the first real test of the storage system. We can thankfully say that the wine industry was much better prepared to handle the earthquake, in part due to the published findings from our work. The wine industry suffered extensive damage, however, further reinforcing the need for competent and energetic civil engineers who are willing to help increase safety and listen to its needs. We will continue to work on this problem for many years to come."

WHAT DOES A CIVIL ENGINEER DO?

If you've ever ridden on a train, driven along a highway, taken an elevator to the very top of a skyscraper, ridden a roller coaster, crossed a bridge, or gone for a stroll through a city park, you've relied on the expertise of a civil engineer. *Civil engineers* get you to work or school on time, as well as take you around the world safely, quickly, and efficiently. They use their knowledge of materials science, engineering theory, economics, and demographics to devise, construct, and maintain our physical surroundings. They apply their understanding of other branches of science—such as hydraulics,

Early Engineering Schools in the United States

1802: United States Military Academy at West Point

1821: Norwich University

1824: Rensselaer Polytechnic University

1833: University of Virginia

1837: University of Alabama

geology, and physics—to design the optimal blueprint for the project.

Feasibility studies are conducted by *surveying and mapping engineers* to determine the best sites and approaches for construction. They extensively investigate the chosen sites to verify that the ground and other surroundings are amenable to the proposed project. These engineers use sophisticated equipment, such as satellites and other electronic instruments, to measure the area and conduct underground probes for bedrock and groundwater. They determine the optimal places where explosives should be placed in order to cut through rock.

Many civil engineers work strictly as consultants on projects, advising their clients. These consultants usually specialize in one area of the industry, such as water systems, transportation systems, or housing structures. Clients include individuals, corporations, and the government. Consultants will devise an overall design for the proposed project, perhaps a nuclear power plant commissioned by an electric company. They estimate the cost of constructing the plant, supervise the feasibility studies and site investigations, and advise the client on whom to hire for the actual labor involved. Consultants are also responsible for such details as accuracy of drawings and quantities of materials to order.

Other civil engineers work mainly as contractors and are responsible for the actual building of the structure; they are known as *construction engineers.* They interpret the consultants' designs and follow through with the best methods for getting the work done, usually working directly at the construction site. Contractors are responsible for scheduling the work, buying the materials, maintaining surveys of the progress of the work, and choosing the machines and other equipment used for construction. During construction, these civil engineers must supervise the labor and make sure the work is completed correctly and efficiently. After the project is finished, they must set up a maintenance schedule and periodically check the structure for a certain length of time. Later, the task of ongoing maintenance and repair is often transferred to local engineers.

Civil engineers may be known by their area of specialization. One of the largest areas of specialization is *transportation engineering. Transportation engineers* plan, design, and operate all means of transport, including streets and highways, transit systems, airports, railroads, shipping ports, harbors, and bicycle paths. In designing these methods of transporta-

tion, they are constantly considering such aspects as safety, efficiency, comfort, convenience, economy, and the environmental friendliness of each project. The six major areas that transportation engineers work in are highways, airways, railways, waterways, conveyors, and pipelines.

Some transportation engineers work in planning. When a project begins, *transportation planners* meet with other transportation professionals, engineers, neighborhood groups, and government officials in order to learn of and address the concerns and challenges a project may have. Typical concerns and challenges include environmental, wildlife, landscaping, special design needs, appearance, and the community impact of a project. Planners for a rapid transit system determine the course of the tracks, where the stops will be, and ease of access by the general public. Planners often must defend or justify a proposed project before neighborhood groups, business leaders, and the media. They often must write long, detailed reports explaining a project or defending it. Planners work closely with government officials and environmental groups to ensure all needs and concerns are addressed.

Design engineers design the methods of transportation for unique situations. For example, they may be challenged to build a highway off-ramp that must avoid a wetlands preserve or enter a suburban area with minimal noise disturbance. Designers build rapid transit systems in already crowded cities and must pay close attention to overall cost and efficiency of their design.

Operations is a very important field in transportation engineering, with safety being one of its largest concerns. These engineers are responsible for how traffic flows, whether the traffic consists of automobiles, bicycles, pedestrians, airplanes, trains, boats, or a combination of these. Factors that transportation engineers look for when designing an operation plan are speed of traffic, how much and what kind of traffic, weather, condition of roads (or railways, sidewalks, ports, etc.), whether or not there is a special event or construction, and countless other factors. Transportation engineers will erect traffic signals, signs, lights, and monitoring devices to conduct and track the flow of traffic.

Research engineers look for ways to improve existing transportation engineering technology and design new tools and methods for the future of the industry. Researchers may study the high accident rate of a certain stretch of highway and come up with ways to minimize hazards. They study the flow and density of traffic and develop a congestion management system to help ease traffic. An important branch of research today is finding ways to reduce pollution resulting from transportation. Other researchers may be involved in designing on-board automobile navigational systems, or a high-speed rapid transit system for a sprawling urban area.

WHAT IS IT LIKE TO BE A CIVIL ENGINEER?

Joshua Marrow has been a civil engineer since 1998. He has held a variety of engineering positions at Simpson Gumpertz & Heger Inc. (SGH) and is the president/CEO of Vingenuity Incorporated, a specialized engineering company that develops earthquake protection products for the California wine industry.

"My particular focus and interest in civil engineering is earthquake, or seismic, engineering," Joshua explains. "I grew up in California, so earthquakes have always been a part of my life. As a result, my professional practice has focused on the aspects of civil engineering related to earthquake hazards and the damage they cause to communities."

Joshua works on a variety of projects for SGH, so his day-to-day duties vary based on the current project(s) that he is assigned. "My primary duties," Joshua says, "include engineering calculations, report writing, development of engineering drawings, and general project management related to the variety of projects I work on here at SGH. My secondary duties include development of engineering and drafting standards within the company, young engineer and new hire training, inside and outside marketing activities, recruiting, involvement in professional organizations, and public education on earthquake-related hazards.

"I probably spend 75 percent of my time working directly with another project manager on a specified project assignment. This project could include development of engineering calculations and drawings for a building design or retrofit, drafting a report for a large company on earthquake risk related to a particular area of their operations, development of presentations for construction litigation disputes, or specialized field investigations for highly technical engineering problems (e.g., settling pipelines, structural collapse, earthquake damage). The remainder of my time is usually spent doing business development, marketing, and training—both internal and with clients."

Joshua usually spends about four days a week in the office and one day out in the field. "It depends greatly on the type of project I have on my desk," he says. "If I am working on a project that is in construction, I may be on the construction site as much as three days a week. When we are on site," he says, "we are typically outside (because the building is not built yet) and wear hard hats and boots at all times. Inside the office we have a pretty relaxed environment. People in the office dress nice, but many wear jeans and boots because they may be heading to a site visit at some point in the day."

Because of the diversity of civil engineering positions, working conditions vary widely. Some civil engineers are assigned to work in remote areas and foreign countries. Most of Joshua's projects, because they are earthquake-related, keep him in California, and mainly in the San Francisco Bay Area. In addition to traveling to job sites in California, Joshua also travels to engineering conferences almost yearly. In the course of his work, he has traveled to conferences in Portland, Seattle, Los Angeles, Long Beach, Chicago, New York, Mexico, Italy, and England.

According to Joshua, there are many pros and few cons to working as a civil engineer. "The pros," he says, "include the

---

To Be a Successful Civil Engineer, You Should . . .

- be curious and creative
- have a passion for mathematics and science
- be good at problem solving
- work well with others
- be able to visualize multidimensional, spatial relationships

---

opportunity to work with many intelligent people (clients and coworkers alike), the broad cross-section of interesting projects, the opportunity to actually stand on the building you designed on paper, and the opportunity to travel to observe firsthand how earthquakes can damage communities (it is life-changing). The cons are limited, but include a long professional ladder one must climb to get to the upper levels of a successful engineering firm and the moderate pay level (civil/structural engineers are generally the lowest paid of all engineering professions, yet we have to be licensed twice—civil and structural licenses—in California, and we spend an equivalent amount of time in college as students in other engineering fields)."

DO I HAVE WHAT IT TAKES TO BE A CIVIL ENGINEER?

To be a successful civil engineer, you should have a combination of strong technical and communication skills. "I think that to be an excellent engineer," Joshua explains, "you need to be technically savvy, to be able to handle the math and science aspects of the civil engineering profession, while still possessing a certain level of interpersonal skills to use in marketing one's skills to another." Civil engineers also need to be able to communicate effectively with engineers and other professionals as they tackle demanding projects. Transportation engineers must have exceptional communication skills since they are often called upon to explain at neighborhood meetings why, for example, a stop sign is or isn't necessary at a particular intersection. Being able to eloquently and persuasively present complex scenarios in front of large groups of people helps the public understand the many issues at stake in the decision-making process.

Due to the fact that so many of their projects affect the general public, civil engineers also must zealously guard against errors of any type or scope. A careless mistake could lead to a breakdown in the system or service, potentially posing risks to any number of people. When mistakes or problems do occur civil engineers need to be able to think calmly and clearly in high stress situations. In addition to levelheadedness, civil engineers should have excellent creative problem-solving strategies.

When solving the various challenges in civil engineering it helps to have a natural curiosity about systems and methods. Innovation is not the by-product of a static, stagnant mind, so civil engineers, like other engineers and scientists, should never shrink from asking questions and delving deeper into an area, no matter how obvious or offbeat that investigation may seem at first. Such healthy skepticism and creativity are also useful when working within the constraints of tight budgets, resourcefulness being yet another desirable quality in civil engineers.

HOW DO I BECOME A CIVIL ENGINEER?
Education

Joshua feels that his training for an engineering career really began when he was a child. "I loved to work with Lego building blocks as a kid," he explains. "I always took things apart and reconstructed them with great fascination for the engineered world. As I hit my senior year in high school, I really had no idea what I wanted to do, but I thought I wanted to be an engineer, whatever that really was. I truly did not have a clue what an engineer really did, I just knew that it would probably be a career that would satisfy my curiosities.

"I started college at College of the Redwoods (CR), a local community college in Eureka, California. I intended to spend two years at CR, and then transfer to a California State or University of California school to finish my engineering education. Initially I studied mechanical engineering, but realized about one year into the curriculum that I was not interested in the practice.

"I transferred to California Polytechnic State University-San Luis Obispo and changed my major to architectural engineering, where I took a particular interest in earthquake engineering and earthquake-resistant building design. The program taught us all facets of structural engineering, including architectural design, structural mechanics, construction methods, and more sophisticated earthquake engineering design and construction techniques.

"While at Cal Poly, I started a research project that focused on assessing the earthquake risks associated with the use of the most popular wine barrel storage system in California. I started the project on my own, with encouragement and support from the staff in my program, solicited funds from the California wine industry ($140,000 in all), and performed a series of basic 'shaking table' studies on model wine barrel stacks. Our work was published almost a dozen times before I graduated from Cal Poly in 1998 with a bachelor of science in architectural engineering.

"I continued my research and my education at the University of California-Berkeley. While at Berkeley, I earned a master's of science in structural engineering and mechanics of materials. I also furthered my engineering research on the barrel storage system with an extensive series of shaking table studies on the second largest (at the time) shake table in the country. The work was challenging and served as the technical basis for a U.S. patent I now hold and the technical basis for the wine industry–based earthquake engineering company of which I am president."

High School

Because a bachelor's degree is considered essential in the field, high school students interested in civil engineering must follow a college prep curriculum. Students should focus on mathematics (algebra, trigonometry, geometry, and calculus), the sciences (physics and chemistry), computer science, and English and the humanities (history, economics, and sociology). Students should also aim for honors-level courses.

Joshua recommends that students interested in civil engineering careers be as active as possible during their high school years. "Get an internship with an architecture or engineering company," he recommends, "or, if you know someone in the industry, get a part-time job with a firm while in high school. First-hand experience is worth so much, over second-hand explanations of the job description." He also recommends that students should "get involved with a contractor or a family member and build a house over a summer. This is an amazing introduction to civil engineering and all the mechanics that go into the practice of building design and construction." Finally, Joshua suggests that young people participate in community-based activity such as the programs sponsored by the American Society of Civil Engineers and the State Structural Engineers Associations. "These programs (often taught within a technical high school course)," he explains, "offer students a nice introduction to the field of engineering."

> ### Most Popular Bachelor Degree Programs in Civil Engineering*
>
> 1. Texas A&M University (http://www.civil.tamu.edu)
>
> 2. Pennsylvania State University (http://www.psu.edu/bulletins/bluebook/major/c_e.htm)
>
> 3. North Carolina State University (http://www.ce.ncsu.edu)
>
> 4. Purdue University (https://engineering.purdue.edu/CE)
>
> 5. Iowa State University (http://www.ccee.iastate.edu)
>
> *in number of bachelor's degrees awarded
>
> Source: American Society for Engineering Education, 2002–03

Postsecondary Training

In addition to completing the core engineering curriculum (including mathematics, science, drafting, and computer applications), students can choose their specialty from the following types of courses: structural analysis; materials design and specification; geology; hydraulics; surveying and design graphics; soil mechanics; and oceanography. Bachelor's degrees can be achieved through a number of programs: a four- or five-year accredited college or university; two years in a community college engineering program plus two or three years in a college or university; or five or six years in a co-op program (attending classes for part of the year and working in an engineering-related job for the rest of the year). About 30 percent of civil engineering students go on to receive a master's degree.

"College engineering programs are difficult, no doubt about it," Joshua says. "Mine required extensive dedication and time to complete the coursework. However if you are interested in the subject matter and dedicated to succeeding, the work does not seem as difficult. College study can be very rewarding, while challenging your limits of stress endurance and self-esteem."

The Accreditation Board for Engineering and Technology (ABET) sets minimum education standards for educational programs in civil engineering. Graduation from an ABET-accredited school is a requirement for becoming licensed in many states, so it is important to select an accredited school. Visit ABET's Web site, http://www.abet.org, for a listing of accredited schools.

Certification and Licensing

The general term in engineering for licensed practitioners is professional engineer (PE). While licensing is usually voluntary for many types of engineering, engineers who approve construction plans are required to be licensed by the state in which the construction will occur. Licensing also ensures employers that their employees meet state legal regulations.

Requirements vary by state, but generally it takes about four to five years to become a licensed PE. States such as California have a two-tier licensing structure, with two years required to become a licensed PE and an additional three years to become a licensed structural engineer, or SE (required to perform work on taller buildings, hospitals, and schools). Students can begin the process while still in college by taking the Fundamentals of Engineering (FE) exam. This is an eight-hour test that covers the basics of everything from mathematics, electronics, chemistry, and physics, to more advanced knowledge of engineering sciences.

The next step to becoming a PE is acquiring four years of progressive engineering experience. Some states require that engineers obtain their experience under the supervision of a PE. After four years, candidates take the Principles and Practice of Engineering (PPE) exam specific to civil engineering (there's one for almost every other major branch of engineering, too). Those who pass the exam are referred to as professional engineers and are accorded all of the privileges and responsibilities that go along with it. Joshua is licensed as a PE by the state of California.

Internships and Volunteerships

Internships are an excellent way to learn more about the demands of a career in civil engineering while you are still in school. Schools requiring an internship usually will set it up with a local or national agency. Internships last between one and two semesters. Students aren't usually paid for their work, but receive credit hours for their participation. The American Society of Civil Engineers offers a list of links to companies that offer intern-

ships to students at its Web site, http:// www.asce.org/careers/internship.cfm.

WHO WILL HIRE ME?

Joshua landed his first civil engineering job while he was still in college—working for John Mitchell, an architect at a small architectural firm in San Luis Obispo. "I got the job," he says, "because I was working in a computer lab on campus at the time, helping to teach a class on Auto-CAD, which was taught as an extended education course for people in the community. One of the people in the course was impressed with my skills, and offered to introduce me to John because he was looking for someone to set up a CAD system in his office. So my first small job on campus turned into a networking opportunity and in turn landed me my first job in the field of architecture and engineering." From his job at John's office, Joshua met two local structural engineers who later hired him to do the same CAD setup in their office. "I worked for these structural engineers for two years as an engineer prior to my graduation from college in 1998," he says.

Slightly more than 40 percent of all civil engineers work for companies involved in engineering consulting services. Nearly one-third work for a government agency at the local, state, or federal level. Construction and manufacturing businesses are also sources of employment, and a small percentage are self-employed, running their own consulting businesses. Approximately 228,000 civil engineers work in the United States.

College career services offices are often the best sources of employment for beginning engineers. Many larger companies send recruiters to college campuses to hold interviews with prospective graduates. Some people get job offers before they even graduate. Those who do not receive offers from the recruiters of large corporations still can expect to move into their profession relatively quickly. There are many smaller companies that don't actively recruit on campus but need young, qualified civil engineers. These positions are posted chiefly at university career services offices, but also in trade journals, in professional association publications, and on the Internet.

You can apply directly to specific companies or government agencies by sending them your resume along with a cover letter detailing your skills and qualifications and why you would like to work for them. The American Society of Civil Engineers publishes a comprehensive list of positions available throughout the United States at its Web site, http://www.asce.org/careers. The Institute of Transportation Engineers also offers job listings at its Web site, http://www.ite.org, and in its monthly magazine, *ITE Journal*. Other engineering-related Web pages provide useful job-hunting information, and allow you to post your resume on their page.

Entry-level jobs usually involve routine work, often as a member of a supervised team. After a year or more (depending on job performance and qualifications), you will become a junior engineer, then an assistant to perhaps one or more super-

vising engineers. Establishment as a professional engineer comes after passing the PE exam.

WHERE CAN I GO FROM HERE?

With at least three to four years of experience under their belts, civil engineers move up to positions of more responsibility, such as managing projects. Transportation engineers with good communication skills will be called on to represent their firm or government at neighborhood meetings where plans are introduced and defended. Other engineers change their area of specialty or become even more focused. For example, with the right training and skills, a transportation planner may move up to a high-tech research position.

Many civil engineers work for government agencies, although it is possible to work as a consultant. For instance, an engineer working at an independent transportation consulting firm may branch off to become self-employed or move up to a more demanding position with a local, state, or federal government agency.

Also, there are those who return to academia to teach high school or college students. For all of these potential opportunities, it is necessary to keep abreast of engineering advancements and trends by reading industry journals and taking courses.

Joshua feels that membership in professional associations is an excellent tool for career advancement. He is a member of national and northern California chapters of the Earthquake Engineering Research

Institute, the Structural Engineers Association of California, and the Structural Engineers Association of Northern California. "I would highly recommend that any new engineer get involved with a professional organization as early as possible in their career—even while in college," he advises. "Most professional organizations have student chapters to help kick-start your career prior to graduation. My involvement in these organizations has made my career advance much more rapidly and has opened many doors for professional development."

WHAT ARE THE SALARY RANGES?

Civil engineers are among the lowest paid in the engineering field; however, their salaries are high when compared to that of workers in many other occupations. The median annual earnings for civil engineers were $66,190 in 2005, according to the U.S. Department of Labor. The lowest paid 10 percent made less than $44,410 per year, and, at the other end of the pay scale, 10 percent earned more than $100,040 annually. Civil engineers working for the federal government had a mean salary of $77,230 in 2005. According to a 2005 survey by the National Association of Colleges and Employers, starting salaries for civil engineers by degree level averaged as follows: bachelor's, $43,679; master's, $48,050; and doctorate, $69,625. As with all occupations, salaries are higher for those with more experience. Top civil engineers earn more than $100,000 a year.

Related Jobs

- airport engineers
- cartographers
- civil engineering educators
- civil engineering technicians
- environmental engineers
- geographic information systems specialists
- geologists
- geophysicists
- hydraulic engineers
- irrigation engineers
- railroad engineers
- sanitary engineers
- structural engineers
- surveying and mapping technicians
- surveyors
- transportation engineers

Civil engineers can usually expect a good benefits package, including paid sick and holiday time, two weeks vacation, personal time, medical coverage, stock options, 401(k) plans, and other perks, depending on the company and industry.

WHAT IS THE JOB OUTLOOK?

The U.S. Department of Labor predicts average employment growth for civil engineers through 2014. There should be a good number of positions available as a result of the need to maintain and repair public works, such as highways, bridges, and water systems. In addition, as the population grows, so does the need for more transportation and pollution control systems, which creates jobs for those who construct these systems. Firms providing management consulting and computer services may also be sources of jobs for civil engineers.

Joshua foresees a strong employment future for civil engineers. "With huge advances in computing technology and material science," he says, "the opportunity to create even more amazing and advanced engineering projects is growing by the day. The major areas of growth include performance-based earthquake-resistant design (high-tech applications to make buildings virtually 'earthquake proof'), environmentally friendly or 'green' design, and highway design (to ease congestion)."

Electrical and Electronics Engineers

SUMMARY

Definition
Electrical and electronics engineers are concerned with developing practical applications of electricity in all its forms. Electrical engineers work with *heavy current* electricity in developing equipment and processes that produce and distribute electricity, such as systems that generate high-power electricity. Electronics engineers work with *light current* electricity in developing virtually anything that uses electricity, from a computer to a digital camera to a satellite.

Salary Range
$47,750 to $73,510 to $114,630+

Educational Requirements
Minimum of a bachelor's degree. Advanced degree recommended.

Certification or Licensing
Required for certain positions

Employment Outlook
Average growth

High School Subjects
Computer science
Mathematics
English (writing/literature)

Personal Interests
Building things
Computers
Figuring out how things work
Fixing things

As an electrical and electronics engineer, Dominique Green has certainly seen his share of challenges since he began working at Accenture, a leading global management consulting, technology services, and outsourcing company.

One of his most challenging projects was with communications giant Verizon. Dominique was responsible for designing and implementing the documentation for a customized trouble-management ticketing and maintenance application designed to replace one of Verizon's older legacy systems.

"A legacy system," Dominique explains, "is essentially an old software application or operating system that is outdated and/or no longer compatible with newer software applications. It also lacks a great deal of enhancements. The documentation I created, which consisted of Server Query Language (SQL), Visual Basic, and some C++ syntax, was used to provide direction for an entire Verizon software development team. It was definitely not an easy task. It required that I have a great deal of provisioning and communication skills to ensure that I could not only create the documentation needed to implement the application, but attend meetings and actually explain and communicate the contents of my documentation and design as well.

"The service I provide as an electrical engineer helped save companies like Verizon time and money by delivering solid technology and business models needed to compete with the next generation of industry leaders. Each of my past and future communications, media, and entertainment clients have received these solutions—giving them the competitive edge they need to grow and expand their business."

WHAT DOES AN ELECTRICAL/ELECTRONICS ENGINEER DO?

Think of the last time your neighborhood experienced a power outage. Things you took for granted such as storing perishable food or heating or cooling your house became impossible. You couldn't even read a book or turn on the television to watch your favorite show. It was pretty difficult to get things done, right? Electricity is truly the blood of modern society. *Electrical and electronics engineers (EEEs)* are the people who keep this electrical "blood" flowing and devise new and creative uses for it in our society.

EEEs use their skills in and understanding of the sciences, engineering, and electricity to develop practical applications of electricity in all its forms. Modern life is unthinkable without the work of electrical and electronics engineers. Their creative ingenuity powers the world. And things aren't changing anytime soon. With the development of new technologies, the widespread use of electronic devices is becoming increasingly prevalent. From pagers to grocery checkout scanners to your neighborhood street lights, this technology is a priceless part of our lives, thanks to the work of EEEs.

Electrical and electronics engineers are distinguished by the comparative strength of the electric currents they work with. Electrical engineers work with *heavy current* electricity in developing equipment and processes that produce and distribute electricity, such as systems that generate high-power electricity. Electronics engineers work with *light current* electricity in developing virtually anything that uses electricity, from a computer to a digital camera to a satellite. However, with recent technological advancements, the line between the two branches is becoming thinner, as each branch uses elements of the other to operate.

EEEs work in many different industries and perform a variety of tasks. Some of the more common industries where EEEs work are consumer electronics, electric power, aerospace, computers, communications, and biomedical technologies. They work in developing things as large as power plants to provide electricity to entire regions of the country, and as small as microprocessors to make your computer run more efficiently. EEEs can be part of a research and development (R&D) team that invents new products and ideas, or part of the design team that actually takes a researcher's concepts and designs the actual product using a computer. EEEs can also be involved in the construction and operation of a design project.

Most engineers choose to specialize in a certain area of electrical and electronics engineering. A complete list of specialties could fill up the rest of this chapter, but some common areas are computer and information engineering, signal processing, electromagnetic compatibility, acoustics, geoscience and remote sensing, lasers and electro-optics, robotics, ultrasonics, ferroelectrics, and biomedical engineering.

Many electronics engineers specialize in the fast-growing area of computer engineering. Computer engineers design the guts of the newest, fastest computers. They use their skills in electronics to develop computer circuitry, information and communications systems, and fundamental computer science applications.

WHAT IS IT LIKE TO BE AN ELECTRICAL/ELECTRONICS ENGINEER?

Dominique Green has been an electrical and electronics engineer since 2001. He currently works as an IT management consultant for Accenture. "My overall goal in working with Accenture," he says, "is to help our clients become a high-per-

Lingo to Learn

ampere The unit of measurement for an electrical current.

capacitor An electrical element used to store electrical energy, consisting of two equally charged conducting surfaces having opposite signs and separated by a dielectric.

circuit A connection of two or more electrical elements to serve a useful function.

dielectric An insulator, or nonconductor of electricity, usually referring to the insulating material between plates of a capacitor.

generator An electromechanical device used to convert mechanical energy into electrical energy.

radiation Energy emitted as electromagnetic waves or subatomic particles from a source or substance.

semiconductor A substance with electrical conductivity, such as germanium or silicon, which is between being a good conductor and a good insulator used in such devices as transistors, diodes, and integrated circuits.

voltage The energy required to move a specific number of electrons across two points.

watt The unit of measurement for electrical power.

formance business and/or government agency."

Although today's engineers wear many hats and are blessed with a great number of abilities, Dominique believes that every engineer must have two important modes:

technical and functional. "The technical," he explains, "is of course the ability to do math and science very well. But then there is the more functional side of engineering, such as creating solutions, designing, problem solving, and working effectively in teams. In my position as an electrical engineer at Accenture, I perform the more functional roles of an engineer. And likewise, I approach my clients and provide solutions based on my engineering background. My strengths in math and science and computer programming have been used to complement my work with clients such as Nextel, Verizon, and federal government agencies."

Dominique's typical day consists of a lot of brainstorming and coming up with solutions that meet his clients' varied needs. "I spend a lot of time provisioning for software upgrades, making changes to our application architectures [the relationships between different applications and operating systems]," he says. "The remainder of my time is spent documenting these changes and responding to questions about my design and troubleshooting in the event that my designs do not work as planned."

Dominique typically works 40 to 60 hours a week. "Since I move around to different projects," he says, "I normally build in time to learn about the project and brainstorm on how to fulfill my obligations and responsibilities in my new role on the project. I have worked weekends to meet deadlines, especially when I do what's called business development work, where Accenture is trying to sell work to a new client."

In many parts of the country, this five-day, 40-hour workweek is still the norm, but it is becoming much less common. Many engineers regularly work five or more hours of overtime a week. Engineers in research and development, or those conducting experiments, often need to work at night or on weekends. Workers who supervise production activities may need to come in during the evenings or on weekends to handle special production requirements. "When I accepted a position with Accenture," Dominique says, "part of my commitment was that I would commit 10 percent overtime to my projects. I actually don't mind the overtime because it gives me a great reason to prepare myself better for each of my projects. Also, it's always hard to imagine doing well on a project without putting in the minimum 10 percent overtime." Many high-tech companies allow flex time, which means that workers can arrange their own schedules within certain time frames.

In addition to the time spent on the job, many engineers also participate in professional associations and pursue additional training during their free time. Dominique is a member of the National Society of Professional Engineers (NSPE) and the Institute of Electrical and Electronics Engineers (IEEE). "NSPE is an organization that guides engineers on how to perform their jobs in an ethical and public-sensitive manner through seminars and industry speakers," he explains. "IEEE is an international organization that links electrical and electronics engineers across the world to share their technologies and insight regarding advancements and innovation around the field of electrical and electronics engineering. Every year, NSPE and IEEE nominate an engineer within their ranks to compete for the National Engineer's Spotlight Award. In 2004, I was fortunate enough to be the recipient." The award was announced during the celebration of National Engineer's Week during the last week in February. "The professional organizations are great because they allow me to experience a less stressful and more interactive part of being an electrical engineer," he says. "Oftentimes, it's also helpful to dialogue with other electrical engineers to discuss some of the new obstacles that affect our discipline and inevitably our careers."

Dominique also dedicates at least two weeks a year to learning a new skill set or updating himself on a previously learned skill set related to communications, wireless communications, leadership skills, communication techniques, goal-setting, and/or networking events. "I also try to attend at least one major function every year that brings electrical engineers across the country together to discuss new technologies and innovation within the field," he says. "It's helpful to stay in tune with the industry so that your knowledge and skills don't become obsolete and force you to pick another career path. I also do computer-based training (CBT), which is offered by my company. CBTs are pretty popular among most companies today because it's an inexpensive way to stay up-to-date on new technologies and information."

Most electrical and electronics engineers work in fairly comfortable environments.

Engineers involved in research and design may work in specially equipped laboratories. Engineers involved in development and manufacturing work in offices and may spend part of their time in production facilities. Dominique works in a high-rise office building and in a project team room. "A project team room," he explains, "is usually a large open area with large desks so that we can lay out designs and client deliverables for review. However, on some projects I've been constrained to a much smaller working area—about the size of an elevator with no windows. Needless to say I always prefer the large project room. But occasionally, I'll be on a project where the client is able to provide us with cube space, which offers some privacy."

Depending on the type of work one does, there may be extensive travel. Engineers involved in field service and sales spend a significant time traveling to see clients. Engineers working for large corporations may travel to other plants and manufacturing companies, both around the country and at foreign locations. In the beginning of his career, Dominique hardly ever traveled, "but as time went on and there became a client-need for increased visibility," he says, "I soon found myself traveling about 85 percent of the time. It's been great to travel and see different parts of the country."

Some electrical and electronics engineers are self-employed. Mary Ellen Randall is the owner of Ascot Technologies, a software and system integration company that specializes in advanced Web solutions and wireless software applications. "We allow realtors to look up information on houses for sale from their cell phone," Mary Ellen explains. "We also allow emergency medical technicians to collect all sorts of information while they are on a call and transmit their condition while en route. It speeds up processing the patient when the ambulance arrives at the hospital."

Owning your own business has both positives and negatives. "The positives are that you can choose what you work on and pick things you find most interesting," Mary Ellen says. "It also provides great freedom to balance family matters. I work even more as a business owner, but can schedule it around doctor's appointments, children's sporting events, and school plays. The challenge is that the buck stops here! As the owner, you are responsible to make payroll and to make sure there is a follow-on project when one finishes up. You must keep an eye on both the short-term goals and the long-term goals. This can be very exciting though."

DO I HAVE WHAT IT TAKES TO BE AN ELECTRICAL/ ELECTRONICS ENGINEER?

Accuracy and precision are the qualities intrinsic to success as an electrical/electronics engineer. This means attending to details, whether the project is a microscopic computer chip or the largest motorized telescope in the world. Besides the obvious professional reasons why precision and accuracy are important in today's fast-paced world, there is an even simpler, more practical reason for crossing every 't' and dotting every 'i'—many projects involve high-voltage electricity;

any error in precision or accuracy resulting in a malfunction also has the potential to be life-threatening. It certainly helps if the electrical/electronics engineers are analytical and systematic in their application of knowledge, from the routine and mundane tasks all the way up to the more extraordinary and unique experiments.

A natural curiosity and interest in science, electronics, and electricity will, of course, pay off in the long run for EEEs, especially when a test or experiment has become frustrating and a great deal of patience is required. In those times, the engineer's inquisitive nature will help to keep him or her involved in the project long after someone else might have given up.

Depending on the industry in which an engineer works, he or she may be involved with the same project for many months, even years; or he or she may be working on different projects every day. This can affect an individual's outlook, so it's important that EEEs be realistic when choosing their area of expertise.

For those students who believe that engineering and other scientific jobs are all about numbers and formulas, they're in for a big surprise. Communicating ideas—whether in the laboratory to other scientists and engineers, or in the boardroom to marketing professionals—is an essential part of the EEE's job. Report- and grant-writing, formal and informal presentations, and concise daily verbal transactions are all fundamental skills and, while they may not always be advertised as such, they are often what distinguishes a mediocre engineer from a successful one.

To Be a Successful Electrical or Electronics Engineer, You Should . . .

- have good computer skills
- be able to communicate your ideas to others
- be attentive to detail
- have patience and tenacity to solve difficult and sometimes complex problems
- be willing to travel

Finally, the nature of the electrical/electronics engineer's work necessitates that he or she travel to construction sites, laboratories, and/or factories, to name but a few destinations, in order to inspect a machine, meet a client, or gauge the amount of work needed to complete a project.

HOW DO I BECOME AN ELECTRICAL/ELECTRONICS ENGINEER?

Dominique Green says that he has always been interested in engineering. "I've always been fascinated with science, math, experiments, and the special effects that come along with putting them together," he says. "I can remember being a youth growing up completely fascinated by science, math, and with programs like *Mr. Wizard* and the many educational programs on PBS. It's funny because I was given an opportu-

nity to work with PBS on one of my many projects with Accenture."

Education

High School

High school classes in mathematics, science, and computer courses are the best way to prepare for further study in electrical/electronics engineering. In fact, the more solid the foundation in the following classes, the easier it will be to assimilate more advanced knowledge later on: algebra, geometry, calculus, trigonometry, physics, chemistry, and computer science. This latter subject is absolutely crucial; the importance of developing top-flight computer skills, from programming to the Internet, cannot be stressed enough. In addition, English, art, speech, and foreign language classes will broaden your range of knowledge and potential applications of your scientific learning. For example, an electronic device might have a decidedly popular and lucrative application in the arts, e.g., an advanced listening system for public libraries and art museums. The EEE who hasn't been exposed to these venues might never think of applying the new device to that area, thus missing the possibility to extend his development to other disciplines. Also, a candidate who possesses good communications skills is much more likely to advance into supervisory and administrative positions where dealing with clients and the public is a crucial part of the job.

High school students are also encouraged to participate in as many extracurricular activities as possible. "As a high school student I worked to involve myself in several extracurricular activities," Dominique says. "Some of my favorite extracurricular activities were engineering competitions and school science fairs. I also joined and held leadership positions in many of my high school's clubs and organizations such as the math club, science club, CHROME (Cooperating Hampton Roads Organization for Minorities in Engineering), TAG (Talented and Gifted), and many other after-school clubs."

Internships are another excellent way to prepare for the field while you are still in high school. While in high school, Dominique participated in hands-on experiments in programs like BEAMS (Becoming Enthusiastic About Math and Science), which was sponsored by the Thomas Jefferson National Laboratory (a research facility managed by the U.S. Department of Energy). "While in that internship I was able to actually meet Secretary O'Leary, who served under President Clinton," he says. "We took several pictures, which still hang at my mother's home." After BEAMS, Dominique participated in a series of internships with Thomas Jefferson National Laboratory, NASA, and the Newport News Shipbuilding, which, Dominique says, helped him to solidify his commitment to math, science, and engineering. "Each internship," he says, "brought with it a deeper understanding of engineering and a stronger understanding of the work required to achieve a career in it—most of which came from my questioning then-professional engineers."

Postsecondary Training

A bachelor's degree in electrical and electronics engineering is generally regarded as the minimum requirement for positions as professional EEEs. Dominique has a bachelor of science degree in electrical and electronics engineering with a concentration in wireless communications and global positioning systems. Some electrical and electronics engineers have degrees in other disciplines. Mary Ellen Randall, for example, has a bachelor of arts degree in mathematics and a master of science degree in computer science. She started as a software engineer, but moved into electronics through experience on the job.

Students should enroll in a four- or five-year degree program at an approved college or university; for information on whether or not a particular program is accredited, contact the Accreditation Board for Engineering and Technology (http://www.abet.org). Currently, there are 150 colleges and universities that offer such programs. Admission requirements generally are strict, with schools accepting only those students with excellent academic records and top scores on college entrance examinations like the SAT (Scholastic Aptitude Test). Competition for admission to the best schools is tough, as is competition for national- and school-sponsored scholarships.

First-year students take general science and math classes like chemistry, physics, and calculus, plus general introduction courses to the field, plus one or more electives. Most colleges and universities require that students take an English composition or technical writing class.

Advice from Mary Ellen Randall to Women Interested in Engineering

Only 16.8 percent of electrical and electronics engineers are women, according to the U.S. Census Bureau. But this percentage is increasing thanks to the work of the Institute of Electrical and Electronics Engineers' Women in Engineering, the Society of Women Engineers, and other professional organizations. Mary Ellen Randall has the following advice for young women who are interested in engineering careers:

- "Seek out other women with similar interests. There are some unique challenges we face as women and engineers. It helps to bounce ideas off other women, particularly when they pertain to balancing work and life. These kindred spirits have been a huge help to me over the years."

- "Seek out mentors. Make sure you have at least one mentor at any point in time. The mentors may be men or women, but they will help you navigate organizational culture. A good mentor also gives you candid feedback so you can continually improve."

- "Keep your skills current and become an expert. If you take time off with your children, make sure to keep up on the latest technological developments. This will give you better problem-solving skills when you return and you will feel great personal satisfaction. People will seek you out for your opinion and knowledge."

Second-year students typically take more advanced science and math classes like differential equations and numerical analysis, and begin to study some field-related classes such as fundamental electronics, circuit analysis, and electromagnetic practice.

Students in their third and fourth years of study begin to specialize, taking classes such as advanced electronics, quantum mechanics, lightwave electronics, digital information circuits, applied radio wave engineering, electrochemistry, engineering ethics, and image engineering. It's a good idea for students to consider early on in their academic careers the area or specialty in which they are most interested, so that they can begin to tailor their education to this niche as soon as possible.

Certification or Licensing

Certification in electrical and electronics engineering is called licensing. Licensed engineers are called PEs (professional engineers). While licensing is generally voluntary, it may be mandatory for some jobs today. Consultants in electrical and electronics engineering are required by law to be PEs. Some employers want to be able to sell their company to clients as one containing only professional engineers. Licensing also assures employers that they meet state legal regulations.

Requirements vary by state, but generally it takes about four to five years to become a licensed PE. Many students begin the process while still in college by taking the Fundamentals of Engineering

(FE) exam. This eight-hour test covers the basics—everything from mathematics, electronics, chemistry, and physics, to more advanced engineering topics.

The next step to becoming a PE is obtaining four years of progressive engineering experience. Some states require that candidates obtain experience under the supervision of a PE. After four years of experience, candidates can take the Principles and Practice of Engineering (PPE) exam specific to electrical engineering (there's one for almost every other major branch of engineering, too). Candidates who pass this final examination are then officially referred to as PEs.

Internships and Volunteerships

Colleges and universities that require an internship as part of their program usually will set up an internship with a local industry. The purpose of these internships, which last between one and two semesters, is to provide students with a "test-run," as well as valuable experiences and networking contacts. Students get the opportunity to see whether the field or specific job is really what they want to be working toward. Often, students redefine their career goals based on their firsthand exposure to the position or workplace. As mentioned earlier, these internships are usually unpaid; instead, students receive credit hours for their work.

The Institute of Electrical and Electronics Engineers (IEEE) offers a variety of internship opportunities, as well as links to other organizations with internship programs. Visit the IEEE's Web site, http://www.ieee.org, for more information.

WHO WILL HIRE ME?

Many colleges and universities with accredited programs are visited yearly by recruiters who are eager to hire qualified graduates. At first, of course, you will have to take part in on-campus interviews during the end of your last semester.

With electrical and electronics engineers being the largest branch of engineering, accounting for roughly 292,000 jobs, there are good employment opportunities for young, skilled, and industrious engineers. Those who do not receive offers from the recruiters of large corporations still can expect to move into their profession relatively quickly. Many smaller companies don't actively recruit, but need qualified electrical and electronics engineers. These positions can be found in trade journals, at your university placement center, in professional association newsletters, and on the Internet. You'll find only a small percentage of the available entry-level jobs in electrical and electronics engineering in newspapers.

Electrical and electronics engineers are employed by a variety of industries, such as manufacturing, computer, aerospace, general engineering and consulting firms, communications and utilities firms, academia, and at government agencies like the Departments of Defense and Energy.

According to Dominique Green, "entering the workforce as an engineer is probably one of the biggest challenges anyone can face. The world of real work and time-sensitive decisions are enough to make even the most steady engineers feel uneasy. This is doubly the case when you know that safety is at stake. As an engineer and a public servant, I always keep one frame of mind which gets me through, and that is hard work complemented with balance. The other thing I keep in mind is to always know who my customer and client are so that I can customize my skills and abilities toward succeeding with that customer/client. One of the saddest things an engineer can do, which will jeopardize his or her career, is to forget that they are providing a service to the public and to their customer."

WHERE CAN I GO FROM HERE?

Most entry-level engineers with bachelor's degrees begin their careers by taking positions as junior assistants with minimal responsibility. They generally report to a more experienced engineer, completing tasks and projects as assigned and gradually accruing experience and increased responsibilities. Simultaneously, they begin to ascend the career ladder. Many EEEs find that their ascension to the more coveted positions is more rapid if they return to school for advanced degrees after working for four or five years. With 5 to 10 years of experience and/or advanced training or licensing, he or she can hope to advance to the positions of supervising engineer, chief engineer, or plant manager. Those hoping for top-level promotions are also those who are the most business savvy; candidates for these positions should consider honing their business skills either by returning once again to school for courses in business administration, or by attending lectures and seminars on developing management skills.

Other paths open to EEEs include teaching and consulting work. Many EEEs take teaching positions at high schools, colleges, and universities, enjoying the rewards of sharing their passion for science and electronics with young people. Still others work for themselves or private companies as consultants. Called in to offer the benefit of their expertise on a project-by-project basis, consultants may work for one company or several, for anywhere from a day to several months or even years. Often, consulting work leads to offers of permanent work. EEEs certainly aren't limited to their own specialty; on the contrary, their unique combination of skills qualifies them to work in many other fields, including environmental control, law, medicine, biomedical specialties, as well as other branches of engineering, like chemical, civil, or mechanical.

WHAT ARE THE SALARY RANGES?

The average starting salary for electrical and electronics engineers varies depending on the field in which they work. The average starting salary for electrical and electronics engineers with a bachelor's degree was $51,888 in 2005, according to a salary survey by the National Association of Colleges and Employers. Electrical and electronics engineers with a master's degree averaged around $64,416 in their first jobs after graduation. And those with a Ph.D. had average starting salaries of

$80,206. Yearly bonuses can increase salary even more.

The U.S. Department of Labor reports that the median annual salary for electrical engineers was $73,510 in 2005. The lowest paid engineers earned less than $47,750 and the highest paid engineers earned more than $110,570 annually. Electronics engineers earned salaries in 2005 that ranged from less than $50,090 to $114,630 or more, with a median salary of $78,030.

Electrical and electronics engineers can usually expect a good benefits package, including paid sick and holiday time, two weeks vacation (and more, the longer they stay with one company), personal time, medical coverage, stock options, 401(k) plans, and many other perks, depending on the company and industry.

WHAT IS THE JOB OUTLOOK?

The U.S. Department of Labor predicts average employment growth for electrical and electronics engineers through 2014, so opportunities for qualified engineers should be good. The growing consumer, business, and government demand for improved computers and communications equipment will create job opportunities for electrical and electronics engineers. Another area of demand should be the development of electrical and electronic goods for the consumer market. The strongest job growth, however, is likely to be in nonmanufacturing industries. This is because more and more firms are contracting for electronic engineering

Related Jobs

- aerospace engineers
- avionics engineers and technicians
- broadcast engineers
- cable engineers
- communications equipment technicians
- electrical and electronics engineering educators
- electrical test engineers
- electrical-design engineers
- electronic sales technicians
- electronics engineering technicians
- electronics service technicians
- electronics technicians
- electronics-design engineers
- electronics-research engineers
- illuminating engineers
- instrumentation technicians
- power-transmission engineers
- printed circuit designers
- studio operations engineers

services from consulting and service firms. Biotechnology is also a growth market, according to Mary Ellen Randall. "Many engineers are learning more about the field so they can apply their skills there," she says.

Engineers will need to stay on top of changes within the electronics industry and will need additional training throughout their careers to learn new technologies. Economic trends and conditions within the global marketplace have become increasingly more important. In the past, most electronics production was done in the United States or by American-owned companies. During the 1990s, this changed, and the electronics industry entered an era of global production. Worldwide economies and production trends will have a larger impact on U.S. production, and companies that cannot compete technologically may not succeed. Job security is no longer a sure thing, and many engineers can expect to make significant changes in their careers at least once. However, since EEEs work in so many different industries, they have the ability to move more freely should one industry be suffering more than others. Of course, they may have to undertake additional training to get up to speed in the new industry.

Engineering Technicians

SUMMARY

Definition
Engineering technicians use engineering, science, and mathematics to help engineers and other professionals in research and development, quality control, manufacturing, and many other fields.

Alternative Job Titles
Varies by specialty

Salary Range
$34,000 to $44,830 to $73,000+

Educational Requirements
Some postsecondary training; associate degree in engineering technology recommended

Certification or Licensing
Recommended

Employment Outlook
About as fast as the average

High School Subjects
Chemistry
Computer science
Mathematics
Physics
Technical/shop

Personal Interests
Building things
Computers
Figuring out how things work

It's early morning and Leo Saenz, a lab supervisor of construction materials testing engineering technicians, is not in the office even five minutes before the phone begins ringing off the hook. On the line: a contractor calling to complain that one of Leo's technician/inspectors is being too critical regarding inspections of some concrete footings being used to hold up structural steel columns at a construction site for a large retail store.

After some discussion, Leo decides to travel to the job site to meet with the unhappy contractor. One look at the con-crete footings tells Leo that his inspector was doing a good job of interpreting the job specifications. He shows the contractor that his technician was using the guidelines established in the project specifications and plans correctly and that the technician was using sound judgment in making sure the bottoms of the concrete footings were stable and acceptable prior to being filled with concrete.

With the issue solved, the contractor happy, and work at the construction site back on schedule, Leo heads back to the office to handle paperwork, monitor his technicians, and be ready to check on other potential problems as they arise.

WHAT DOES AN ENGINEERING TECHNICIAN DO?

Engineering technicians assist engineers, scientists, and other workers in a variety of tasks. They are highly trained workers with strong backgrounds in a specialized technological field, such as aerospace, civil, materials, and many other types of engineering. In short, engineering technicians can be found supporting engineers and other workers in any engineering discipline. They bridge the gap between the engineers who design the products, structures, and machines, and those who implement them.

Engineering technicians play a role in almost every part of our daily lives. We can thank engineering technicians (along with engineers, scientists, and other workers) for safer cars and planes, drugs that work effectively when we are sick, well-constructed buildings and highways, clean water and air, and the computer games we play for hours, among many other things that we take for granted.

Approximately 478,000 engineering technicians are employed in the United States, according to the U.S. Department of Labor. Some of the major technician specialties include electrical and electronics engineering, civil engineering, industrial engineering, and mechanical engineering. The following paragraphs provide more information on these and other engineering technician specialties.

Aeronautical and aerospace engineering technicians design, construct, test, operate, and maintain the basic structures of aircraft and spacecraft, as well as propulsion and control systems. They work with scientists and aeronautical aerospace engineers. Many aeronautical and aerospace engineering technicians assist engineers in preparing equipment drawings, diagrams, blueprints, and scale models. They collect information, make computations, and perform laboratory tests.

Biomedical engineering technicians use engineering and life science principles to help biomedical engineers and scientists research biological aspects of animal and human life. They help design and construct health care instruments and devices and apply engineering principles to the study of human systems.

Chemical engineering technicians assist chemists and chemical engineers in the research, development, testing, and manufacturing of chemicals and chemical-based products.

Civil engineering technicians help civil engineers design, plan, and build public as well as private works to meet the community's needs. Civil engineers and technicians work together for the community, providing better, faster transportation; designing and developing highways, airports, and railroads; improving the environment; and constructing buildings, bridges, and space platforms. These engineering professionals work in one of the seven main civil engineering areas: structural, geotechnical, environmental, water resources, transportation, construction, and urban and community planning. The work is closely related, so a technician might work in one or many of these areas. A variety of subspecialties are available, including structural engineering technicians, geotechnical engineering technicians, materials technicians, urban and community planning technicians, research engineering technician, sales engineering technician, transportation technicians, highway technicians, rail and waterway technicians, and construction engineering technicians.

Electrical and electronics engineering technicians work individually or with engineers to help design, produce, improve, maintain, test, and repair a wide range of electronic equipment. Equipment varies from consumer goods like televisions, computers, and home entertainment components, to industrial, military, and medical goods, such as radar and laser equipment. Electronic devices play a part in practically every business and even many leisure activities found around the globe. Such diverse activities as NASA space missions, sophisticated medical testing procedures, and car and airplane travel would be impossible without the use of electronic equipment. The products made by the electronics industry can be divided into four basic categories: government products (which include missile and space guidance systems, communications systems, medical technology, and traffic control devices), industrial products (which include large-scale computers, radio and television broadcasting equipment, telecommunications equipment, and electronic office equipment), consumer products (which include televisions, DVD players, and radios), and components (which comprises the smaller pieces that make up all electronics, such as capacitors, switches, transistors, relays, and amplifiers). Subspecialties in this career field include electronics development technicians, electronics drafters, cost-estimating technicians, electronics manufacturing and production technicians, and electronics service and maintenance technicians.

Environmental engineering technicians help environmental engineers and scientists design, build, and maintain systems to control waste streams produced by municipalities or private industry. Environmental engineering technicians typically focus on one of three areas: air, land, or water.

Industrial engineering technicians assist industrial engineers in their duties: they collect and analyze data and make recommendations for the efficient use of personnel, materials, and machines to produce goods or to provide services. They may study the time, movements, and methods a worker uses to accomplish daily tasks in production, maintenance, or clerical areas. The kind of work done by industrial engineering technicians varies depending on the size and type of company for which they work. A variety of subspecialties are available, including methods engineering technicians, materials handling technicians, plant layout technicians, work measurement technicians, time-study technicians, production-control technicians, and inventory control technicians.

Materials engineering technicians work in support of materials engineers and scientists. These jobs involve the production, quality control, and experimental study of metals, ceramics, glass, plastics, semiconductors, and composites (combinations of these materials). Metallurgical technicians may conduct tests on the properties of the aforementioned materials, develop and modify test procedures and equipment, analyze data, and prepare reports.

Mechanical engineering technicians work under the direction of mechanical engineers to design, build, maintain, and modify many kinds of machines, mechanical devices, and tools. They work in a wide range of industries and in a variety of specific jobs within every industry. Technicians may specialize in any one of many areas, including biomedical equipment, measurement and control, products manufacturing, solar energy, turbo machinery, energy resource technology, and engineering materials and technology.

Petroleum engineering technicians help petroleum engineers and scientists improve petroleum drilling technology, maximize field production, and provide technical assistance.

Robotics technicians assist robotics engineers in a wide variety of tasks relating to the design, development, production, testing, operation, repair, and maintenance of robots and robotic devices.

Engineering technicians work in a variety of conditions depending on their field of specialization. Technicians who specialize in design may find that they spend most of their time at the drafting board or computer. Those who specialize in manufacturing may spend some time at a desk but also spend considerable time in manufacturing areas or shops.

Lingo to Learn

computer-aided drafting (CAD) Also called computer-aided design, or computer-aided design drafting; the use of computer software to draw or design such items as machine parts, products, or even buildings.

computer-aided manufacturing (CAM) The use of computers to run the machines that make specific parts and products.

computer-integrated manufacturing (CIM) An overall approach to planning, manufacturing, and selling and distributing products, where computers are used to track raw materials, produce the products, and track inventory and shipping in order to increase efficiency and reduce costs and inventory.

nanotechnology Controlling individual atoms and molecules to create devices such as computer chips that are thousands of times smaller than what current technologies permit.

schematic A diagram, plan, or drawing created and used by engineers.

thermodynamics The science concerned with the relations between heat and mechanical energy or work, and the conversion of one into the other.

Conditions also vary according to industry. Some industries require technicians to work in foundries, die-casting rooms, machine shops, assembly areas, or punch-press areas. Most of these areas, however, are well lighted, heated, and ventilated. Moreover, most industries employing mechanical engineering technicians have strong safety programs.

WHAT IS IT LIKE TO BE AN ENGINEERING TECHNICIAN?

Leo Saenz is a lab supervisor of construction materials testing engineering technicians for HBC/Terracon in Austin, Texas. He has been an engineering technician for 24 years. "My primary duty," he explains, "is supervising technicians, and my secondary duty is to perform inspections and materials tests on construction sites."

On a typical day, Leo gets to his office anywhere from 6:00 to 6:30 A.M. "When I first get to the office," he says, "I check to make sure all our technicians have gotten to their assignments. Between our dispatcher and myself we send our technicians out in the field to perform concrete, soils, hot mix, masonry, structural steel, through firestop systems, pier/cassion, wood truss, reinforcing steel, and post tension cable inspections. A lot of our projects start very early in the morning or during the night. I talk with our dispatcher to make sure there are no problems, and then I go to my office to check for any messages and e-mails. After that, I spend the rest of my day checking on how jobs are going; reviewing and signing paperwork; handling phone calls from irate contractors, owners, or developers; and addressing any problem situations that come up during the day. On occasion, when our schedule is overbooked, I go out into the field to do either some concrete, soils, reinforcing steel, or hot mix inspection. Then, late in the afternoon, I coordinate with the dispatcher to make sure all upcoming work is scheduled and covered for the next day."

To Be a Successful Engineering Technician, You Should . . .

- be able to communicate and work well with others to solve problems
- be curious about how things work
- have an understanding of math and the sciences
- enjoy using tools and electronic equipment; have strong manual dexterity
- be enthusiastic about keeping up with technological advances
- be very detail oriented and accurate in your work
- have problem solving skills

Engineering technicians may be required to travel to different states or even different countries as a requirement of their jobs. Leo spends nearly all of his time working within a 100-mile radius of Austin, Texas, his employer's headquarters.

DO I HAVE WHAT IT TAKES TO BE AN ENGINEERING TECHNICIAN?

Kurt Schuler, General Manager of the American Society of Certified Engineering Technicians (ASCET), and an engineering technician for 31 years, believes ethics is the most important professional quality for engineering technicians, "since," he explains, "many of the jobs performed by engineering technicians affect the health, safety, and welfare of the general public." He notes that other important professional qualities are, "attention to detail, a determination to always look for better ways to do things or improve products, and a quest for continuing education to keep up with changes in the state of the art."

All engineering technicians are relied upon for solutions and must express their ideas clearly in speech and in writing. Good communication skills are important for a technician in the writing and presenting of reports and plans. These skills are also important for working alongside other technicians and professionals, people who are often from many different backgrounds and skilled in varying areas of engineering.

Engineering technicians need mathematical and mechanical aptitude. They must understand abstract concepts and apply scientific principles to problems in the shop, laboratory, or work site.

Many tasks assigned to engineering technicians require patience and methodical, persistent work. Good technicians work well with their hands, paying close attention to every detail of a project. Some technicians are bored by the repetitiveness of some tasks, while others enjoy the routine. "I think that the most important qualities for an engineering technician are patience and a willingness to learn," Leo Saenz says. "One has to always keep an open mind and be willing to get along with others both in the office and the field.

Most of what we learn is by trial and error. This is a very interesting field, but one in which it takes many years to master. There is nothing too difficult in what we do, and it is very repetitious at times, so what we are looking for are dependable, energetic, and easygoing people who are willing to go out and work long hours."

Individuals planning to advance beyond the technician's level should be willing to and capable of pursuing some form of higher education.

HOW DO I BECOME AN ENGINEERING TECHNICIAN?
Education
High School

Preparation for this career begins in high school. Although entrance requirements to associate programs vary somewhat from school to school, mathematics and physical science form the backbone of a good preparatory curriculum. Classes should include algebra, geometry, science, trigonometry, calculus, chemistry, mechanical drawing, shop, and physics. Because computers have become essential for engineering technicians, computer courses are also important.

English and speech courses provide invaluable experience in improving verbal and written communication skills. Since some technicians go on to become technical writers or teachers, and since all of them need to be able to explain technical matter clearly and concisely, communication skills are important.

Top Colleges: Engineering Technology Degrees Awarded

1. Ferris State University (Big Rapids, Michigan)
2. Purdue University School of Technology (West Lafayette, Indiana)
3. Wentworth Institute of Technology (Boston)
4. Indiana University
5. Purdue University–Indianapolis
6. DeVry University–Phoenix
7. Rochester Institute of Technology (Rochester, New York)
8. Texas A&M University (College Station, Texas)
9. University of Southern Mississippi (Hattiesburg, Mississippi)
10. State University of New York Institute of Technology–Utica

Source: ASEE Profiles of Engineering and Engineering Technology Colleges, 2003 Edition

Postsecondary Training

While some current engineering technicians enter the field without formal academic training, it is increasingly difficult to do so. Most employers are interested in hiring graduates with at least a two-year degree in engineering technology. Technical institutes, community colleges, vocational schools, and universities all offer this course of study.

The Technology Accreditation Commission of the Accreditation Board for Engineering and Technology (http:// www.abet.org) accredits engineering technology programs.

Some engineering technicians decide to pursue advancement in their field by becoming engineer technologists. Others decide to branch off into research and development or become engineers. These higher-level and higher-paid positions typically require the completion of a bachelor's degree in engineering technology (for engineering technologists) or at least a bachelor's degree in engineering (for technicians interested in research and development and becoming engineers).

Certification or Licensing

Certification and licensing requirements vary by specialty. Check with the your state's department of labor and professional associations within your field for further information.

Many engineering technicians choose to become certified by the National Institute for Certification in Engineering Technologies. To become certified, you must combine a specific amount of job-related experience with a written examination. Certifications are offered at several levels of expertise. Such certification is generally voluntary, although obtaining certification shows a high level of commitment and dedication that employers find highly desirable.

Electronics engineering technicians may obtain voluntary certification from the International Society of Certified Electronics Technicians and the Electronics Technicians Association International. This certification is regarded as a demonstration of professional dedication, determination, and know-how.

Engineering technicians are encouraged to become affiliated with professional groups, such as the ASCET, that offer continuing education sessions for members. Kurt Schuler believes that membership in organizations such as ASCET offer technicians "the ability to network with their peers in not only their discipline, but with those in other disciplines, as well as continued professional development and training."

Additionally, some engineering technicians may be required to belong to unions.

Internships and Volunteerships

Community college and technical school students may be able to secure off-quarter or part-time internships with local employers through their college placement office. Internships for people not in school are difficult to find. You should look in the help wanted sections of local newspapers and magazines in search of opportunities. You might also contact the personnel department of potential employers and governmental agencies for information. Some internship opportunities may be included in job lists published by professional organizations and associations.

You should also pursue part-time and summer positions. It's a great way to learn more about your prospective career.

WHO WILL HIRE ME?

Leo Saenz landed his first job for Brytest, a geotechnical civil engineering firm in Bryan, Texas, in 1981. "I ran a satellite office and performed concrete and soils tests and inspections," he says.

Most technical schools, community colleges, and universities have career services offices. Companies actively recruit employees while they are still in school or are nearing graduation. Because these job services are the primary source of entry-level jobs for engineering technicians, you should check out a school's placement rate for your specific field before making a final decision about attending.

Another way to obtain employment is through direct contact with a particular company. It is best to write to the personnel department and include a resume summarizing your education and experience. If the company has an appropriate opening, a company representative will schedule an interview with you. There are also many excellent public and commercial employment organizations that can help graduates obtain jobs appropriate to their training and experience.

Newspaper want ads and employment services are other methods of getting jobs. Professional or trade magazines often have job listings and can be good sources for job seekers. Professional associations compile information on job openings and publish job lists. For example, the International Society of Certified Electronics Technicians offers lists of job openings around the country at its Web site. Information about job openings can also be found in trade magazines. Professional organizations are also good for networking with other technicians and are up to date on industry advancement, changes, and areas of employment.

WHERE CAN I GO FROM HERE?

As engineering technicians remain with a company, they become more valuable to the employer. Opportunities for advancement are available if you are willing to accept greater responsibilities either by specializing in a specific field, taking on more technically complex assignments, or assuming supervisory duties. Some technicians advance by moving into technical sales or customer relations. Others pursue advanced education to become engineering technologists or engineers.

WHAT ARE THE SALARY RANGES?

The earnings of engineering technicians vary widely depending on skills and experience, the type of work, geographical location, and other factors. The U.S. Department of Labor reports the following median earnings for engineering technicians by specialty in 2005: aerospace engineering, $52,450; civil engineering, $39,210; electrical and electronic engineering, $48,040; environmental engineering, $39,810; and mechanical engineering, $44,830. Salaries ranged from less than $34,000 to $73,000 or more annually.

Engineering technicians generally receive premium pay for overtime work on Sundays and holidays and for evening and nightshift work. Most employers offer benefits packages that include paid holidays, paid vacations, sick days, and health insurance. Companies may also

offer pension and retirement plans, profit sharing, 401(k) plans, tuition assistance programs, and release time for additional education.

WHAT IS THE JOB OUTLOOK?

According to the *Occupational Outlook Handbook*, employment of engineering technicians is expected to increase about as fast as the average for all occupations through 2014. Computer-aided design allows individual technicians to increase productivity, thereby limiting job growth. Those with training in sophisticated technologies and those with degrees in technology will have the best employment opportunities. Faster than average employment growth is predicted for environmental engineering technicians as a

---

Related Jobs

- computer-aided design drafters and technicians
- construction workers
- drafters
- engineering technology educators
- fluid power technicians
- geological technicians
- instrumentation technicians
- iron and steel industry workers
- laboratory testing technicians
- tool designers

result of increasing focus on the protection of the environment.

Kurt Schuler predicts that the future for the engineering profession is limitless. "The infrastructure," he explains, "of this country needs a major update and automation is continually changing the way we live and do business and will continue to do so for many years. Just these two areas require engineers and engineering technicians from almost every discipline because almost every change in one discipline effects that of another."

Environmental Engineers

SUMMARY

Definition
Environmental engineers design, build, and maintain systems to reduce or prevent damage to the environment by municipal or industrial wastes.

Alternative Job Titles
Public health engineer
Sanitary engineer
Waste management engineer

Salary Range
$42,570 to $68,090 to $104,610+

Educational Requirements
Minimum of a bachelor's degree. Advanced degree recommended.

Certification or Licensing
Recommended

Employment Outlook
Much faster than the average

High School Subjects
Biology
Chemistry
Earth science
English (writing/literature)
Mathematics
Physics

Personal Interests
Building things
Environment
Science

One of the most interesting projects that environmental engineer Jennifer Puffer has worked on was improving the quality of water for the 300,000 people who live in the Des Moines, Iowa, metropolitan area.

Her employer, Des Moines Water Works (DMWW), gets its water from the Des Moines and Raccoon Rivers, but both of these rivers flow through a large agricultural area before they reach Des Moines. "The water quality in these rivers is impacted by the agricultural practices that occur in their watersheds," Jennifer explains. "The main contaminant is nitrate that comes from fertilizers used on crops. The amount of nitrate in drinking water is regulated by the federal government because at high levels nitrate can cause adverse health effects. The levels of nitrate in the rivers regularly exceeded the amount allowed in drinking water."

To solve the problem, the DMWW installed an ion exchange system at its drinking water treatment plant that removed nitrate from the water. However, this system is expensive to operate, and Jennifer's assignment was to come up with a plan to reduce the nitrate levels in the river so the system would not have to be used at all. "The challenge this posed," says Jennifer, "was working with the farmers along these rivers to help them understand how their farming practices impacted the rivers and what things they could do to protect the water quality in the rivers. We worked with a few professors from the local university who had been studying the transport of nitrate and asked them to share their research findings with the farmers. The information helped everyone better understand how their own activities affected the water quality in the rivers. The farmers were encouraged to use their nitrate fertilizer only during times of the year when the crop actually needed it and to only apply the amount that was needed. These efforts would help reduce the amount of nitrate that entered the rivers while not reducing the farmers' crop yields—a win for all involved."

While the efforts mentioned above have been completed, Jennifer says it will take some time before it is known if their work was successful in reducing the nitrate level in the rivers. "The process we went through has already been valuable in that it allowed a relationship to be built between our utility and the agricultural community in the watersheds," she says. "We will be in a better position to work together down the road as other obstacles arise."

WHAT DOES AN ENVIRONMENTAL ENGINEER DO?

Environmental engineers are responsible for the systems that are basic to our survival—clean air and water, and treatment of wastes. Environmental engineering is an exceptionally diverse field. Environmental engineers work in many different circumstances and concentrate on many different challenges. Some develop systems to purify water and wastewater. Others design systems to dispose of hazardous waste. Still others are responsible for developing and enforcing environmental regulations. No matter where they work, however, all environmental engineers use scientific principles to design, implement, and maintain systems that protect or restore the environment.

In order to design systems, environmental engineers must combine knowledge from various disciplines. They must understand biology, chemistry, architecture, and economics. An environmental engineer must, for example, know how various chemicals will behave when released into groundwater or soil, how they might affect living organisms, and how long they may take to degrade. The same environmental engineer must know how to design an effective system for removing chemicals or for preventing them from leaking into the environment in the first place. Finally, the engineer must be able to design cost-effective systems, using materials that are both reliable and affordable.

Because environmental engineers must have such a breadth of knowledge, most specialize in one of the many distinct areas of environmental engineering, including air pollution control, hazardous waste management, industrial hygiene, public health engineering, radiation protection, solid waste management, water supply engineering, and wastewater control. Depending on where they work, environmental engineers may concentrate on regulatory compliance, regulatory testing and enforcement, remediation, or research.

Environmental engineers who are responsible for helping companies comply with environmental regulations and design systems that enable their clients or employers to dispose of waste and emissions in a responsible manner. Each environmental engineering challenge is unique, however—there is no "cookie-cutter" solution to waste management problems. Environmental engineers must evaluate the type of waste; risks posed to living organisms, surrounding population, soil and water characteristics; and cost of materials and procedures. In some circumstances, an environmental engineer might decide to incinerate waste.

Environmental engineers responsible for developing and enforcing environmental regulations may conduct research to assess the impact of various chemicals or materials on the environment. They also may be responsible for testing the emissions and waste streams created by companies or communities. An environmental engineer might, for instance, take samples of emissions from a company's smokestack. If these samples contain chemicals that are dangerous to the environment or to surrounding communities, the engineer will order the company to eliminate the harmful chemicals from their emissions.

Some environmental engineers design and build systems to pump the ground-water or surface water (lakes, rivers, etc.) to a community's water treatment plant. Others design and build systems that will remove contaminants from the waters. Filtration is a common treatment process. Environmental engineers must constantly monitor the systems and quality of water to ensure that communities receive safe drinking water.

Environmental engineers who focus on remediation efforts must begin by analyzing the type of environmental contamination and track down its source. This can be a painstaking process. If, for example, an environmental engineer finds traces of a commonly used industrial solvent in a community's water supply, he or she must trace the contamination back to the waste's source. The engineer must then identify nearby companies that might use the solvent. Once he or she has narrowed the possibilities, the engineer might have to test the waste streams of several companies to locate the source of the contamination. When the source has been identified, the company must move quickly to redesign its systems to cease the contamination.

In the meantime, the environmental engineer must wrestle with the problem of eliminating the contamination that has already occurred. Environmental engineers today have many methods from which to choose. Before selecting the appropriate method, an environmental engineer must evaluate the chemical contaminant. Some contaminants degrade quickly and can be allowed to degrade naturally. Others break down into chemicals that are more dangerous than the original contaminants. Once the engineer has selected an effective, safe method for removing the contamination, he or she must design the system, oversee its implementation, and monitor its operation.

Some environmental engineers are employed by two- and four-year colleges and universities to teach students and conduct research. Demetrios Moschandreas is a Professor of Environmental Engineering at the Illinois Institute of Technology in Chicago, Illinois. "I have taught full time since 1990; before that time, I taught on and off as an adjunct ever since I received my doctorate in 1972. The two major advantages of being a professor are: (1) You are always around young, vigorous individuals full of life and full of ambition. This vigor empowers professors to deal with teaching and research issues and indeed their personal life positively. (2) A professor is his or her own boss; there is no one who has the actual power to ask 'What have you done for me lately?' I spent about 20 years as a research consultant, the last six as a research director of a large research institute, and I was subjected and later subjected others to this question. At the university environment, a professor is autonomous (I started as full professor), his or her failures are related to his or her inability to perform what is supposed to be performed."

WHAT IS IT LIKE TO BE AN ENVIRONMENTAL ENGINEER?

Jennifer Puffer has been an environmental engineer for more than six years. "I became

---

Lingo to Learn

biodegradation The use of bacteria or other living organisms to decompose contaminants.

Comprehensive Environmental Response, Compensation, and Liability Act (CERCLA) A 1980 law (known as "Superfund") that mandated cleanup of private and government-owned hazardous waste sites.

EPA U.S. Environmental Protection Agency—federal agency responsible for overseeing the implementation of environmental laws, including those designed to monitor and control air, water, and soil pollution. State EPAs help carry out these laws.

hazardous waste Any discarded substance, usually chemicals, that can cause harm to humans.

National Priorities List U.S. EPA list of the worst hazardous waste sites in the country needing cleanup.

remediation The process by which environmental problems are remedied or redressed.

septic Anaerobic (without air) decomposition typically accompanied by an unpleasant odor.

---

an environmental engineer because I wanted to make the world a better place by improving the quality of life for society and protecting the environment," she says. "My academic strengths in high school were in math and science, and in addition I have always liked to watch things being built."

Jennifer's current project involves the design of a new drinking water treatment plant. "This will be a 10-million-gallon-per-day plant that uses membrane technology and is scheduled to be on-line next year," she says. "The main tasks I do involve coordinating with the other engineers working on the project to make sure their portions of the project are staying on schedule. If one area of the plant design gets behind schedule, it is important to get it back on track so the whole project doesn't get behind. It is a problem-solving kind of exercise; if one thing takes longer than expected, you have to figure out how to make up that time in another area."

Most environmental engineers spend time working both indoors and outdoors. The majority of environmental engineers spend up to three-fourths of their time in an office, though a small number do work primarily outdoors. "When I am not at my desk (I work in a regular office setting)," Jennifer says, "I am primarily at either the treatment plant facilities or a construction project site. The treatment plant facilities may include a pump station, a treatment process system, or the operations control center. A construction project site for me may include a new water main installation project, a remodel project on one of our buildings, or an inspection of one of our water towers."

Environmental engineers who work for multinational corporations may travel extensively, while those who work for local companies or government agencies may stay in one geographic region. Most environmental engineers work closely with other professionals, including architects, builders, hydrogeologists, laboratory technicians, and chemists.

To Be a Successful Environmental Engineer, You Should . . .

- be organized and detail-minded
- be a good problem solver
- have good oral and written communication skills
- be mechanically inclined
- have integrity and be committed to doing what's right for the environment

DO I HAVE WHAT IT TAKES TO BE AN ENVIRONMENTAL ENGINEER?

Environmental engineers must be good problem solvers. "An environmental engineer has to like working on unique, challenging projects, and enjoy problem solving," Jennifer Puffer says. "One has to like working with numbers, equations, and the sciences—like chemistry, biology, and physics." Environmental engineers must be able to organize information and identify relationships between a multitude of details. They are the sleuths of the environmental industry.

Because environmental engineers usually work within teams of professionals, they also must be cooperative and flexible. They must be able to listen to and evaluate suggestions from a disparate group of professionals. Excellent leadership and communications skills are essential.

Most importantly, environmental engineers must have integrity. Environmental engineers sometimes find themselves in situations that require them to strike an appropriate balance between achieving an employer's objectives and protecting the environment.

HOW DO I BECOME AN ENVIRONMENTAL ENGINEER?

Many environmental engineers can and do enter the profession immediately after obtaining a bachelor's degree. Because the body of knowledge and the technological capabilities within this field are constantly growing, however, many environmental engineers today choose to pursue master's or doctoral degrees. An increasing number of environmental engineers also opt to specialize in one area of environmental engineering.

To prepare for this career, Jennifer Puffer took dual credit courses in math, science, and English while in high school. After she graduated, Jennifer attended the University of Iowa where she received her bachelor of science degree in civil and environmental engineering. In 2001, she received a master of business administration from Drake University.

Education

High School

High school students who hope to pursue a career in environmental engineering should concentrate on math and science courses. Algebra, calculus, biology, chemistry, and physics all are important classes for the future environmental engineer. Students should also take as many computer courses as possible.

Since environmental engineers must draw the designs for various systems, students also may find drafting courses helpful, although the computer has largely replaced the drafting table and instruments. Laboratory classes can help students become familiar with mechanical equipment and develop an understanding of how things are put together. Classes such as English and speech can help students develop the communication skills that are so essential to a successful career in this field.

Postsecondary Training

At the college level, you should major in environmental engineering. About 20 schools offer an undergraduate degree in environmental engineering. You should supplement this course of study with chemistry and biology courses and you should continue to study computer programming. Since environmental engineers often must translate highly technical information into language that nontechnical people can understand, you also should take any available technical writing courses.

There is no tried and true formula of personal characteristics that will ensure success in college. If you were a good, conscientious student in high school, you will obviously carry these traits to your postsecondary career. But even if you were a successful student in high school, there is always room for improvement. Krishna Pagilla, an associate professor of environmental engineering at the Illinois

Institute of Technology in Chicago, Illinois, says that the most successful students "have strong interpersonal skills and are quick learners, motivated for lifelong learning, and focused and dedicated in achieving their goals."

After completing an undergraduate program, you should at least consider pursuing a master's degree in environmental engineering.

Another educational possibility is to earn a civil engineering, mechanical engineering, industrial engineering, or other traditional engineering degree with an environmental focus. You could also obtain a traditional engineering degree and learn the environmental knowledge on the job, or obtain a master's degree in environmental engineering.

The Accreditation Board for Engineering and Technology (ABET) sets minimum education standards for engineering educational programs. Graduation from an ABET-accredited school is a requirement for becoming licensed in many states, so it is important to select an accredited school. Visit ABET's Web site, http://www.abet.org, for a listing of accredited schools.

Internships and Volunteerships

Outside of class, students should look for opportunities to learn more about the profession by interviewing environmental engineers or by seeking unpaid intern experiences. Such volunteer positions are available, but students have to show initiative to find them. The Student Conservation Association (http://www.sca-inc.org) offers internships to high school students who are interested in environmental careers.

Jennifer Puffer participated in two internships during her summer breaks from college. "The first one was with McHan Construction," she says, "where I worked as a construction laborer. I helped build a large concrete tank that was to be used to store drinking water in my hometown. This work involved building formwork, tying rebar, and pouring concrete. This was a labor-intensive job, but it allowed me to better understand how things are actually built, which has aided me in my design efforts as an engineer." Jennifer's second internship was with the Cass County (Iowa) Engineering Department. "This experience allowed me to see what type of work a government entity is involved with," she explains. "In that position I worked on a survey team and helped oversee the installation of a new bridge on a rural road."

Certification or Licensing

Though licensing is not required, it is extremely valuable for environmental engineers. Licensed environmental engineers have considerably more authority to approve and implement system designs.

In order to obtain licensing as professional engineers, graduates must sit for an eight-hour exam immediately after completing their undergraduate degree. Students who pass this exam earn the engineer-in-training designation. They must then complete four years of on-the-job experience before taking another eight-hour test. Engineers who have four or more years of experience and have successfully completed both examinations are licensed professional engineers, and may use the initials PE (professional engineer) after their names.

The American Academy of Environmental Engineers offers additional certification opportunities. Environmental engineers can take additional examinations to obtain certification in seven areas of specialization: air pollution control; hazardous waste management; industrial hygiene; general environmental engineering; radiation protection; solid waste management; and water supply and wastewater engineering. Environmental engineers also may strive to become diplomate environmental engineers. Diplomate environmental engineers are those who have eight years of engineering experience, four of them in a supervisory capacity, and have passed written and oral examinations. Environmental engineers who have met these qualifications may use the initials DEE after their names.

WHO WILL HIRE ME?

Professor Demetrios Moschandreas advises new graduates to "convince your potential employer that you are well equipped to deal with the environment as a unit. Environmental engineers are not just air or water or food pollution experts; they are, and should be, all of the above. In my view, specialization is attained after the M.S. degree." He believes that it is also important to "convince the potential employer that you are an engineer in search of the truth and an efficient solution to the problem at hand and not an advocate of a point of view. Environmental engineers deal with sensitive issues and they must assess them without any preconceived notions and biases."

Associate Professor Krishna Pagilla advises environmental engineering students to "be prepared with necessary course work and projects before you graduate. Know what talent, skills, and knowledge you have to offer to the employer. Be truthful. You must also convey to the employer that you are willing and looking to make a long-term career in the company/organization, not just looking for a job."

It is difficult to generalize about where the approximately 47,000 environmental engineers who are employed in the United States work. Because the field has so many possible applications, career opportunities are extremely diverse.

The consulting industry is currently the largest employer of environmental engineers. Environmental engineers who work as consultants typically have a broad spectrum of responsibilities. They help large companies comply with environmental regulations and they design systems for waste disposal. They serve municipalities by developing systems to test and treat water to ensure that the drinking supply is safe. They sometimes help government agencies enforce regulations by testing the emissions or waste streams created by various companies or communities. They also plan, implement, and oversee remediation efforts. Environmental engineers who serve as consultants often are responsible for marketing their services, for maintaining budgets, and for managing vendors and support staff in addition to their engineering responsibilities.

Many industrial manufacturers and utility companies hire full-time environmental engineers to help them comply with environmental regulations, to design operations that will create minimal waste, and to plan and implement efficient remediation efforts. Government entities employ environmental engineers to develop and enforce environmental regulations. The armed forces employ environmental engineers to develop systems to dispose of the hazardous and radioactive waste created by munitions plants.

Academic institutions also hire environmental engineers to teach and conduct research.

In addition to the more obvious sources of employment, environmental engineers may find opportunities in a number of seemingly unrelated fields. Legal firms, for example, may hire environmental engineers to review the remediation efforts undertaken by one or more parties to a lawsuit. Investment firms may ask environmental engineers to assess the environmental risks involved in various investments. Companies that manufacture and sell environmental technology may hire environmental engineers for advice about the design of, or need for, various pieces of equipment. Municipalities or highway departments may ask environmental engineers to assess the potential impact of a proposed development on the surrounding environment.

WHERE CAN I GO FROM HERE?

Not surprisingly, environmental engineers can advance their careers and increase their earning potential by obtaining additional education, earning licensure, or becoming certified in one or more areas of specialty. Continuing education is extremely important to advancement in this field because the body of relevant knowledge is constantly growing and evolving.

Environmental engineers can also advance by assuming managerial responsibilities. This is true of environmental engineers who work for government agencies, private industry, consulting firms, and academic institutions. Most employers will offer individuals higher compensation for assuming responsibility for a department's performance, budget, and administrative duties. Because environmental engineers who become managers usually must sacrifice some of the time they might ordinarily dedicate to design and field work, individuals who truly love these aspects of the job may find greater satisfaction in nonmanagerial positions.

Jennifer Puffer says that she would like to stay in the water industry and continue to learn more about how we can improve the quality of our drinking water. "As more research is conducted on water quality," she says, "there will always be improvements we can make to the treatment of drinking water. Safe drinking water is important to everyone; it is one of life's most basic needs, and I would like to continue to make sure our community has an adequate supply."

WHAT ARE THE SALARY RANGES?

The salaries for environmental engineers depend on the individual's level of education and experience and on the type and location of employment. An environmental engineer who works for an industrial giant, for example, usually will earn more than one who works for a local governmental agency. Environmental engineers who work in major metropolitan areas typically earn more than those who work in more rural settings.

The U.S. Department of Labor reports that median annual earnings of environmental engineers were $68,090 in 2005. Salaries ranged from less than $42,570 to more than $104,610. According to a 2005 salary survey by the National Association of Colleges and Employers, bachelor's degree candidates in environmental/environmental health engineering received starting offers averaging $47,384 a year.

Fringe benefits vary widely depending on the employer. Many jobs may include, for example, two weeks of vacation, health insurance, tuition reimbursement, use of company vehicles for work, and similar perks. In-house or consulting positions may add additional benefits to lure top candidates.

WHAT IS THE JOB OUTLOOK?

Environmental engineering is a field that is driven by government regulation. "The market for environmental engineers is a function of the administration in Wash-

Related Jobs

- air quality engineers
- architects
- biochemists
- ceramic engineers
- chemists
- civil engineers
- drafters
- ecologists
- electro-optical engineers
- environmental engineering educators
- environmental technicians
- geologists
- groundwater professionals
- hazardous waste management specialists
- hazardous waste management technicians
- hydraulic engineers
- industrial engineers
- marine biologists
- mechanical design engineers
- naturalists
- oceanographers
- renewable energy workers
- sanitary engineers
- soil conservationists and technicians
- soil scientists
- transportation engineers
- wastewater management engineers
- wastewater treatment plant operators and technicians

ington, D.C.," Professor Demetrios Moschandreas explains. "The discipline, like all other disciplines, experiences considerable market variation, yet environmental integrity interests all of us and the environmental engineer should be able to find a job with relative ease."

The U.S. Department of Labor projects that there will be much faster than average employment growth for environmental engineers through 2014. They will be needed to clean up existing hazards and help companies comply with government regulations. The shift toward prevention of problems and protecting public health should create job opportunities.

Environmental engineering is a field that is always changing. "The best way [for students] to keep track of changes," advises Associate Professor Krishna Pagilla, "is to join professional organizations such the Water Environment Federation, Air and Waste Management Association, American Water Works Association, and others. Often the memberships are free, and the professional meetings help students understand the trends in the field and where to concentrate for the future."

Industrial Engineers

SUMMARY

Definition
Industrial engineers use their knowledge of various disciplines—including systems engineering, management science, operations research, and fields such as ergonomics—to determine the most efficient and cost-effective methods for industrial production. They are responsible for designing systems that integrate materials, equipment, information, and people in the overall production process.

Alternative Job Titles
Management Analysts
Management Engineers

Salary Range
$43,620 to $66,670 to $97,000+

Educational Requirements
Minimum of a bachelor's degree. Advanced degree recommended.

Certification or Licensing
Required for certain positions

Employment Outlook
About as fast as the average

High School Subjects
Computer science
Mathematics

Personal Interests
Building things
Computers
Figuring out how things work

Night was falling, the UPS delivery truck was loaded with packages, and John Ripley had a problem.

The UPS industrial engineer was out in the field training a driver to use his company's new Delivery Information Acquisition Device (DIAD)—the small handheld computer device you see UPS drivers using today when they deliver a package.

The initial DIAD didn't have a screen that was back-lit. As a result, it was taking John and the driver a long time to input customer information—slowing delivery times. And, John thought to himself, if you multiply this one instance by the 13 million packages delivered each day by UPS, this could make for a lot of unhappy customers.

John spotted a hardware store on their way to the next delivery. He ran in and bought a small battery-powered light. After making a few minor adjustments, he affixed it to the DIAD to allow them to see the screen and speed up the deliveries.

John's temporary fix became one of the recommended short-term solutions for the DIAD roll-out until the next version of DIAD was manufactured with a back-lit screen.

Helping delivery systems become as efficient as possible is just one of the many tasks John is responsible for as an industrial engineer.

WHAT DOES AN INDUSTRIAL ENGINEER DO?

Industrial engineers are involved with the development and implementation of the systems and procedures that are utilized by many industries and businesses. In general, they figure out the most effective ways to use the three basic elements of any company: people, facilities, and equipment.

Although industrial engineers work in a variety of businesses, the main focus of the discipline is in manufacturing, also called industrial production. Primarily, industrial engineers are concerned with process technology, which includes the design and layout of machinery and the organization of workers who implement the required tasks.

Industrial engineers have many responsibilities. With regard to facilities and equipment, engineers are involved in selecting machinery and other equipment and then in setting them up in the most efficient production layout. They also develop methods to accomplish production tasks, such as the organization of an assembly line. In addition, they devise systems for quality control, distribution, and inventory.

Industrial engineers are responsible for some organizational issues. For instance, they might study an organization chart and other information about a project and then determine the functions and responsibilities of workers. They devise and implement job evaluation procedures

as well as articulate labor-utilization standards for workers. Engineers often meet with managers to discuss cost analysis, financial planning, job evaluation, and salary administration. Not only do they recommend methods for improving employee efficiency but they may also devise wage and incentive programs.

Industrial engineers evaluate ergonomic issues, the relationship between human capabilities and the physical environment in which they work. For example, they might evaluate whether machines are causing physical harm or discomfort to workers or whether the machines could be designed differently to enable workers to be more productive.

In industries that do not focus on manufacturing, industrial engineers are often called *management analysts* or *management engineers.* In the health care industry, such engineers are asked to evaluate current administrative and other procedures. They also advise on job standards, cost-containment, and operations consolidation. Some industrial engineers are employed by financial services companies. Because many engineering concepts are relevant in the banking industry, engineers there design methods to optimize the ratio of tellers to customers and the use of computers for various tasks and to handle mass distribution of items such as credit card statements.

WHAT IS IT LIKE TO BE AN INDUSTRIAL ENGINEER?

John Ripley is a district industrial engineering manager at UPS. He has been an industrial engineer for 17 years. "My typical day," he says, "involves balancing many different activities throughout the day. It usually involves, in no certain order, looking at what is currently happening in the operation and in the market place and proactively planning for the future by creating effective operational plans. I work cross-functionally with all departments to seek input, ideas, and feedback from people at all levels within UPS to promote teamwork, ownership, and cooperation for various on-going projects. I monitor results daily through operational reports to ensure operations adjust their plans accordingly. Areas that are off plan are generally reviewed in scheduled weekly meetings and sometimes daily conference calls."

To achieve his company's goals, John sometimes visits customers to manage their concerns and conducts audits to ensure safety and service goals are met. "I seek out information and keep current on all issues, trends, and technology that affect my group's success," he says.

One of John's responsibilities is to manage a team of industrial engineers. "For those industrial engineers who report to me I audit their work, usually consisting of worksheets and other reports to ensure their accuracy and I monitor group progress in working towards achieving established timelines and other commitments for our projects. I work closely with my people to ensure I have identified those people with high potential and develop them to assume greater responsibility within the company."

How does John manage to keep all these tasks straight? "I use a PDA for scheduling these various tasks, meetings, work reviews, and for travel and business expenses, when necessary," he explains.

Industrial engineers often work in offices at desks and computers, designing and evaluating plans, statistics, and other documents. John spends the majority of his workday indoors. "However," he explains, "my indoor time is split between office work and working in an operational environment such as a package sorting facility, otherwise known as a hub operation at UPS. By spending time in the operations environment, I can help create operating plans to assist our facility managers in making operational changes to either improve our service, performance, or cost. The plan is not created in the office and then sent to operations to implement. It is a joint effort, which is what makes the job rewarding."

Overall, industrial engineering is ranked above other engineering disciplines for factors such as employment outlook, salary, and physical environment. However, industrial engineering jobs are considered stressful because they often entail tight deadlines and demanding quotas, and jobs are moderately competitive. Engineers work an average of 46 hours per week. John typically works 9 to 10 hours a day and roughly spends the following percentages of time on various duties: developing/implementing proposals, 40 percent; operation visits/project evaluations, 30 percent; answering e-mail/voicemail and reviewing reports, 10 percent; participating in cross-functional meetings/conference calls, 10 percent; and training/travel, 10 percent.

Since many of today's companies are global in nature, many industrial engineers travel extensively for their jobs. "My previous assignments," John says, "have included travel to Europe and Central and South America. In addition to traveling when required, I have moved numerous times with UPS—including relocating from Montana to Alaska, Florida, and Louisville, Kentucky."

Asked about the pros and cons of his job, John offers many pros and only one con. "One of the biggest pros of an industrial engineering job," he says, "is that you are usually at the forefront of change going on within a company. You are involved with strategic direction, coordination of project implementations, and making a vision reality. I also enjoy the ability to manage my own projects, directing a group of industrial engineers to complete various projects, working with all levels of company employees, working on various projects over time with the same company without having to change jobs, traveling to various areas of the U.S. and the world, and providing both career opportunities and a chance to develop my skills. Other pros would be hands-on participation in operational projects, a good benefits and salary package, industry recognition for our company's continued productivity and technological improvements, and the respect you feel when you tell people you work for UPS.

"The only con of my job," John continues, "would have to be non-typical working hours, which at certain times can have

To Be a Successful Industrial Engineer, You Should . . .

- like to solve problems
- be able to work as a member of a team
- have strong communication skills—both oral and written
- be organized and detail-minded
- be creative and inventive

an impact on you or your family. However, in today's global marketplace I don't know if the word typical applies anymore. You may be working on a logistics solution that involves coordinating internal and external customers whom are in Europe or Asia or even the West Coast and East Coast for that matter. You may need to work in the warehouse implementing a new process on the night shift. Or the operation requiring help is the weekend shift. You learn to plan accordingly when you are assigned projects of this nature."

HAVE I GOT WHAT IT TAKES TO BE AN INDUSTRIAL ENGINEER?

Industrial engineers enjoy problem solving and analyzing things as well as being a team member. The ability to communicate is vital since engineers interact with all levels of management and workers. Being organized and detail-minded is important because industrial engineers often handle large projects and must bring them in on time and on budget. Since process design is the cornerstone of the field, an engineer should be creative and inventive.

HOW DO I BECOME AN INDUSTRIAL ENGINEER?

Education

High School

John recommends that high school students who are interested in this field take mathematics, finance, computer classes, and extra-curricular activities that will help you develop your interpersonal skills. "I have seen some very intelligent engineers," John says, "not be successful in the workplace because they were too technical in their approach and did not have the ability to communicate effectively with operations employees and other management."

John also recommends that students study a foreign language. "Our workforce today is more diverse than ever," he says. "Having bilingual language skills starts separating job candidates who may appear equal otherwise. Combine technical, language, and people skills into one package and you will see an industrial engineer who will be very successful in today's global marketplace."

In addition, since engineers often have to convey ideas graphically and may need to visualize processes in three-dimension, you should take courses in graphics, drafting, or design.

Postsecondary Training

A bachelor's degree from an accredited institution is usually the minimum requirement for professional positions. The Accreditation Board for Engineering and Technology (ABET) accredits schools offering engineering programs, including industrial engineering. A listing of accredited colleges and universities is available on the ABET Web site (http://www.abet.org), and a visit there should be one of your first stops when you are deciding on a school to attend. Colleges and universities offer either four- or five-year engineering programs. Because of the intensity of the curricula, many students take heavy course loads and attend summer sessions in order to finish in four years.

During your junior and senior years of college, you should consider your specific career goals, such as in which industry to work. Third- and fourth-year courses focus on such subjects as facility planning and design, work measurement standards, process design, engineering economics, manufacturing and automation, and incentive plans.

Many industrial engineers go on to earn a graduate degree. These programs tend to involve more research and independent study. Graduate degrees are usually required for teaching positions.

Certification and Licensing

Licensure as a professional engineer is recommended since an increasing number of employers require it. Even those employers who do not require licensing will view it favorably when considering new hires or when reviewing workers for promotion. Licensing requirements vary from state to state. In general, however, they involve having graduated from an accredited school, having four years of work experience, and having passed the eight-hour Fundamentals of Engineering exam and the eight-hour Principles and Practice of Engineering exam. Depending on your state, you can take the Fundamentals exam shortly before your graduation from college or after you have received your bachelor's degree. At that point you will be an engineer-in-training (EIT). Once you have fulfilled all the licensure requirements, you receive the designation "Professional Engineer" (PE).

John is not a certified industrial engineer. "Though this is a necessary requirement for some engineering jobs," he explains, "the many different training courses and work experiences through continued employment with my company have provided me with the tools I need to successfully complete any projects that I am assigned."

Internships and Volunteerships

Most industrial engineering programs will require that you participate in an internship program with a company that employs industrial engineers. Some programs may require you to take two internships. Schools with degree programs that require an internship usually will have a partnership set up with local industry. What are the benefits of internships? Internships will offer you an opportunity to make valuable contacts as well as learn more about the field from experienced engineers. Internships can last anywhere from four months to a year.

WHO WILL HIRE ME?

John began working at UPS during his first year of college to help pay for his education. After he graduated, he interviewed at UPS and was hired as an air industrial engineering supervisor. "My job," he says, "was to make sure the operation successfully sorted and loaded our customers' packages on time into airplanes departing to the different cities that we served. At the time, this operation was not based in a facility and involved working outside on the airport ramp during rain, snow, and freezing temperatures."

Industrial engineers hold approximately 194,000 jobs in the United States. Although a majority of industrial engineers are employed in the manufacturing industry, related jobs are found in almost all businesses, including transportation, communications, electric, gas and sanitary services, government, finance, insurance, real estate, wholesale and retail trade, construction, mining, agriculture, forestry, and fishing. Also, many work as independent consultants.

The typical qualification for an entry-level job is a bachelor's degree in industrial engineering, although some industrial engineers may earn degrees in related fields. Accredited college programs generally have job openings listed in their placement offices. Entry-level industrial engineers find jobs in various departments, such as computer operations, warehousing, and quality control. As engineers gain on-the-job experience and familiarity with departments, they may decide on a specialty such as work measurement standards, shipping and receiving, cost control, engineering economics, materials handling, management information systems, mathematical models, and operations. Others may move on to administrative positions. Many who choose industrial engineering as a career find its appeal in the diversity of sectors that are available to explore.

WHERE CAN I GO FROM HERE?

After having worked at least three years in the same job, an industrial engineer may have the basic credentials needed for advancement to a higher position. In general, positions in operations and administration are considered high-level jobs, although this varies from company to company. Engineers who work in these areas tend to earn larger salaries than those who work in warehousing or cost control, for example. If one is interested in moving to a different company, it is considered easier to do so within the same industry.

Industrial engineering jobs are often considered stepping-stones to management positions, such as is in John's case, even in other fields. Engineers with many years' experience frequently are promoted to higher level jobs with greater responsibilities. Because of the field's broad exposure, industrial engineers are generally considered better prepared for executive roles than are other types of engineers.

WHAT ARE THE SALARY RANGES?

According to the U.S. Department of Labor, the median annual wage for industrial engineers in 2005 was $66,670. The lowest paid 10 percent earned less than $43,620 annually. However, as with most occupations, salaries increase as engineers gain more experience. Very experienced engineers can earn more than $97,000. According to a survey by the National Association of Colleges and Employers, the average starting salary for

Related Jobs

- civil engineers
- cost estimators
- environmental engineers
- ergonomists
- engineering engineering educators
- fire protection engineers
- industrial designers
- industrial engineering technicians
- management analysts and consultants
- manufacturing engineers
- quality control engineers
- quality control technicians
- robotics engineers
- robotics technicians
- safety engineers
- standards engineers
- time-study engineers

industrial engineers with a bachelor's degree was $49,567 in 2005, while those with a master's degree had average starting offers of $56,561 a year.

In addition to salary, most industrial engineers receive paid vacation time, holidays, insurance and retirement plans, and tuition assistance for work-related courses.

WHAT IS THE JOB OUTLOOK?

The U.S. Department of Labor anticipates that employment for industrial engineers will grow about as fast as the average for all occupations through 2014. The demand for industrial engineers will continue as manufacturing and other companies strive to make their production processes more effective and competitive. Engineers who transfer or retire will create the highest percentage of openings in this field.

John Ripley feels that the employment outlook for industrial engineers is very bright. "Technology," he says, "continues to develop at a very rapid pace across all industries. Some technologies are advertised as being the solution to various opportunities that exist within industry today. The challenge, not only for me, but for all industrial engineers, will be how we are able to integrate this technology within our particular business environment to ensure the technology provides real value to the company. Success will be determined by how data, information systems, and business processes are all combined to maximize efficiency in the workplace. Because this area provides the greatest challenge, it will also provide the greatest opportunity for industrial engineers going forward. Potential growth areas should include industrial and facility engineers who can evaluate emerging technology and make it affordable for the workplace."

Materials Engineers

SUMMARY

Definition
Materials engineers extract, process, create, design, and test materials—such as metals, ceramics, plastics, semiconductors, and combinations of these materials called composites—to create a wide variety of products.

Alternative Job Titles
Ceramic engineer
Chemical engineer
Metallurgical engineer

Metallurgist
Plastics engineer
Polymer engineer
Semiconductor engineer

Salary Range
$44,090 to $69,660 to
  $105,330+

Educational Requirements
Minimum of a bachelor's
  degree. Advanced degree
  recommended.

Certification or Licensing
Required for certain positions

Employment Outlook
Average growth

High School Subjects
Computer science
Mathematics
Physics

Personal Interests
Building things
Computers
Figuring out how things
  work

You probably don't think of *CSI* when you hear "materials engineer." So you might be surprised to learn that these engineering professionals use many of the same investigative tools as the experts on the hit television show. No, materials engineers don't analyze DNA, blood, and fingerprints to nab murderers, but they do use optical microscopy, scanning electron microscopes, and other equipment and techniques to help manufacturers determine why critical parts and equipment fail under a variety of circumstances. Their work keeps our everyday world functioning and you safe in your car, home, and countless other settings.

WHAT DOES A MATERIALS ENGINEER DO?

Materials engineers extract, process, create, design, and test materials—such as metals, ceramics, plastics, semiconductors, and combinations of these materials called composites—to create a wide variety of products. These products include television screens, automotive parts, computer chips, ceramic tiles for the

Lingo to Learn

additive A compound or substance added to a polymer at some point during its processing to effect a desired change in the polymer.

ceramic Something that relates to the making of products made from nonmetallic elements (like clay) taken from the earth.

electroplating This process involves the deposition of one metal into another by electrolytic action.

grades Refers to polymers that belong to the same chemical family and are produced by the same manufacturer.

heat treatment Processes in which metals are subjected to specific time-and-temperature cycles in order to modify their physical properties.

kiln A heated enclosure, like an oven or a furnace, that is used for burning, firing, and drying ceramics or glass.

metallography Study of the structure of metals and alloys by various methods, but especially light and electronic microscopy.

metallurgy Technology and science of metallic materials. As a branch of engineering, it is concerned with the extraction and production of metals and alloys, their adaptation to use, and their performance in a particular usage.

monomer Molecules of an organic substance that are the basic structural unit of polymers. Monomers must be bonded together to form polymers.

plastic A synthetic or naturally occurring organic substance, which at some point in its formation or manufacturing process becomes formable or pliable. Plastics are generally made up of polymers.

polymer A substance formed by a chemical reaction in which chemical units (mers) join together in a line to form repeating smaller units. Polymers joined together (with other substances) are what make the varieties of plastics.

semiconductors Sometimes called microchips, these tiny devices are made from silicon and produced in high-tech manufacturing environments.

space shuttle, and golf clubs, among many others. Several types of engineering subspecialties exist under the umbrella term "materials engineer." These include *metallurgical engineers; ceramic engineers;* and *polymer,* or *plastics, engineers.*

Metallurgical Engineers

Metals are at the core of every manufacturing society. Parts made from metal are incorporated in a wide variety of products, from steel and iron used in building materials and automobile parts, to aluminum used in packaging, to titanium used in aerospace and military aircraft applications like bulkheads, fasteners, and landing gear. Metallurgy is the art and science of extracting metals from ores found in nature and preparing them for use by alloying, shaping, and heating them.

Metallurgical engineers are specialists who develop extraction and manufacturing processes for the metals industry. Metallurgical engineers develop new types of metal alloys and adapt existing materials to new uses. They manipulate the atomic and molecular structure of materials in controlled manufacturing environments, selecting materials with desirable mechanical, electrical, magnetic, chemical, and heat-transfer properties that meet specific performance requirements. Metallurgical engineers are sometimes also referred to as *metallurgists.*

There are basically three categories in which metallurgical engineers work. *Extractive metallurgists,* also known as *chemical metallurgists,* are concerned with the methods used to separate metals from ores, and the reclamation of materials from solid wastes for recycling. As part of their responsibilities, they may supervise and control concentrating and refining processes in commercial mining operations. They may determine the methods used to concentrate the ore by separating minerals from dirt, rock, and other unwanted materials. Many of these separation methods are performed at a treatment plant or refinery. There the extractive metallurgist may supervise and control both the separation processes and final purification processes.

Extractive metallurgists also develop ways to improve the current methods of separating minerals. To do this, the extractive metallurgist processes small batches of ores in a laboratory and analyzes the efficiency of each operation and the feasibility of adapting the operations to commercial use. Extractive metallurgists also research ways to use new sources of metals, such as the reclamation of magnesium from seawater.

Extractive metallurgists often are involved in the design of treatment plants and refineries and the equipment and processes used within them. They may determine the types of machines needed, supervise the installation of machinery, train refinery workers, and closely observe processing operations. They monitor operations and suggest new methods and modifications needed to improve efficiency.

Because minerals are becoming depleted in the environment, extractive metallurgical engineers are constantly searching for new ways to take metals from low-grade ores and to recycle metals that are considered scrap material. During the last 20 years, many of the refining processes have greatly improved, lessening environmental damage from waste materials.

Physical metallurgists, on the other hand, focus on the scientific study of the relationship between the structure and properties of metals and devise uses for metals. These engineers begin their job after metals have been extracted and refined. At that point, most such metals are not yet useful, so they must be

Failure Analysis: Making Automobiles Safe for the Consumer

All automotive manufacturers perform accelerated testing of their vehicles to insure that the individual components can withstand the rigors of 10 to 15 years of normal driving. If a problem is discovered during testing, the manufacturer sends the part to a materials engineer, such as Toby Padfield, to conduct a failure analysis project.

Toby recently conducted a failure analysis project on a suspension coil spring that fractured during accelerated testing. In the following paragraphs, he details how he and his team of materials engineering professionals tackled and solved the problem.

"We began our analysis with a visual inspection of the suspension coil spring to see if there were any signs of abnormal use, corrosion, and to generally document the appearance of the part. At this stage the fracture surface showed the appearance of red rust and the presence of small blisters on the paint coating used to prevent corrosion.

"Next, we evaluated the fracture surface using optical microscopy, and photographs were taken of the results. The type of optical microscopy used for observing fracture surfaces is capable of magnifying the image up to ~ 25x.

"We used a scanning electron microscope to perform our next evaluation. This instrument is capable of much higher resolution, up to a magnification of 10,000x. The results from this analysis showed the failure was a result of fatigue, meaning that a crack initiated relatively early in the testing, and then propagated over time, weakening the steel coil spring and ultimately causing it to fail.

"We needed to determine why the fatigue failure initiated, so we tested the base material (a steel alloy) of the coil spring and the corrosion protective coating (an epoxy-based coating similar to ordinary paint, but harder and more corrosion resistant) to verify that they met the specified requirements. This was done by removing a section of the failed spring some distance away from the fractured area.

"We tested the chemical composition of the steel and found it to be within the specified range. The hardness and microstructure of the steel were also found to meet the specified requirements. The coating was measured for thickness and adhesion, and both met the requirements. The only problems were some small blisters near the fracture area as well as near an adhesive label used for identifying the manufacturer's part number.

"Once we determined that the steel and coating properties met the specification requirements, another review was held with the automotive manufacturer to discuss the test conditions, any failures that may have occurred to other parts of the suspension, and routine maintenance that was performed.

"We discovered that the vehicle had experienced a problem with the rear brakes, and therefore some maintenance had been performed, including draining of the brake fluid. Brake fluid is an extremely aggressive chemical, and can degrade a

(continued on next page)

(continued from previous page)

number of organic materials, such as the epoxy paint used for coating the coil spring. We then performed an accelerated test on a similar spring to determine whether or not exposure to brake fluid would cause paint blistering and subsequent fatigue failure of the coil spring. This testing confirmed that exposure to brake fluid would indeed cause blistering and initiate fatigue failure in the coil spring.

"We still had to confirm that the coil spring had actually fractured on the test vehicle due to brake fluid exposure. We took a very small sample of the blistered coating and tested it using Fourier Transform Infrared Spectroscopy. This method is capable of determining the chemical composition of any organic substances (meaning carbon-based, not metals or ceramics). Testing of the small blistered coating sample confirmed the presence of brake fluid. This allowed us to make the conclusion that the coil spring fractured due to fatigue that was initiated by degradation of the coating after exposure to brake fluid. The brake fluid had apparently come into contact with the spring coating in a number of locations (hence the small blisters) as well as the identification label, allowing prolonged exposure that ultimately led to the failure."

improved by being blended with other metals and nonmetals to produce alloys.

Physical metallurgists may conduct X-ray and microscopic experiments on the metals to determine their physical structure and other characteristics, such as the amount of alloys and base metals present. These engineers also test the materials for impurities and defects and determine whether they can be used in thermal, electrical, or magnetic applications. The results of the studies and tests determine what the metal will be used for and how long it is expected to last.

Using the data gained during research, physical metallurgists also develop new applications for metals. They devise processes that transform the metals so they have desired characteristics such as hardness, corrosion resistance, malleability, and durability. These processes include hot working, cold working, foundry methods, powder metallurgy, nuclear metallurgy, and heat treatment. After the metals have been processed, they can be transformed into commercial products.

Lastly, *process metallurgical engineers,* or *mechanical metallurgical engineers,* take metals and, by melting, casting, and mechanically processing them, produce forms that will be sold for a multitude of applications, such as automotive parts, satellite components, and coins. The field of process metallurgy is quite broad, involving such methods as welding, soldering, plating, rolling, and finishing metals to produce commercially standard products.

Ceramic Engineers

When we refer to ceramics we often think only of objects made of clay, like cups and saucers. Thousands of years ago, ceramics makers were limited by a dependence on this one raw material. Today, basic ceramic materials such as clay and sand are being used not only by artists and craftspeople but also by engineers to create a variety of products—memory storage, optical communications, and electronics. Ceramic engineers are working with more advanced materials as well (many produced by chemical processes), including high-strength silicon carbides, nitrides, and fracture-resistant zirconias.

Ceramic engineers work with nonmetallic elements such as clay and inorganic elements such as zirconia. They are part of the ceramics and glass industry, which manufactures such common items as tableware and such highly technical items as ceramic tiles for the space shuttle. These engineers perform research, design machinery and processing methods, and develop new ceramic materials and products. Like other materials engineers, ceramic engineers work toward the development of new products. They also use their scientific knowledge to anticipate new applications for existing products.

Ceramic research engineers conduct experiments and perform other research. They study the chemical properties (such as sodium content) and physical properties (such as strength) of materials as they develop the ideal mix of elements for each product's application. Many research engineers are fascinated by the chemical, optical, and thermal interactions of the oxides that make up many ceramic materials.

Ceramic design engineers take the information culled by the researchers and further develop actual products to be manufactured. In addition to working on the new products, these engineers may need to design new equipment or processes in order to produce the products. Examples of such equipment include grinders, milling machines, sieves, presses, and drying machines.

Ceramic test engineers test materials that have been chosen by the researchers to be used as sample products, or they might be involved in ordering raw materials and making sure the quality meets the ceramics industry standards. Other ceramic engineers are involved in more hands-on work, such as grinding raw materials and firing products. Maintaining proper color, surface finish, texture, strength, and uniformity are further tasks that are the responsibility of the ceramic engineer.

Beyond research, design, testing, and manufacturing, there are the *ceramic product sales engineers*. The industry depends on these people to anticipate customers' needs and report back to researchers and test engineers on new applications.

Ceramic engineers often specialize in an area that is associated with selected products. For example, a ceramic engineer working in the area of glass may be involved in the production of sheet or window glass, bottles, fiberglass, tableware, fiber optics, or electronic equipment parts. Another engineer may specialize in whitewares, which involves production of pottery, china, wall tile, plumbing fixtures, electrical insulators, and spark plugs.

Other segments of the industry—advanced, or technical, ceramic—employ a great number of specialized engineers. Areas workers are involved in include engineered ceramics (for things such as engine components, cutting tools, and military armor), bioceramics (for things such as artificial teeth, bones, and joints), and electronic and magnetic ceramics (for products such as computer chips and memory disks).

Plastics Engineers

Plastics are used everywhere—in the clothes we wear, the cars we drive, the buildings in which we work and live, to name but a few of the more common applications. Either as a part or ingredient, or as the entire product itself, the manufacture of plastics has escalated since the late 19th century when John W. Hyatt first created celluloid as his entry in a contest to invent substitutes for the ivory used in billiard balls. Today, synthetic polymers—chains of hydrocarbon molecules—represent a multimillion dollar business as either the main ingredient or the item itself in building and construction, clothing, packaging, aerospace, and consumer products. In addition, plastics have had a stunning effect on the automotive, biomedical, communications, electrical and electronic fields, in some cases breathing new life into them. Since plastic is man-made, relatively inexpensive to produce, highly durable, recyclable, and does not drain natural resources, one of its most common uses is in replacing products and parts made of tradi-tional materials like wood, metals, and glass.

Plastics engineers perform a wide variety of duties depending on the type of company they work for and the products it produces. Plastics engineers, for example, may develop ways to produce clear, durable plastics to replace glass in areas where glass cannot be used. Others design and manufacture lightweight parts for aircraft and automobiles, or create new plastics to replace metallic or wood parts that have come to be too expensive or hard to obtain. Others may be employed to formulate less-expensive, fire-resistant plastics for use in the construction of houses, offices, and factories. Plastics engineers may also develop new types of biodegradable molecules that are friendly to the environment, reducing pollution and increasing recyclability.

Plastics engineers perform a variety of duties. Some of their specific job titles and duties include: *plastics application engineers,* who develop new processes and materials in order to create a better finished product; *plastics process engineers,* who oversee the production of reliable, high quality, standard materials; and *plastics research specialists,* who use the basic building blocks of matter to discover and create new materials.

In the course of their day, plastics engineers must solve a wide variety of internal production problems. Duties include making sure the process is consistent to ensure creation of accurate and precise parts and making sure parts are handled and packaged efficiently, properly, and cheaply. Each part is unique in this respect.

Computers are increasingly being used to assist in the production process. Plastics engineers use computers to calculate part weight and cycle times; for monitoring the process on each molding press; for designing parts and molds on a computer-aided design system; for tracking processes and the labor in the mold shop; and to transfer engineering files over the Internet.

Plastics engineers also help customers solve problems that may emerge in part design—finding ways to make a part more moldable or to address possible failures or inconsistencies in the final design. Factors that may make a part difficult to mold include: thin walls, functional or cosmetic factors, sections that are improperly designed that will not allow the part to be processed efficiently, or inappropriate material selection which results in an improperly created part.

Plastics engineers also coordinate mold-building schedules and activities with tool vendors. Mold-building schedules consist of the various phases of constructing a mold, from the development of the tool and buying of materials (and facilitating their timely delivery), to estimating the roughing and finishing operations. Molds differ depending on the size of the tool or product, the complexity of the work orders, and the materials required to build the mold.

Most importantly, plastics engineers must take an application that is difficult to produce and make it (in the short period of time allowed) profitable to their company, while still satisfying the needs of the customer.

To Be a Successful Materials Engineer, You Should . . .

- understand the properties of the material in which you work
- have an inquisitive mind and an eye for detail
- have strong oral and written communications skills
- be able to work as a member of a team
- be able to adjust and adapt well to changes in the industry

WHAT IS IT LIKE TO BE A MATERIALS ENGINEER?

Toby Padfield is a senior materials engineer at ZF Sachs Automotive of America in Northville, Michigan. He has been a materials engineer for approximately 10 years.

"I primarily work," he says, "with design engineers to determine what materials (steel, plastic, etc.) and processes (sheet metal stamping, plastic injection molding, welding, painting, etc.) are used to make automotive suspension parts with respect to strength, cost, corrosion resistance, durability, and other issues. A second part of my job is to coordinate testing and failure analysis activities on components that have fractured, corroded, or are no longer functioning properly. This involves working with internal and external laboratories to determine the chemical composition, strength, and other characteristics of the various materials that are used. I also support our manufacturing, purchasing, and quality departments in developing new suppliers, troubleshooting processing issues, and reviewing materials-related data/documentation." Toby says he spends approximately 50 percent of his time on materials and process selection, 25 percent on failure analysis, and 25 percent on other projects.

Working conditions in materials engineering positions vary depending on the specific field and department in which one works. Hands-on engineers work in plants and factories. Researchers work mainly in laboratories, research institutes, and universities. Those in management positions work mostly in offices; teachers, of course, work in school environments. Toby works in a normal office environment with a desk and computer, but he does spend some time in various testing labs. "Part of my job is to work with our manufacturing plants and component suppliers," he says, "so this entails visiting many different manufacturing facilities that range from extremely large steel mills to small companies that specialize in machining, painting, or testing."

Most materials engineers work a 40-hour week. Occasionally, evening or weekend work may be necessary to complete special projects or work on experiments.

Depending on their job responsibilities, some materials engineers are required to travel. Toby averages about one trip every one to two months. "Most of the trips are confined to the Midwest (many automotive suppliers are located in Michigan, Ohio, Indiana, Illinois, Pennsylvania, and Kentucky)," he says, "but I also travel to Germany and Mexico since we have operations in both countries. I consider it a reasonable amount of travel that provides me with the opportunity to gain a wide range of experience on how things are made and to meet new people with different backgrounds and cultures."

Other materials engineers work as teachers at the secondary and postsecondary levels. John Hellmann has been a professor of ceramic science and engineering at Pennsylvania State University for 19 years. "My primary job duties," he says, "concern instruction in thermal properties, composite materials, and engineering methodology and design. In addition, I lead a vigorous research enterprise, incorporating a half dozen graduate students and several undergraduates, in developing new ceramics, intermetallics, and composites for thermostructural applications (such as for aerospace propulsion and airframes, materials for energy systems, and high wear/corrosion/erosion applications). I also am the associate head for undergraduate instruction, with primary responsibility for engineering accreditation, recruiting, curriculum development, cooperative education, mentoring, and professional development opportunities for our undergraduates. On top of all of this, I serve on numerous department, college, and university committees, such as curriculum development, faculty advisory board for engineering accreditation, the University Faculty Senate, scholarships, and as adviser for several student groups." In addition to his job responsibilities, Professor Hellmann serves as a member of the Board of Directors and chairman of the Education and Outreach Committee of the American Ceramic Society, president of the National Institute of Ceramic Engineers, and a frequent coordinator for technical symposia and meetings.

DO I HAVE WHAT IT TAKES TO BE A MATERIALS ENGINEER?

With new products being developed daily, materials engineers are constantly under pressure to integrate new technology and science. Having the imagination to consider all of the possibilities and then being versatile enough to adapt one application of a metal, ceramic, polymer, or other material to another situation are, perhaps, the most essential qualities for materials engineers. To accomplish this, materials engineers must first learn how the material may be applicable to their industry or product line, and then decide how to adjust their current manufacturing process to incorporate it.

In addition to having a good mechanical aptitude for developing parts and tooling, one of the more basic qualities for any student considering a career in materials engineering is a solid understanding of the properties of the material they work with—be it metals, ceramics, polymers, or a composite of these materials.

As in every scientific endeavor, there are always a varying number of factors that influence the outcome of the experiment, and the chemical configurations of a specific material is no different. It takes an individual with an extraordinary amount of patience, focus, and determination to notice precisely what factors are achieving the desired results. Successful materials engineers pay attention to the smallest detail, note the nuances between experiments, and then use that information to develop further tests or theories. Having a certain amount of critical distance helps materials engineers step back from the minutia and reassess the direction in which they're headed.

Materials engineers need to be inquisitive, take creative steps toward improvements by constantly asking questions, and take a fresh look at familiar practices.

Good communication skills are vital for success in engineering. You may be required to write reports and present your research before a large audience at industry seminars.

Toby Padfield believes that the most important personal and professional qualities for materials engineers are "good communication skills (both written and verbal), a good work ethic, taking pride in your job and the way that you do it, and continuing education." He is active in several professional societies such as ASM International, SAE International, and TMS. "I have benefited enormously from my involvement," he says. "I have pursued educational opportunities such as attending conferences and seminars, writing technical papers, and participating in technical committees. I also read

Know Your Plastics!

polyacrylamide A tough clear plastic that compact discs are made from.

polyethylene The soft clear kind of plastic that plastic baggies are typically made out of.

polystyrene A stiffer, often white plastic, that your milk is "bottled" in.

trade publications and journals in order to keep up with current trends and future developments."

HOW DO I BECOME A MATERIALS ENGINEER?

Education

High School

While few courses at the high school level are directly related to materials engineering, the basic foundation for engineering includes a wide range of math and science courses. If you are interested in pursuing a career in this field you should invest in an education steeped heavily in math and science, including geometry, algebra, trigonometry, calculus, chemistry, biology, physics, and computer programming. Materials engineers who will also be designing products will need drafting skills, so mechanical drawing and art classes are an excellent choice. "I never participated in anything related to cars or vocational training (metal shop, drafting, etc.)," Toby Padfield says, "but certainly the latter would have been beneficial. Most scientific and engineering work requires at some point working with mechanical drawings and manufacturing methods."

English, speech, and foreign language classes will help you develop strong communication skills and provide you with the opportunity to learn how to better express yourself. "Pay attention to your writing and composition courses," Professor John Hellmann advises. "Communication skills are very important! And don't forget geography and social sciences; you will need these to work in a global economy."

Ancillary interests should not be overlooked. In addition to providing you with possible ways of applying your scientific knowledge in enjoyable, recreational activities, exploring personal hobbies can also develop crucial personal and professional qualities and skills, such as patience, perseverance, and creative problem solving.

Postsecondary Training

If your career goal is to become a materials engineer, you will need a bachelor of science degree in materials, metallurgical engineering, ceramic engineering, plastics engineering, or a related field. Degrees are granted in many different specializations by more than 80 universities and colleges in the United States.

There are a wide variety of programs available at colleges and universities, and it is helpful to explore as many of these programs as possible, especially those that are accredited by the Accreditation Board for Engineering and Technology (http://www.abet.org). Some programs prepare students for practical design and production work; others concentrate on theoretical science and mathematics.

More than 50 percent of materials engineers begin their first job with a bachelor's degree. The materials science and engineering curriculum at Penn State University, where Professor Hellmann teaches, starts with a two-year sequence of chemistry, physics, mathematics, communications, writing, and general arts and sciences courses. "These are followed," he says, "by a junior and senior year with emphasis on crystal chemistry; experimental techniques; kinetics and thermodynamics; electric, optical, thermal, and mechanical properties of materials; statistical experimental design; and courses on engineering design and scientific methodology. This culminates in a senior capstone assignment, generally in the form of independent research published in a bound, archived thesis. Job opportunities are generally robust, and students with B.S. degrees are highly sought for a wealth of positions such as process engineer, research technician, technical sales representative, field engineers, metallurgists, and ceramic engineers."

Many engineers continue on for a master's degree either immediately after graduation or after a few years of work experience. A master's degree generally takes two years of study. A doctoral degree requires at least four years of study and research beyond the bachelor's degree and is usually completed by engineers interested in research or teaching at the college level. "Graduate degrees enhance the students' ability to find employment in research settings, as technical managers, and in national laboratories and academia," Professor Hellmann says.

Certification or Licensing

Licensing is not generally required for most materials engineering professions. However, licensing is recommended to enhance your credentials and make yourself open to more job opportunities.

In general, the licensing process for all branches of engineering results in the formal designation of Professional Engineer (PE). Requirements vary from state to state but generally it takes about four to five years to become a licensed PE. Many engineers begin the process while still in college by taking the Fundamentals of Engineering (FE) exam, an eight-hour test that covers everything from electronics, chemistry, mathematics, and physics to the more advanced engineering issues.

Once a candidate has successfully passed the FE exam, the next requirement to fulfill is to acquire four years of progressive engineering experience. Some states require that materials engineers obtain experience under the supervision of a PE. Once a candidate has four years of on-the-job experience, he or she then takes another exam specific to their engineering area (each branch of engineering has its own specialized, upper-level test). Candidates who successfully complete this examination are officially referred to as professional engineers. Without this designation, engineers aren't allowed to refer to themselves as PEs, or function in the same legal capacity as PEs.

Toby does not have a professional license. "It is not required in the materials field," he says, "especially if you work in the automotive industry. However, it certainly is a worthwhile pursuit if you plan to become an independent consultant, to work in the testing field, and especially if you become involved in litigation activities like expert witness testimony."

Internships and Volunteerships

Most materials engineering programs require that students participate in an internship program with a company employing materials engineers; some programs may require you to take two internships. "Our students are highly encouraged to supplement their classroom experience with research internships in university, industrial, and national laboratories," Professor Hellmann says. Schools with degree programs that require an internship usually will have a partnership set up with local industry. Internships will give you a chance to make valuable contacts as well as learn more about the field from experienced engineers. Internships can last anywhere from four months to a year.

WHO WILL HIRE ME?

Toby Padfield landed his first job through a friend that had graduated a year before him. "We were both involved in an extracurricular student design project sponsored by SAE International," he explains, "and he recommended that I interview with his company for a full-time job. I had worked with the on-campus recruiting office to arrange several other interviews, and ended up receiving five employment offers. It was a difficult decision to choose between the final two, one in the aerospace field and one in the automotive

field, but my love of cars won out, and I took the job working with my friend at a small automotive design and research company in suburban Detroit."

As a high school senior, you might want to inquire with established manufacturing companies about internships and summer employment opportunities. College career services offices can also help you find employers that participate in cooperative education programs, where high school students work at materials engineering jobs in exchange for course credits.

Most materials engineers find their first job through their colleges' career services office. Technical recruiters visit universities and colleges annually to interview graduating students and possibly offer them jobs. Materials engineers can also find work by directly applying to companies through job listings at state and private employment services or in classified advertisements in newspapers and trade publications.

Upon graduation most materials engineers go to work in industry. In industry, materials engineers fall into five main employment groups: manufacturing (where the products are made and tested), material applications and development, machinery/equipment (which requires advanced knowledge of mechanical engineering), government positions, and consulting (where you will need your Professional Engineer licensing). According to the *Occupational Outlook Handbook,* approximately 68 percent of the 24,000 materials engineers in the United States work in manufacturing, mainly in computer and electronic products, fabricated metal products, transportation equipment, machinery manufacturing, and primary metal production.

Other materials engineers may continue their studies and go on to teach in higher education. Most materials programs have advanced programs for master's and doctoral studies.

WHERE CAN I GO FROM HERE?

In general, advancing through the ranks of materials engineers is similar to other disciplines. Working in entry-level positions usually means executing the research, plans, or theories that someone else has originated. With additional experience and education, materials engineers begin to tackle projects solo or, at least, accept responsibility for organizing and managing them for a supervisor. Those materials engineers with advanced degrees (or, at this point in time, a great deal of experience) can move into supervisory or administrative positions within any one of the major categories, such as research, development, or design. Eventually, those materials engineers who have distinguished themselves by consistently producing successful projects, and who have polished their business and managerial skills, will advance to become the directors of engineering for an entire plant or research division.

Engineers should keep current on technological advances in their chosen specialty throughout their careers. Many materials engineers join professional associations such as ASM International and the Minerals, Metals, and Materials Society. These associations hold annual conferences and meetings, in addition to other activities, which keep members up to date on recent developments and events within the industry. Special recognition—awards, scholarships, grants, and

Related Jobs

- automotive engineers
- biomedical engineers
- ceramic technicians
- chemical engineers
- chemists
- civil engineers
- electrical and electronics engineers
- environmental engineers
- geologists
- geophysicists
- industrial engineers
- iron and steel industry workers
- materials engineering educators
- materials engineering technicians
- mechanical engineers
- metallographers
- mining engineers
- nondestructive testers
- plastics products manufacturing workers
- plastics technicians
- safety engineers

fellowships—are often given to those who demonstrate outstanding achievement in the field. For example, the Application to Practice Award is presented by the Minerals, Metals, and Materials Society to individuals who excel in translating their research work into practical manufacturing applications.

WHAT ARE THE SALARY RANGES?

Materials engineers are among the highest paid engineers in the engineering professions. The U.S. Department of Labor reports a median annual income for all materials engineers of $69,660 in 2005. At the low end of the scale, 10 percent of materials engineers earned less than $44,090 annually. The highest paid 10 percent had annual incomes of more than $105,330 during this same time period. Starting salaries for those with bachelor's degrees in materials engineering averaged approximately $50,982 in 2005, according to a survey by the National Association of Colleges and Employers. Salaries for government workers are generally less than those who work for private companies.

Materials engineers can expect a good benefits package, including paid sick, holiday, vacation, and personal time; medical coverage; stock options; 401(k) plans; and other perks, depending on the company and industry.

WHAT IS THE JOB OUTLOOK?

Toby Padfield feels that the future outlook is good for materials engineering—especially for the specific areas of electronic materials (semiconductors, computer chips, etc.) and biomedical applications. "The traditional jobs in primary raw materials production (steel, aluminum, etc.) and metal-related manufacturing (forging, heat treating, wire and tube production, etc.) are on the decline," he says, "but the increased government spending in military and space programs has resulted in more jobs in these fields."

Professor John Hellmann also sees strong employment prospects in materials engineering. "Materials engineering is a very well-camouflaged discipline," he says. "Everyone has heard of electrical, chemical, industrial, mechanical, or nuclear engineering. But very few people hear of materials science and engineering before they get to college. It is a very exciting and rewarding discipline because no other engineering field can advance without materials scientists and engineers inventing new materials, processes for manufacturing them, and developing ways to improve other products and processes by incorporating advanced materials."

Overall employment growth for all materials engineers is predicted by the U.S. Department of Labor to grow as fast as the average through 2014.

Mechanical Engineers

SUMMARY

Definition
Mechanical engineers design, test, build, and maintain all kinds of mechanical devices, components, engines, and systems. One of their chief concerns is the production, transmission, and use of power.

Alternative Job Titles
None

Salary Range
$50,236 to $67,590 to $120,000+

Educational Requirements
Minimum of a bachelor's degree. Advanced degree recommended.

Certification or Licensing
Required for certain positions

Employment Outlook
Average growth

High School Subjects
Computer science
Mathematics
Physics
Shop (trade/vo-tech education)

Personal Interests
Building things
Computers
Figuring out how things work

Mechanical engineer Matthew Robinson is working with a firm to design a crane concurrently with engineers designing a building. During one of the 3D model reviews, one of the system integration engineers notices a conflict between the diverter mechanism that aligns the umbilical cable in its cable tray, close to the runway support beams.

The runway could be cut short, Matthew and his colleagues reason, but the crane would no longer be able to lift items through the maintenance hatch. A quick team is assembled to discuss options to correct the oversight with a minimal impact to all those involved. Matthew and his fellow engineers ask themselves the following questions: Can part of the structural steel that supports the crane rail be cut out during construction to allow the diverter to pass without impacting the integrity of the beam? Is the cable flexible enough for the diverter to be slightly moved without relocating the cable spool or cable tray? Are there other options for lifting items into the area?

These questions and others will be answered as a team effort between Matthew and the other engineers designing the structure steel and rails, the engineers responsible for purchasing the diverter assembly, the engineers responsible for designing the steel plates embedded in the concrete walls to anchor items into the building, the system integration engineers, the crane technical experts, and the crane supplier.

If this type of brainstorming and problem-solving scenario sounds interesting, then you might be interested in a career as a mechanical engineer.

WHAT DOES A MECHANICAL ENGINEER DO?

Mechanical engineers design and manufacture a variety of items, primarily tools and machines, which generate, transmit, or use power. The items created by mechanical engineers may be used within their own field, but a great deal of mechanical engineering involves designing tools that other specialist engineers or professionals use in their areas of expertise. The mechanical engineer's work falls into the general areas of energy, manufacturing, and engineering-design mechanics.

Beginning with a basic problem—say, how to transport a great number of people through an urban environment quickly and cheaply, how to deter sea mammals from swimming into commercial fishing nets, or how to dissect a single-nerve cell under a microscope—the mechanical engineer researches the existing strategies of solving these problems to determine if there are alternative solutions. In addition to research, he or she conducts experiments and creates models.

Based on the information gleaned from his or her research, the mechanical engineer next creates alternative solutions, complete with new experiments, models, and formulations to test his or her hypotheses. From these tests come the mechanical engineer's designs for a new, partially submerged railway, an ultrasonic device that transmits high-pitched sounds to warn dolphins and seals, or a laser-based microscopic scalpel. Often, part of the design process also includes coming up with the means of manufacturing or producing the solution. In addition, mechanical engineers design instruments, controls, and power-producing engines such as internal combustion engines, steam and gas turbines, and jet engines.

Even after designing a new device, tool, or machine, the mechanical engineer again submits his or her creations to further testing. Improvements and modifications to the original design are made, and even more testing occurs, both in the laboratory and in the field.

Once the design or theory has been put through many tests and is reasonably, if not completely, error-free—or "bug-proof"—the mechanical engineer then assists in the manufacturing process. He or she selects the proper raw materials, equipment, machines, and systems necessary to make the best product, whether that product is a railway system, an ultrasonic device, or a micro probe. In addition, the mechanical engineer is responsible for supervising the setup, start-up, and safe operation of the product's manufacture.

Finally, the mechanical engineer oversees the day-to-day operation and maintenance of the manufacturing process: supervising technicians and machine operators, assessing the safety and efficiency of the system, and guiding the repairs and regular maintenance of the machines and equipment.

The above aspects of the mechanical engineer's job could easily be performed by one individual; this is often the case in smaller companies or projects. On the other hand, large manufacturers can more readily afford to employ many individuals with specialized knowledge to work on specific tasks or areas; in this way a research/development team of 10 mechanical engineers are all working on alternative fuel sources, while another 10 mechanical engineers are devoted to the design of a machine that could deliver an alternative fuel, while yet another 10 mechanical engineers are concerned with testing the machines developed by the design team . . . and so on and so forth through the various stages of the manufacturing process—from concept to product. Most mechanical engineers are employed in one of the following areas of concentration: research, development, design, testing, manufacturing, operations and maintenance, and sales. As these areas tend to overlap, and as it is necessary to share information and ideas in order to solve mechanics-based problems, engineers in each area will work closely with one another to create successful solutions.

Mechanical engineers are employed in industries as diverse as automotive, computers, heating and air-conditioning, farm equipment, petroleum, metals, and utilities, among others. Depending on the industry in which they work, mechanical

---

Lingo to Learn

conduction The process by which heat travels through a substance.

convection The process by which heat is transferred by the movement of fluids.

gear A toothed wheel, cylinder, or other machine element that, when turned, fits with another toothed element to transmit motion, or to change speed or direction.

generator A device, consisting of a magnet and coil of wire, which transforms mechanical energy into electrical energy.

mechanism A part of a machine containing two or more parts arranged so that motion of one part compels the motion of the others.

momentum The measurement of the motion of a body, determined by multiplying its mass by its velocity.

---

engineers provide a wide array of services; in fact, mechanical engineering is considered the broadest category of engineering, encompassing the widest variety of tasks and functions. However, many mechanical engineers end up specializing in one area, such as applied mechanics, design engineering, heat transfer, power plant engineering, pressure vessels, and underwater technology.

WHAT IS IT LIKE TO BE A MECHANICAL ENGINEER?

Matthew Robinson has been a mechanical engineer for nearly six years. He is employed by Bechtel National, Inc. in

Richland, Washington. Matthew says that the best part about being an engineer is that you rarely do the same thing from one day to the next. "Today, for example, I worked with several other engineers as well as nontechnical specialists in budgeting, scheduling, and quality to plan the procurement of a special crane being built in Philadelphia, incorporating a large spool designed in the United Kingdom that holds a 3.5" thick power cable from Germany. Last week, I was meeting with safety engineers to establish guidelines on how to design similar cranes so they could be operated without the risk of injury to the operator or the public. Last year, I was reviewing designs against the customer design basis. The year before that, I was designing tools to remotely repair contaminated equipment from behind a three-foot-thick concrete wall."

Working conditions for mechanical engineers vary. Most work indoors in offices, research laboratories, or production departments of factories and shops. Depending on the job, however, a significant amount of work time may be spent on a noisy factory floor, at a construction site, or at another field operation. Matthew works indoors, but travels during the job process to ensure that everything goes smoothly. "When we initially place an order for equipment," he says, "I travel to the manufacturer's shop to make sure their engineers understand what I need. When they have completed manufacturing, I'll likely return to watch the factory acceptance test. After the equipment is delivered, there is a good chance that I will transfer to the construction site to help install the equipment. After all of the equipment has been installed, I could be involved in the commissioning of the equipment (making sure that it operates like it did in the manufacturer's shop, as well as with all the interfacing equipment)."

Mechanical engineers have traditionally designed systems on drafting boards, but since the introduction of sophisticated software programs, design is increasingly done on computers.

Engineering is for the most part a cooperative effort. While the specific duties of an engineer may require independent work, each project is typically the job of an engineering team. Such a team might include other engineers, engineering technicians, and engineering technologists.

Mechanical engineers generally have a 40-hour workweek; however, their working hours are often dictated by project deadlines. They may work long hours to meet a deadline, or show up on a second or third shift to check production at a factory or a construction project. Matthew typically 40 hours a week, although he works overtime about once a month to keep his projects on schedule. "The nice thing about working for a construction company," he says, "is that the engineers are paid for their overtime, which isn't typical of the engineering profession."

Mechanical engineering can be a very satisfying occupation. Engineers often get the pleasure of seeing their designs or modifications put into actual, tangible form. Conversely, it can be frustrating when a project is stalled, full of errors, or even abandoned completely.

What Is a Machine?

What comes to mind when you think of a machine? A car engine? A sewing machine? A movie projector? Indeed, these are all machines, but so is a hammer, a screwdriver, a wheel, a crowbar; anything that helps you do work is a machine. There are six so-called "simple machines" upon which mechanical engineering is traditionally based. They are the lever, the pulley, the wheel and axle, the inclined plane, the screw, and the gear. We use these simple machines alone and combined, forming "complex machines" for five general purposes: to transform energy, to transfer energy, to multiply force, to multiply speed, and to change the direction of force.

DO I HAVE WHAT IT TAKES TO BE A MECHANICAL ENGINEER?

An innate sense of curiosity is probably the most essential requirement for mechanical engineers. They work with numbers and theories, so having a compelling interest in the results is key to enjoying the work and being successful at it. Without that natural desire to figure out how things work, the job of a mechanical engineer would quickly grow dry and boring. "Engineers are problem solvers," Matthew says, "and the solution to the problems aren't always readily apparent. So I would have to say curiosity and perseverance are important traits."

Technically, mechanical engineers also should be the kind of individuals who pay scrupulous attention to their projects, from the slightest detail to the organizing principles. Calculations must be flawless, specifications must be accurate, and all drawings must be complete. A misplaced decimal point on a drawing can be devastating to a project. Mechanical engineers need to be willing to devote the extra time it takes to thoroughly and exhaustively research any and all possibilities, and then analyze them for their potential.

Second only to analytical skills is the ability to be decisive under pressure. One of the toughest parts of this job is to make the correct or best decision when several viable options are available. Confidence helps in this regard, and that is only developed through experience and hard work; knowing that all possible solutions and strategies have been endlessly reworked and revisited in order to ensure that the final solution really is the best solution.

A knack for resourcefulness is also a crucial quality for the successful mechanical engineer. Many projects are tied to strict budgets, so the mechanical engineer who consistently comes up with cost-effective alternatives is certain to find himself or herself in high demand.

Finally, ideas are only as good as they sound. If you can't communicate your earth-shattering discovery, guess what? It will go unnoticed, or worse, someone else who can better communicate its impact will take all the credit for it. Learn to

To Be a Successful Mechanical Engineer, You Should . . .

- have an inquisitive mind
- have good written and oral communication skills
- be interested in figuring out how things work
- have an aptitude for math and science
- be attentive to details and a good problem solver
- have the ability to make decisions and stick to them

speak clearly and concisely, and people will listen.

HOW DO I BECOME A MECHANICAL ENGINEER?

Education

Matthew, like many college students, found his way to an engineering career through a slightly unconventional path. "My first year of college," he explains, "I was determined to find a career that dealt with my broad interests in art, science, and math. When I tried to find the architecture department, I found out the university I attended didn't offer that degree, but they did have a program in mechanical engineering technology. I was hooked after the first class."

High School

If you are interested in pursuing a career in mechanical engineering, you should get off to a solid start by taking as many science, mathematics, and computer science courses as are offered, especially algebra, geometry, calculus, trigonometry, physics, and computer science. Mechanical engineers do far less hand-drafting than before, but good drafting skills are still highly recommended. "Technical drawing or 'drafting' is an excellent place to start," Matthew recommends. "Auto shop would be good too, if available." In addition, taking a course in computerized drafting is a good idea. English, literature, and speech classes are also important for building strong communication skills. Knowing one or more foreign languages could feasibly triple the number of jobs available to you.

In addition to school subjects, you should pursue whatever hobbies, groups, or projects that intrigue you. These very same interests may one day turn out to be your life's work; at the very least, a hobby or interest can offer the chance to develop related skills and personal qualities, such as perseverance and precision. Matthew enjoys building things. He designed and built a timed underground sprinkler system for his house, as well as miscellaneous furniture (bookshelves, picture frames, a headboard, a desktop, and a workbench). "I'm also a bit of a computer junkie, playing games and piecing together systems," he says. "It doesn't seem like it would tie in so much with engineering, but it develops a level of comfort with office automation tools such as word processors, spreadsheets, databases, and solid modeling/CAD—all of which are additional items in an engineers problem-solving toolbox."

Postsecondary Training

The core of the mechanical engineer's work is based in the mechanical sciences. Each mechanical engineer must have a broad understanding of these sciences, and he or she must be able to apply them to practical uses. The typical course of study includes dynamics, which is concerned with the relation between forces in motion; and thermodynamics, which is concerned with the relationships between the forms of heat, energy, and power. The other areas are automatic control, heat transfer, fluid flow, lubrication, and the basic properties of materials. While these topics and subjects are covered in high school, they are covered in much greater depth in college-level courses.

A bachelor's degree in mechanical engineering or mechanical engineering technology is the minimum educational level required to work in this field; it is also the first step toward becoming a professional engineer. Matthew has a bachelor of science degree in mechanical engineering technology, which, he says, "equates to approximately four years of school in a very diverse set of classes: math through calculus (a mechanical engineering degree would go even higher), a full year of physics, then a more in-depth look at the way things work, from basic electric circuits, to the way heat, fluid, and air moves. The classes are definitely challenging, but if you were meant to be an engineer, they will only answer the questions you've been asking all your life."

Many colleges and universities with programs in mechanical engineering follow an approved course of study as set forth by the Accreditation Board for Engineering and Technology (http://www.abet.org). Programs do exist that are not accredited, however. Potential students of mechanical engineering should verify that the programs they are considering are accredited. The typical program lasts four years, although some may last longer and/or require that students continue with graduate work in the field.

The first two years of most mechanical engineering programs are typically devoted to mathematics, physics, and chemistry. Students take such math courses as calculus, sequences and series, linear algebra, and elementary differential equations; they also take basic engineering courses like mechanics, thermodynamics, fluid mechanics, material sciences, and electrical sciences.

In the junior and senior years students study advanced mechanical engineering, covering areas such as dynamics, design of elements, heat transfer, computer integrated manufacturing, lasers, pulmonary mechanics, stress analysis, and air-conditioning and refrigeration. Many programs require that students also take classes in computer programming. In addition, students are generally asked to fulfill core requirements in supporting fields such as the humanities and communications.

A graduate degree is a prerequisite for becoming a university professor or researcher. It may also lead to a higher level job within an engineering department or firm. Some companies encourage their employees to pursue graduate education by offering tuition-reimbursement programs. Because technology is rapidly developing, mechanical engineers need to continue their education, formally or informally, throughout their careers. Conferences, seminars, and professional journals serve to educate engineers about developments in the field.

Certification or Licensing

Engineers whose work may affect the life, health, or safety of the public must be registered according to regulations in all 50 states and the District of Columbia. Licensed engineers are called professional engineers (PEs). While licensing is generally voluntary, it may be mandatory for some jobs today. For example, consultants in mechanical engineering are required by law to be PEs. Licensing also assures employers that job applicants meet state legal regulations. Licensing is also tied to higher salaries, better jobs, more responsibilities, and timely promotions.

Requirements vary from state to state but it generally takes about four to five years to become a licensed PE. Many mechanical engineers begin the process while still in college by taking the Fundamentals of Engineering (FE) exam, an eight-hour test that covers everything from electronics, chemistry, mathematics, and physics to more advanced engineering issues.

Once a candidate has successfully passed the FE exam, the next requirement to fulfill is to acquire four years of pro-gressive engineering experience. Some states require that you obtain your experience under the supervision of a PE. Once a candidate has four years of on-the-job experience, he or she then takes another exam—the Principles and Practice of Engineering (PPE)— which is specific to mechanical engineering (each branch of engineering has its own specialized, upper-level test). Candidates who successfully complete this examination are officially referred to as Professional Engineers. Without this designation, mechanical engineers aren't allowed to refer to themselves as PEs, or function in the same legal capacity as PEs.

Matthew is licensed as a PE, qualified in mechanical engineering. To become licensed, he successfully took and completed the FE and the PPE exams. "The tests are difficult, and many engineers fail or don't even try," he says.

Certification is also granted by a technical or professional organization for the purpose of recognizing and documenting an individual's abilities in a specific engineering field. For example, the Society of Manufacturing Engineers offers the following designations to mechanical engineers who work in manufacturing and who meet education and experience requirements: certified manufacturing engineer and certified engineer manager.

Internships and Volunteerships

An internship may be required as part of your college curriculum. This hands-on work experience at a company employing mechanical engineers will give you a chance to work side-by-side with mechanical engineers on real-life problems and projects. This experience allows students to gain valuable exposure to the field and practical applications of their studies, as well as providing them with future networking contacts. Internships routinely last 4 to 12 months and are usually arranged for by the school, especially when the internship is a requirement for the degree. They are usually nonpaying, but do count toward semester credit hours.

The American Society of Mechanical Engineers also offers a list of companies that offer internships at its Web site, http://www.asme.org/Communities/Students.

WHO WILL HIRE ME?

Approximately 215,000 mechanical engineers are employed in the United States, according to the U.S. Department of Labor. All large industries employ mechanical engineers, so depending on your interests and particular skills, you have many options. Some of the major industries employing mechanical engineers include automobile, heavy and light machinery, machine tool, construction equipment, transportation, heating and refrigeration, and power and energy, as well as engineering or consulting firms, and government laboratories and agencies.

Jobs for mechanical engineers are usually advertised in the multitude of industry trade magazines. Some major cities have a large engineering jobs section in their classified pages where employers advertise openings. Increasingly, jobs are posted on the Internet. The American Society of Mechanical Engineers offers a large jobs section on its Web site, http://www.asme.org.

Many mechanical engineers find their first job through their college or university career services office. Many companies send recruiters to college campuses to interview and sign up engineering graduates. Other students might find a position in the company where they had a summer or part-time job. Newspapers and professional journals often list job openings for engineers. Job seekers who wish to work for the federal government should contact the nearest branch of the Office of Personnel Management.

WHERE CAN I GO FROM HERE?

Many career avenues are open to the mechanical engineer, perhaps more so than any other engineering discipline. Career paths in mechanical engineering resemble those in other branches of engineering in that mechanical engineers can pursue a technical career in research and development; a teaching and research post at a major research university; a corporate position in the sales department of a manufacturer; or a supervisory/managerial position directing the work of other mechanical engineers in the design and manufacture of products. Matthew sees his career path leading toward project management (managing the people that manage the people doing the design). "If I find that I don't like being that far away from the engineering activities," he says, "then I'll take a step back and do technical management [manage the people doing the design]."

Clearly, an ambitious candidate in each of these scenarios will rise to these roles with the right education level, experience, and hard, disciplined work, but other qualities can make the difference between a stellar career and a mediocre one; again, it depends on the industry in which the person works and the person's area of specialization. For instance, the person with excellent business skills, even an advanced degree in business administration, will be more likely to move into an upper-level position.

Mechanical engineers entering the job market with only a bachelor's degree will find that without further education and training their possibilities for advancement may be more difficult. On the other hand, mechanical engineers with advanced degrees and the Professional Engineer (PE) designation will qualify for higher-level, supervisory positions.

WHAT ARE THE SALARY RANGES?

Mechanical engineers are among the highest-paid engineers. The National Association of Colleges and Employers reports the following 2005 starting salaries for mechanical engineers by educational achievement: bachelor's degree, $50,236; master's degree, $59,880; and Ph.D., $68,299. The U.S. Department of Labor reports that experienced mechanical engineers earned median annual salaries of $67,590 in 2005, with the top 10 percent earning $101,660 or more. Also, earning your certification as a PE will boost your salary. Engineers in management positions with 25 years of experience can earn $120,000 and more.

Mechanical engineers can usually expect a good benefits package, including

Related Jobs

- aerospace engineers
- automotive engineers
- biomedical engineers
- ceramic engineers
- civil engineers
- computer-aided design drafters and technicians
- electrical and electronics engineers
- environmental engineers
- industrial engineers
- mechanical engineering educators
- mechanical engineering technicians
- metallurgical engineers
- optomechanical engineers
- packaging engineers
- petroleum engineers
- plant engineers
- plastics engineers
- robotics engineers and technicians
- safety engineers
- structural engineers
- tool and die designers
- transportation engineers

paid sick, holiday time, vacation, and personal time; medical coverage; stock options; 401(k) plans; and other perks, depending on the company and industry.

WHAT IS THE JOB OUTLOOK?

Employment of mechanical engineers is expected to grow more slowly than the average through 2014, according to the U.S. Department of Labor (USDL). Engineers will be needed to meet the demand for more efficient industrial machinery and machine tools. The USDL also predicts good opportunities for mechanical engineers who are involved with new technologies such as biotechnology, nanotechnology, and materials science. It should also be noted that increases in defense spending in the wake of the terrorist attacks of September 11, 2001 may create improved employment opportunities for engineers within the federal government.

SECTION 3

Do It Yourself

On July 20, 1969, a human being walked on the pocked, chalky-white surface of the moon for the very first time. As he dropped to the surface from the last rung of the lunar module, Neil Armstrong's historic words were immediately transmitted back to earth: "That's one small step for a man, one giant leap for mankind." Millions of people sat motionless before their radios and televisions, trying to wrap their minds around the enormity of what he had just uttered and, more importantly, from where his voice came.

In the years since Armstrong, Buzz Aldrin, and Michael Collins made that incredible journey to the moon and back, much has changed about our world, and some of those very changes are a direct result of the engineering genius that, through years of research, design, and development, sent three Americans to the moon. Today, for instance, government and private communications satellites orbit the earth, transmitting live broadcasts from all around the world; food products are sealed into special containers that don't require cooling—helping people who live in hot, isolated regions with no electricity; special, lightweight, synthetic materials protect mountain climbers and Indy 500 auto racers alike from exposure to heat and cold; and computers that used to be housed in several large rooms now fit inside a business executive's pocket (the chips which power them fit on the head of a pin). Even now, scientists are working to perfect a way of "farming" on space stations the antidotes to deadly viruses that are too expensive to produce on Earth.

The fantastic discoveries and developments that resulted from space exploration are, however, only one example of how the work of engineers affects our lives. Even something as seemingly simple as hopping on a bike for an afternoon ride demonstrates the degree to which engineering is involved with nearly every instant and every aspect of our lives. From the gears on your bicycle to the reflective, plastic swoosh on your tennis shoes to the dense Styrofoam padding the inside of your bike helmet to the LCD display on your watch—these were once the newfangled gadgets of the future, a brainstorm in the mind of an engineer somewhere. Engineers turn problems into solutions, setbacks into progress. If you see opportunities where others see only obstacles, perhaps you're cut out to be an engineer.

Are you naturally curious, always asking questions? When something at home breaks, do you take it to a mechanic or repair technician, or do you pull out your toolbox and try to fix it yourself? Do you enjoy taking things apart even if they're not broken just so you can see what the insides look like? Just to see if you can put it back together again? Do you actually look forward to solving problems and feel exhilarated when you solve them?

John Stasey's father is a mechanical engineer. At age 14, John already knows he wants to follow in his dad's footsteps. John has made a hobby out of taking things apart and putting them back together again. He scours garage sales, looks in second-hand stores, even scouts out the trash, searching for old, broken mechanical objects—toasters, wall clocks, light fixtures, and lawn mowers. Once he finds them, he tries to repair them. This is often much easier than it might seem; in a disposable society people are so used to tossing something out once it stops working, rather than trying to fix it, that often, the device or machine needs little more than a little oil to lubricate the working parts. After taking them apart, John gives each item a complete overhaul, cleaning all of the individual pieces, oiling them as necessary. With certain items, John waits for his father's help, but he learns quickly, and rarely has to have his father show him how to make a repair twice. More and more, John works alone, saving the stubborn problems for when his father has time to help him. Once the items are repaired John saves them for the family's annual summer garage sale. At the last sale John made $230.

John's financial success quickly prompted a couple of his friends to join him in his hobby. Together, they work in John's basement after school and on the weekends, figuring that as a group they can collect more salvageable items, fix them faster, learn from each other's projects, and make a bigger profit at this summer's garage sale. Occasionally they work on items that they just simply can't fix, and often they don't realize this until they've spent a couple of days working on the problem. Although John admits this can be very frustrating, he emphasizes that it's definitely not a waste of time. "We learn as much or more from the things we can't fix as we learn from the things we do fix," he says.

At first glance, it might seem like John is just having a good time monkeying around with old, broken-down machines, and making a little spending money. Look a bit more closely and you'll realize that John is well on his way to becoming an engineer, if not a prosperous businessman. He has a working knowledge of machines and mechanics, is developing problem-solving and troubleshooting skills, and, now that he's working with a group of friends, he is developing the teamwork and communication skills crucial for success as an engineer. His hobby is helping him attain his dream of one day becoming a mechanical engineer. What are you doing to realize your dreams? What can you do now?

❑ WHAT CAN YOU DO?

More than you may realize. There are many ways young people can get involved in the field of engineering. As you can see from the number of chapters in this book, engineering is not just a single career, although each and every branch of engineering is based on the same fundamental understanding of science and math. No matter which branch of engineering they want to specialize in, most engineers start by acquiring solid math and science skills, as well as some sort of experience that allows them to apply their math and science knowledge in a practical, hands-on manner. Depending on what type of engineer you want to be, your opportunities for experience and exploration will vary.

If you look in the right places and are creative, you will see that it isn't difficult to locate many fun and helpful opportunities to learn engineering and science skills or, like John did, even create your own opportunities.

Books and Periodicals

Looking for detailed information on engineering? One great place to start is your local or high school library, which contain countless books and periodicals about engineering specialties, competitions, famous engineers, the history of engineering, groundbreaking inventions, and almost any other engineering-related topic you can think of. For a great list of books and periodicals about engineering, check out the "Read a Book" chapter in Section 4 of this book.

Surf the Web

You probably don't ever stop to realize how much easier our lives have become as a result of the Internet. Information that we once had to gather via visits to the library, snail mail, or phone calls can now be accessed almost instantaneously by the click of a mouse. What engineering materials are available on the Internet? A better question is what is *not* available on the Internet? In short, you can surf the Web to find engineering associations, discussion groups, competitions, educational programs, glossaries, company information, worker profiles and interviews, and the list goes on and on. So log on and begin educating yourself about engineering! To help get you started, check out the "Surf the Web" chapter in Section 4 for more info.

Math

The first thing you can do is pay close attention in math class. All engineering fields use math. Lots of it. Math ability is key to success in engineering, so if this isn't your favorite subject and you think you may want to be an engineer, then it's time to go in for extra help after class. No matter how good you are at fixing things or understanding complex problems, if your math skills are poor, you can't be an engineer. Why? The scientific principles which govern engineering rely on the accurate execution of, you guessed it, mathematical equations and formulas. You can't do one without the other. Don't worry, though, with a little hard work and determination you can certainly conquer math. The more you do it, the easier it gets. Better yet, try and find ways to use your math skills, polished or not. Using practical, real examples to which you can apply the math is one of the best ways to make any subject come alive.

If you're already a whiz at math (maybe you even feel a tingle in your spine when you solve that crazy problem that has everyone else stumped), then you're well on your way. Keep it up. But don't grow complacent and let your spark fizzle; keep pushing yourself, keep giving your math-savvy mind new challenges.

Math, Science, & Engineering Clubs

Joining a science club, such as the Junior Engineering Technical Society, can provide hands-on activities and opportunities to explore scientific topics in depth. Student members can join competitions and design structures that exhibit scientific know-how.

Many junior high and high schools have math and science clubs that meet after school. These are great places to advance your math and science skills beyond the classroom. And how about fueling a little healthy competition? Some clubs even participate in competitions with other local high schools. Talk to the math and science teachers at your school about getting involved. If your school doesn't already have a science or engineering club, start one yourself. Enlist the help of one of your math or science teachers; most likely, they'll be overjoyed to find a group of kids who are willing and interested in exploring math and science in more depth. They will probably be happy to assist, or at least steer you in the right direction. Like other school clubs or teams, a math, science, or engineering club needs the leadership of a teacher, especially if you're thinking of conducting experiments using school equipment and facilities. Just stop and think about that for a moment.

Imagine the super-cool experiments you and your fellow club members can conduct. You're in charge, so whatever you're interested in exploring, studying, proving—you can do. And because of the wide scope of engineering, there should be no shortage of topics your club can study and perform experiments on, topics like physics, electricity, chemistry, mechanics. Working with others on projects like these helps you develop teamwork and problem-solving skills.

Among the projects which math, science, and engineering clubs have explored are alternative and experimental means of transportation (flying cars), fuel (solar power), and elaborate Mousetrap-like games that demonstrate different fundamentals of science.

Randy Clifton found a project his high school engineering club could solve that would gain him the respect of his principal, the janitors, the basketball team, and the whole student body. It also impressed the school superintendent so much that Randy's club was granted extra funds to buy some equipment they would need to perform more experiments. Here's how it happened.

The high school had a relatively old electronic scoreboard in their gym for basketball games. The scoreboard had analog numbers that were controlled electronically. Over the summer it broke down, and when one of the janitors went to take a look at it, he only made matters worse. A repairman was finally brought in to fix it, but the repair cost was too high for the school's budget at the time. The repair technician recommended that the school buy a new scoreboard. But that, too, was out of the question.

When school started that fall, just a few months before basketball season, Randy, along with his science teacher, the club's supervisor, persuaded the principal to let them have a look at the scoreboard. "It was a mess," Randy remembers. "It hadn't been properly maintained over the years so there was all kinds of crud and rust inside." Not to mention the additional damage done by the janitor.

Every day after school for a month the club's seven members went to work on the scoreboard. They pinpointed and identified the problems. They cleaned it and removed worn or damaged parts, replacing them with parts they made themselves in the shop room, or bought from the hardware store with money the principal donated. In the end repair costs were only $57—five times less than the repair technician estimated it would cost. The scoreboard went back up just days before the first game of the season. The crowd rewarded Randy and his engineering club with a big round of grateful applause.

Museums

Many cities have science museums where young people and adults can participate in interactive exhibits that teach principles of science and engineering. Talk to one of your teachers about a field trip to the museum—maybe volunteer to coordinate a field trip with a particular lesson. Of course, you can always go on your own or with some friends on a weekend or day off. In these museums you can find fun and exciting exhibits that demonstrate principles of electricity, chemistry, and the environment; show the inner mechanics of complex machines; and explore the intricacies of space travel.

Museums often provide opportunities for the curious young scientist and engineer beyond the museum's in-house exhibits. Some sponsor science clubs where you can have a much more active role in designing and running experiments. Some of the larger museums like the Museum of Science and Industry (http://www.msichicago.org) in Chicago have

teen volunteer programs in which qualified teens work in facilitating museum-organized activities for younger children. This is a great way to get involved in the museum, to really learn a subject, and to meet people in the industry. In addition to jobs in the major industries, museums also employ engineers and scientists to make creative exhibits that will keep the attention of visitors of all ages.

Lanna Jackson visited Chicago's Museum of Science and Industry with her family a couple times a year when she was in grade school. In junior high, she often visited the museum with friends on the weekends. Eventually Lanna and two of her friends decided to join one of the science clubs. The club met every Saturday and conducted a variety of experiments that were determined by the 15 club members and supervised by two adults. In June the current club ended festivities with the annual Science Club Network Jamboree, where other clubs from museums, schools, and community groups met for a day of science-related competitions. Lanna says that she made so many new friends and learned so much more that she plans on joining the club next year, too.

Familiarize Yourself with Engineering Tools

Many tools used by engineers are highly complex and expensive, and won't be available for you for study. But you can find many of the basic engineering tools in your family's workroom or garage. Try out these tools to get a better understanding of the daily work of engineers:

wrenches, screwdrivers, hammers, pliers, measuring tape, levels, chisels, vices, clamps, wire cutters, and saws. You might also purchase a microscope or ask your science teacher to show you how to use one. And don't forget computer and electronic tools such as calculators, software (such as CAD/CAM drafting programs), and Personal Digital Assistants (PDAs).

Experiments/Exercises

Trying your hand at engineering-related experiments and exercises is a fun and challenging way to get involved in engineering right now. For example, if you are interested in electrical engineering, you can build a radio or central processing unit of a computer. If you are interested in aerospace engineering, you could try working on cars and boats, which will provide you with a good opportunity to discover more about aerodynamics and physics. If you'd like to be a mechanical engineer, you could study and repair broken appliances and other equipment. If chemical engineering is your thing, you could purchase a starter chemistry kit and tackle some basic experiments. You get the idea!

Association Membership

Many professional engineering associations offer membership to high school and college students. Membership benefits include the chance to participate in association-sponsored competitions, seminars, and conferences; subscriptions to magazines (some of them geared specifically toward students) that provide the latest industry information; mentor-ing and networking opportunities; and access to financial aid. See the "Look to the Pros" chapter in Section 4 for more information on associations that offer student membership.

Summer Programs

An excellent way to get your feet wet when it comes to engineering is to participate in engineering and science summer programs at colleges and universities. Such activities will allow you to meet other young people who are interested in the field and help you to learn more about engineering specialties. After all, what better place is there to learn about engineering and educational opportunities than at a college or university! Summer programs usually consist of workshops, seminars, experiments, and other activities that introduce you to engineering. You'll also get a chance to talk with engineering students and faculty—so have your list of questions about the field ready. Summer programs are covered in depth in Section 4.

Internships

High school is not too soon to start looking for work related to engineering. One of the best ways to locate valuable, hands-on experience is to work as an intern, either after school, on the weekends, or during the summer. To be perfectly honest, there are many more internships available for college students. That shouldn't prevent you from trying to find a local company, museum, or manufacturer who would be willing to exchange experience for a little extra help. Start with the obvious places.

Ask your science and math teachers if they know of any companies in the area that offer internships or might be interested in having another pair of eyes, ears, and hands to help with projects. Contact adults you, your parents, or teachers know who are engineers. Where do they work? Could their company or workplace use your help? Be as enterprising as possible. If these leads turn up nothing, move on to less obvious places. For example, look through the summaries of the chapters included in this book. What is the basic role of each engineer? Focus on the verbs used to describe their work. Transportation engineers, for instance, coordinate many different aspects of traffic. What other companies or workplaces are involved with the coordination of events? How about the mayor's Special Events Office? Or the Philanthropy Committee for the local college? The scheduling office at an arena or convention center? You get the idea. Brainstorm all of the different possibilities, and then ask your parents and friends for their ideas and suggestions. The key to learning always lies in how well you can apply your knowledge. Where you intern and what the company produces are less important than learning how to apply the basic, elemental aspects of engineering in a real-world scenario. In the end, your initiative and creative thinking will go miles toward proving to your next employer what an asset you will be.

Information Interviews/Job Shadowing

Talking with engineers and shadowing them for a day will help you learn more about the pros and cons of being an engineer. Information interviews consist of a phone or in-person conversation with an engineer about his or her job. You can learn more about why they chose their specialty, their daily tasks, the tools and other equipment they use to do their job, what skills are required, and how best to prepare for the field. Remember to do the following when conducting an information interview: dress and act appropriately; arrive or call on time; have written questions prepared; listen closely and don't interrupt the subject while he or she is talking; have a notepad and pen ready to record the subject's responses; don't overstay your welcome (if the subject has volunteered 20 minutes of his or her time, than stick to that time frame), and be sure to thank the subject both verbally and in writing (send a thank you via mail soon after the interview) for his or her time.

Job shadowing simply means observing someone at their job. In the case of engineers, you might shadow them as they work in offices, laboratories, factories, construction sites, and other locales. Remember to do the following when shadowing a worker: dress and act appropriately, arrive on time, take plenty of notes, be positive (if the job seems boring, don't say so), follow the ground rules established by the subject, and thank the subject both verbally and in writing for the opportunity.

Ask your math or science teacher to help you arrange an information interview or job shadowing opportunity. Perhaps one of your parents has an engineer friend you could job shadow. You could also take the initiative and call or e-mail the public relations department of an engineering company near you to see if they can refer you to an engineer. Some engineering associations may also offer these opportunities to student members.

Employment

Take your internship experiences to the next level and look for paid jobs that not only use your blossoming engineering experience, but also provide you with the opportunity to add to your existing knowledge. Challenge yourself. Start by contacting the same firms you used to search for internships. Now that you have some practical experience under your belt, they may be more inclined to offer you an internship or, better yet, a paying position.

Don't think small, but be realistic. As hard as it is to get internships as a high school student, it's even more difficult to get jobs. If you're finding that employers are saving those choice positions for college students, aim just a little bit lower. Let employers know how interested you are in learning from the ground up and you just might find yourself learning how to operate a tool-and-die machine—and taking home a nice paycheck.

Technician-level jobs, or positions as apprentices to technicians, are another good place to look for work. Keep in mind that you will be competing with men and women who have trained in technical schools for some of these jobs, but with solid grades and an obvious desire to learn, your chances are good.

If you still turn up empty-handed, resort to the same tactics that helped you locate more unusual opportunities for internships. Brainstorm the specific tasks which different engineers complete. Mechanical engineers work with moving parts, engines, and machine repair. Try calling repair and automotive shops, and the service departments of companies or organizations that use equipment; inquire if they have any openings in maintenance or service/repair. Hospitals, golf courses, apartment buildings, and factories, for instance, all use specific types of machines and devices, and these places all need someone to help repair and maintain the equipment. You might find you have to work for free for a probationary period until you learn the ropes, but in the end, you'll have a paying job that will give you valuable experience.

SECTION 4

What Can I Do Right Now?

Get Involved: A Directory of Camps, Programs, and Competitions

Now that you've read about some of the different careers available in engineering, you may be anxious to experience this line of work for yourself, to find out what it's really like. Or perhaps you already feel certain that this is the career path for you and want to get started on it right away. Whichever is the case, this section is for you! There are plenty of things you can do right now to learn about engineering careers while gaining valuable experience. Just as important, you'll get to meet new friends and see new places.

In the following pages you will find programs designed to pique your interest in engineering and start preparing you for a career. You already know that this field is complex and highly technical, and that to work in it you need a solid education. Since the first step toward an engineering career will be gaining that education, we've found more than 40 programs that will start you on your way. Some are special introductory sessions, others are actual college courses—one of them may be right for you. Take time to read over the listings and see how each compares to your situation: how committed you are to engineering, how much of your money and free time you're willing to devote to it, and how the program will help you after high school. These listings are divided into categories, with the type of program printed right after its name or the name of the sponsoring organization.

❑ THE CATEGORIES

Camps

When you see an activity that is classified as a camp, don't automatically start packing your tent and mosquito repellent. Where academic study is involved, the term "camp" often simply means a residential program including both educational and recreational activities. It's sometimes hard to differentiate between such camps and other study programs, but if the sponsoring organization calls it a camp, so do we!

College Courses/Summer Study

These terms are linked because most college courses offered to students your age must take place in the summer, when you are out of school. At the same time, many summer study programs are sponsored by colleges and universities that want to attract future students and give them a head start in higher education. Summer study of almost any type is a good idea because it keeps your mind and your study skills sharp over the long vacation. Summer study at a college offers any number of additional benefits, including giving you the tools to make a well-informed decision about your future academic career. Study options, including some impressive college and university programs, account for most of the listings in this section—primarily because higher education is so crucial to every engineering career.

Competitions

Competitions are fairly self-explanatory, but you should know that there are only a few included here, for two reasons: one, a number of engineering competitions are part of general science contests too numerous to mention, and two, many engineering competitions are at the local and regional levels and so again are impractical to list here. What this means, however, is that if you are interested in entering a competition, you shouldn't have much trouble finding one yourself. Your guidance counselor or math and science teachers can help you start searching in your area.

Conferences

Conferences for high school students are usually difficult to track down because most are for professionals in the field who gather to share new information and ideas with each other. Don't be discouraged, though. A number of professional organizations with student branches invite those student members to their conferences and plan special events for them. Some student branches even run their own conferences; check the directory of student organizations at the end of this section for possible leads. This is an option worth pursuing because conferences focus on some of the most cur-

rent information available and also give you the chance to meet professionals who can answer your questions and even offer advice.

Employment and Internship Opportunities

As you may already know from experience, employment opportunities for teenagers can be very limited. This is particularly true in engineering, which requires workers with bachelor's and even graduate degrees. Even internships are most often reserved for college students who have completed at least one or two years of study in the field. Still, if you're very determined to find an internship or paid position in engineering, there may be ways to find one. See Section 3 "Do It Yourself," in this book for some suggestions.

Field Experience

This is something of a catch-all category for activities that don't exactly fit the other descriptions. But anything called a field experience in this book is always a good opportunity to get out and explore the work of engineering professionals.

Membership

When an organization is in this category, it simply means that you are welcome to pay your dues and become a card-carrying member. Formally joining any organization brings the benefits of meeting others who share your interests, finding opportunities to get involved, and keeping up with current events. Depending on how active you are, the contacts you make and the experiences you gain may help when the time comes to apply to colleges or look for a job.

In some organizations, you pay a special student rate and receive benefits similar to regular members. Many organizations, however, are now starting student branches with their own benefits and publications. As in any field, make sure you understand exactly what the benefits of membership are before you join.

Finally, don't let membership dues discourage you from making contact with these organizations. Some charge dues as low as $10 because they know that students are perpetually short of funds. When the annual dues are higher, think of the money as an investment in your future and then consider if it is too much to pay.

Incidentally . . .

We have included in these pages a few listings for localized programs and activities that are actually connected to larger movements or organizations. For example, some programs listed here are run by university branches of the Society of Women Engineers (SWE)—a national organization. Others are part of the Minority Introduction to Engineering (MITE) program. If you're interested in SWE or MITE, check with the colleges and universities that interest you to see if they have a branch of their own.

❑ PROGRAM DESCRIPTIONS

Once you've started to look at the individual listings themselves, you'll find that they contain a lot of information. Naturally, there is a general description of each program, but wherever possible we also have included the following details.

Application Information

Each listing notes how far in advance you'll need to apply for the program or position, but the simple rule is to apply as far in advance as possible. This ensures that you won't miss out on a great opportunity simply because other people got there ahead of you. It also means that you will get a timely decision on your application, so if you are not accepted, you'll still have some time to apply elsewhere. As for the things that make up your application—essays, recommendations, etc.—we've tried to tell you what's involved, but be sure to contact the program about specific requirements before you submit anything.

Background Information

This includes such information as the date the program was established, the name of the organization that is sponsoring it financially, and the faculty and staff who will be there for you. This can help you—and your family—gauge the quality and reliability of the program.

Classes and Activities

Classes and activities change from year to year, depending on popularity, availability of instructors, and many other factors. Nevertheless, colleges and universities quite consistently offer the same or similar classes, even in their summer sessions. Courses like Introduction to Mechanical

Engineering and Physics 101, for example, are simply indispensable. So you can look through the listings and see which programs offer foundational courses like these and which offer courses on more variable topics. As for activities, we note when you have access to recreational facilities on campus, and it's usually a given that special social and cultural activities will be arranged for most programs.

Contact Information

Wherever possible, we have given the title of the person whom you should contact instead of the name because people change jobs so frequently. If no title is given and you are telephoning an organization, simply tell the person who answers the phone the name of the program that interests you and he or she will forward your call. If you are writing, include the line "Attention: Summer Study Program" (or whatever is appropriate after "Attention") somewhere on the envelope. This will help to ensure that your letter goes to the person in charge of that program.

Credit

Where academic programs are concerned, we sometimes note that high school or college credit is available to those who have completed them. This means that the program can count toward your high school diploma or a future college degree just like a regular course. Obviously, this can be very useful, but it's important to note that rules about accepting such credit vary from school to school. Before you commit to a program offering high school credit, check with your guidance counselor to see if it is acceptable to your school. As for programs offering college credit, check with your chosen college (if you have one) to see if they will accept it.

Eligibility and Qualifications

The main eligibility requirement to be concerned about is age or grade in school. A term frequently used in relation to grade level is "rising," as in "rising senior"—someone who will be a senior when the next school year begins. This is especially important where summer programs are concerned. A number of university-based programs make admissions decisions partly in consideration of GPA, class rank, and standardized test scores. This is mentioned in the listings, but you must contact the program for specific numbers. If you are worried that your GPA or your ACT scores, for example, aren't good enough, don't let them stop you from applying to programs that consider such things in the admissions process. Often, a fine essay or even an example of your dedication and eagerness can compensate for statistical weaknesses.

Facilities

We tell you where you'll be living, studying, eating, and having fun during these programs, but there isn't enough room to go into all the details. Some of those details can be important: what is and isn't accessible for people with disabilities, whether the site of a summer program has air-conditioning, and how modern the laboratory and computer equipment are. You can expect most program brochures and application materials to address these concerns, but if you still have questions about the facilities, just call the program's administration and ask.

Financial Details

While a few of the programs listed here are fully underwritten by collegiate and corporate sponsors, most of them rely on you for at least some of their funding. Prices and fees given here were current at time of publication, but you should bear in mind that costs rise slightly almost every year. You and your parents must take costs into consideration when choosing a program. We always try to note where financial aid is available, but really, most programs will do their best to ensure that a shortage of funds does not prevent you from taking part.

Minorities

In the not-so-distant past, engineering was a field populated almost solely by Caucasian males—that is most certainly not the case today. Still, colleges and universities are working to promote even more diversity in the field, so there are any number of programs encouraging applicants of every gender, race, and ethnic background. However, when an engineering department bills its summer session as a "minority program," you must determine just who is a minority. If you are of Asian descent, you are a minority in the U.S. population, but not necessarily in engineering: Asian-Americans are so well represented in the field that the MITE program, among others, does not include them. In short, if you are interested in minority programs, make sure you know how they define the term.

Residential Versus Commuter Options

Simply put, some programs prefer that participating students live with other participants and staff members, others do not, and still others leave the decision entirely to the students themselves. As a rule, residential programs are suitable for young people who live out of town or even out of state, as well as for local residents. They generally provide a better overview of college life than programs in which you're only on campus for a few hours a day, and they're a way to test how well you cope with living away from home. Commuter programs may be viable only if you live near the program site or if you can stay with relatives who do. Bear in mind that for residential programs especially, the travel between your home and the location of the activity is almost always your responsibility and can significantly increase the cost of participation.

Finally . . .

Ultimately, there are three important things to bear in mind concerning all of the programs listed in this book. The first is that things change. Staff members come and go, funding is added or withdrawn, supply and demand determine which programs continue and which are terminated. Dates, times, and costs vary widely because of a number of factors. Because of this, the information we give you, although as current and detailed as possible, is just not enough on which to base your final decision. If you are interested in a program, you simply must write, call, fax, or e-mail the organization concerned to get the latest and most complete information available. This has the added benefit of putting you in touch with someone who can deal with your individual questions and problems.

Another important point to keep in mind when considering these programs is that the people who run them provided the information printed here. The editors of this book haven't attended the programs and don't endorse them: we simply give you the information with which to begin your own research. And after all, we can't pass judgment because you're the only one who can decide which programs are right for you.

The final thing to bear in mind is that the programs listed here are just the tip of the iceberg. No book can possibly cover all of the opportunities that are available to you—partly because they are so numerous and are constantly coming and going, but partly because some are waiting to be discovered. For instance, you may be very interested in taking a college course but don't see the college that interests you in the listings. Call their admissions office! Even if they don't have a special program for high school students, they might be able to make some kind of arrangements for you to visit or sit in on a class. Use the ideas behind these listings and take the initiative to turn them into opportunities!

❑ THE PROGRAMS

American Chemical Society

Competitions, Employment and Internship Opportunities, Field Experience, Membership

The American Chemical Society (ACS), formed in 1876, runs a number of educational and career-related programs for high school students interested in chemistry and chemical engineering, including an essay competition, the National Olympiad, tech prep programs, and summer employment opportunities for disadvantaged students. The ACS also publishes *ChemMatters,* a magazine for high school chemistry students, and even has high school curricula of its own. If you're interested in the chemical aspects of engineering, get in touch with the American Chemical Society.

American Chemical Society
1155 16th Street, NW
Washington, DC 20036
800-227-5558
help@acs.org
http://www.chemistry.org

American Indian Science & Engineering Society
Conference, Membership

The American Indian Science & Engineering Society (AISES) is a nonprofit organization founded in 1977 to encourage young American Indians to pursue careers in science, technology, and engineering. AISES welcomes students from kindergarten to 12th grade (whom they refer to as "pre-college students") as members; dues are only $10 per year. Pre-college student members can participate in many special programs, including the National American Indian Science and Engineering Fair, and attend the annual AISES Annual Conference, which features High School Day and a career fair. AISES also has a number of programs designed for entire classes and their teachers, so talk to your science or math teacher about getting involved with the Society. You can also contact them yourself or visit their Web site for more information.

American Indian Science & Engineering Society
PO Box 9828
Albuquerque, NM 87119-9828
505-765-1052
http://www.aises.org

The Center for Excellence in Education
Field Experience
The goal of the Center for Excellence in Education (CEE) is to nurture future leaders in science, technology, and business. And it won't cost you a dime: all of CEE's programs are absolutely free. Since 1984, the CEE has sponsored the Research Science Institute, a six-week residential summer program held at the Massachusetts Institute of Technology. Seventy-five high school students with scientific and technological promise are chosen from a field of more than 700 applicants to participate in the program, conducting projects with scientists and researchers. You can read more about specific research projects online.

The Center for Excellence in Education
8201 Greensboro Drive, Suite 215
McLean, VA 22102
703-448-9062
cee@cee.org
http://www.cee.org

Challenge Program at St. Vincent College
College Course/Summer Study
The Challenge Program, offered by St. Vincent College, is just what its name implies. Challenge gives gifted, creative, and talented students in grades 9 through 12 the opportunity to explore new and stimulating subjects that most high schools just can't cover. If you qualify for this program and are highly motivated, you can spend one week in July on the campus of St. Vincent College taking courses like robotics and aviation. Should you choose, you may live on campus, meeting and socializing with other students who share your ambitions and interests. Resident students pay a total of about $600 for the week while commuters pay closer to $500. For more information about Challenge and details of this year's course offerings, contact the program coordinator. There is a similar Challenge program for students in the sixth through ninth grades, usually held one week before the high school session.

Challenge Program at St. Vincent College
300 Fraser Purchase Road
Latrobe, PA 15650
412-532-5093
http://www.stvincent.edu/challenge_home

College and Careers Program
College Course/Summer Study
The Rochester Institute of Technology (RIT) offers its College and Careers Program for rising seniors who want to

experience college life and explore career options in engineering. The program, started in 1990, allows you to spend a Friday and Saturday on campus, living in the dorms and attending four sessions on the career areas of your choice. Each year, some sessions focus on the liberal arts and sciences, but between 10 and 20 sessions focus on engineering and technology. Topics vary but generally include introductions to civil, electrical, mechanical, and manufacturing engineering, among others. In each session, participants work with RIT students and faculty to gain some hands-on experience in the topic area. This residential program is held twice each summer, usually once in mid-July and again in early August. The registration deadline is one week before the start of the program, but space is limited and students are accepted on a first come, first served basis. For further information about the program and specific sessions on offer, contact the RIT admissions office.

College and Careers Program
Rochester Institute of Technology
Office of Admissions
60 Lomb Memorial Drive
Rochester, NY 14623-5604
585-475-6631
https://ambassador.rit.edu/careers2006/

Cornell University Summer College
College Course/Summer Study

As part of its Summer College for High School Students, Cornell University offers an Exploration in Engineering for students who have completed their sophomore, junior, or senior years. The Summer College session runs for six weeks from late June until early August. It is largely a residential program designed to acquaint you with all aspects of college life. The Exploration in Engineering seminar is one of several such seminars Cornell offers that allows students to survey various disciplines within the field and speak with working professionals. The seminar meets several times per week and includes laboratory projects and field trips. In addition, Summer College participants take two college-level courses of their own choosing, one of which should be in computer science or mathematics to complement the engineering focus. You must bear in mind that these are regular undergraduate courses condensed into a very short time span, so they are especially challenging and demanding. Cornell University awards letter grades and full undergraduate credit for the two courses you complete. Residents live and eat on campus and enjoy access to the university's recreational facilities and special activities. Academic fees total around $4,785, while housing, food, and recreation fees amount to an additional $2,465. Books, travel, and an application fee are extra. A very limited amount of financial aid is available. Applications are due in early May, although Cornell advises that you submit them well in advance of the deadline; those applying for financial aid must submit their applications by April 1. Further information and details of the application procedure are available from the Summer College office.

Cornell University Summer College for High School Students

Summer College
B20 Day Hall
Ithaca, NY 14853-2801
607-255-6203
http://www.sce.cornell.edu/sc

Explorations in Engineering, Women in Engineering, and Summer Youth Programs

College Course/Summer Study

Michigan Technological University (MTU) offers three different opportunities for high school students to explore engineering in a college setting. The residential Explorations in Engineering Program is for minority or economically disadvantaged students; freshmen, sophomores, and juniors are eligible. While living on campus for one week, participants engage in informational discussions and technical projects with MTU faculty and other professional engineers. The program is usually held in June or July, and applications are due in April. The only cost for the program is a $50 registration fee. The Women in Engineering Program is almost identical to the Minorities Program except, of course, that only female students are eligible. Finally, Michigan Technological University offers the Summer Youth Program for all students in the grades of 6 through 11. Participants attend one of four weeklong sessions usually held during the months of July or August, choosing either to commute or to live on campus. Students undertake an Exploration in one of many career fields—including engineering—through laboratory work, field trips, and discussions with MTU faculty and other professionals. The cost of the Summer Youth Program is $510 for the residential option, $300 for commuters. Applications are accepted up to one week before the Explorations program begins.

Explorations in Engineering, Women in Engineering, and Summer Youth Programs

Michigan Technological University
Youth Programs Office, Alumni House
1400 Townsend Drive
Houghton, MI 49931-1295
906-487-2219
888-773-2655
http://youthprograms.mtu.edu

Women in Engineering at the University of Maryland

College Course/Summer Study

The University of Maryland at College Park (UMCP) runs Exploring Engineering at the University of Maryland for Women for one week in July. (The program is called EE^2@UMD for short.) Rising juniors and seniors who are considering careers in engineering learn more about the various disciplines within the field by participating in fun activities, experiments, interesting workshops, and talking with professional engineers. Participants live on the UMCP campus. The program costs about $200 and does not include spending money or the cost of transportation to and from UMCP.

Scholarships are available. To be considered for the program, the university must receive a completed application form, a letter of recommendation, and a high school transcript by early April. For more information, contact the program directly.

EE²@UMD

Women in Engineering Program
University of Maryland
1134G Glenn L. Martin Hall
College Park, MD 20742
301-405-3931
http://www.eng.umd.edu/wie

Eye On Engineering and Computer Science

College Course/Summer Study

The Catholic University of America (CUA) offers rising seniors the chance to participate in Eye On Engineering and Computer Science. Students in the program explore the opportunities available to them in this field and even consider an undergraduate engineering degree as a solid foundation for graduate studies in law, medicine, and business. During the weeklong program held each July, participants take part in two research projects from a selection of subjects like robotics and artificial intelligence, computer graphics, and surveying and construction. Participants also take an active role in discussions with CUA engineering faculty and students about such topics as engineering curricula and careers, and professional ethics. There is also time to take advantage of CUA's many recreational facilities and to explore campus life while living in the dormitories. Applicants to Eye On Engineering and Computer Science must submit a completed form, transcript, and one letter of recommendation by the end of April. Participants are selected primarily on the basis of their achievements in science and mathematics. The cost is about $500, which does not include transportation to and from the school. For an application and further information, contact the program.

Eye On Engineering and Computer Science

The Catholic University of America
School of Engineering
Washington, DC 20064
202-319-5160
eyeonengineering@cua.edu
http://engineering.cua.edu/activities/
   Engr2002

FIRST

Competition

The nonprofit organization FIRST—For Inspiration and Recognition of Science and Technology—wants to generate an interest in science and engineering in high school students. One way they do this is by sponsoring an annual robot-building contest. Each year the rules of the competition are different, and details are kept top-secret until a kick-off workshop. After the workshop, students team up with engineers from corporations and universities for six weeks to brainstorm, design, construct, and test their robots. Contact FIRST to get more information.

FIRST

200 Bedford Street
Manchester, NH 03101
603-666-3906
http://www.usfirst.org

Frontiers at Worcester Polytechnic Institute

College Courses/Summer Study

Frontiers is an on-campus research and learning experience for high school students who are interested in science, mathematics, and engineering. Areas of study include aerospace engineering, biology and biotechnology, computer science, electrical and computer engineering, mathematics, mechanical engineering, physics, and robotics. Participants attend classes and do lab work Monday through Friday. Participants also have the opportunity to try out one of five communication modules: creative writing, elements of writing, music, speech, and theater. In addition to the academic program, you will attend evening workshops, live performances, field trips, movies, and tournaments. Applications are typically available in January and due in March. Tuition is about $2,000; this covers tuition, room, board, linens, transportation, and entrance fees to group activities. A $500 nonrefundable deposit is required. For more information, contact the program director.

Worcester Polytechnic Institute

Frontiers Program
100 Institute Road
Worcester, MA 01609-2280
508-831-5286
frontiers@wpi.edu
http://www.admissions.wpi.edu/
   Frontiers

Future Scientists and Engineers of America

Membership

Future Scientists and Engineers of America (FSEA) is a nonprofit organization on the order of Future Farmers of America, working to encourage early participation in a chosen career field. The FSEA encourages young people in 4th through 12th grade to found student chapters in their schools. Each chapter needs a sponsor from the local community, a teacher to act as an adviser, a parent coordinator, two mentors from the local scientific or engineering community, and up to 25 student members. Naturally, with these people involved, the students in each FSEA chapter learn about the professional world and gain hands-on experience in science and engineering. If you'd like more information about the FSEA or about starting a chapter, write to them or visit their Web site.

Future Scientists and Engineers of America

8441 Monroe Avenue
Stanton, CA 90680
714-229-2224
fsea@fsea.org
http://www.fsea.org

G.R.A.D.E. Camp

Camps

The Cullen College of Engineering at the University of Houston offers G.R.A.D.E

Camp (Girls Reaching and Demonstrating Excellence) for female high school freshmen, sophomores, juniors, and seniors in the Houston area. The week-long commuter program, offered several times in the summer, offers girls the chance to explore engineering by participating in fun, hands-on activities. Program cost is about $200; some financial aid is available. Applications are due in early April. For more information, contact the program director.

GRADE Camp Director
Educational Grants Manager
Cullen College of Engineering
University of Houston
E316 Engineering Building 2
Houston, TX 77204-4009
713-743-5939
grade@egr.uh.edu
http://www.egr.uh.edu/grade/
  ?e=camp

Hila Science Camp
Camp

Hila Science Camp offers both residential and day camps in the Ottawa Valley, close to Beachburg, Ontario. Established in 1984, Hila features a variety of programs with an emphasis on science and technology. You choose a major program as your focus; options include engineering and technology, rocketry, and computer science. You can build an advanced model rocket, construct and fly a balsa model aircraft, and construct electronic circuits using circuit boards, solder, and a soldering iron. The computer science program shows you how to create digital computer images, set up your own Web page, and write computer programs. In addition to your major program, you can collect specimens, go on archaeological digs, hunt for fossils, and gaze at the stars through Hila's eight-foot reflecting telescope. Residential camp lasts one week, from Sunday afternoon through the following Friday. Campers sleep in large dome-style tents, and Hila facilities include a dining hall, basketball court, rocketry and aircraft shop, computer room, and a flying field. Day camp runs Monday through Friday, 9:00 A.M. to 5:00 P.M. Hila offers seven camp sessions, beginning in late June, and all programs are offered in all sessions. A week of day camp at Hila costs about $335; contact Hila for current prices for residential camp. Kits and equipment for various programs cost extra. Supplies for the engineering and technology program, for example, cost an extra $115. Each program enrolls a maximum of 34 students on a first come, first served basis. If you live in the Ottawa Valley, some scholarships are available. Hila is happy to provide you with more details on all matters.

Hila Science Camp
382 Hila Road
RR #2
Pembroke, Ontario, Canada K8A 6W3
613-582-3632
hila@hilaroad.com
http://www.hilaroad.com

Idaho JEMS Summer Workshop
College Course/Summer Study

The University of Idaho College of Engineering sponsors Idaho JEMS (Junior

Engineering Math & Science program) each summer for rising seniors. During Idaho JEMS, first introduced in 1967, students live on the university campus for two weeks and take classes with College of Engineering professors. Such classes may include engineering design, human factors, computer programming, and engineering problem solving. Successful completion of the classes leads to college engineering credits from the University of Idaho. In addition to course work, participants explore engineering through lab exercises, field trips, and guest speakers. You can experience college life to the fullest while living and dining on campus by using the university's recreational facilities and touring its colleges. There are also special barbecues and dances to promote an active social life during the Idaho JEMS program. Applicants must have at least a 3.0 GPA and three years of mathematics; you must submit a high school transcript, brief resume, and essay along with your application form. The cost of the program is about $550 including room and board, and some financial aid is available. Female and minority students are especially encouraged to apply, but the program is open to all qualified applicants. For more information and an application, contact the program director.

Idaho JEMS Summer Workshop
University of Idaho
College of Engineering
PO Box 441011, JEB B40
Moscow, ID 83844-1011
208-885-4934
isgc@uidaho.edu
http://www.uidaho.edu/engr/jems

Intel Science Talent Search
Competition
Since 1942, Science Service has held a nationwide competition for talented high school seniors who plan to pursue careers in science, engineering, math, or medicine. Those who win find themselves in illustrious company: former winners have gone on to win Nobel Prizes, National Medals of Science, MacArthur Foundation fellowships, and memberships in the National Academy of Engineering. High school students in the United States and its territories, as well as American students abroad, are eligible to compete for more than $1 million in scholarships and prizes awarded to participants, including the top one for $100,000. If you'd like to enter the next competition, contact the Talent Search for more information.

Intel Science Talent Search
1719 N Street NW
Washington, DC 20036
202-785-2255
http://www.sciserv.org/sts

International Bridge Building Competition
Competition
The International Bridge Building Competition is an annual opportunity to test your ability to construct a model bridge based on sound engineering principles and a set of specifications. Once your bridge is built to specification, it must withstand a certain amount of weight and be fully functional. Bridges are judged for efficiency, and the most efficient bridge wins. The contest, which originated at

Illinois Institute of Technology in 1977, is held regionally across the United States. Each region sends its two top winners to the International Bridge Building Competition, held in a different location every year. There is no cost to enter the competition, although certain regions may charge a small amount for a bridge kit containing everything you need to build your bridge. You must enter the competition through your school, and schools must be registered with a region. Some schools and regions allow for teams, but only one person can be declared the winner at the international level. First-place winners can take advantage of a four-year scholarship to the Illinois Institute of Technology. Other prizes vary from year to year. All participants receive medals and a trophy for their school. For details and a list of regions, contact the International Bridge Building Competition at the Illinois Institute of Technology.

International Bridge Building Competition
Illinois Institute of Technology
Chicago, IL 60616
kallend@itt.edu
http://www.iit.edu/~hsbridge/data-base/search.cgi/:/public/index

Junior Engineering Technical Society (JETS)
Competition, Field Experience
The Junior Engineering Technical Society (JETS) offers several different opportunities for young people in grades 9 through 12 to test and strengthen their aptitude for engineering before mak-

ing college and career decisions. One of their most interesting and direct means of testing aptitude is administrating the National Engineering Aptitude Search+ (NEAS+) exam. The NEAS+ is a self-assessment of your thinking, reasoning, and understanding processes, which you can take at any point during your high school career. This not only reveals whether your skills are generally suited to an engineering career, but also what your weaknesses are so that you can work to improve them before starting college. To take this exam, you need only request the NEAS+ kit (which includes career guidance materials) from JETS; the cost is about $15.

If some of your friends share your interest in engineering, you may want to participate in JETS' Tests of Engineering Aptitude, Mathematics, and Science (TEAMS). The TEAMS program is a one-day assessment of your ability to work with others on engineering problems; results determine if your group is ranked at the local, state, or national levels. High school groups can also participate in JETS' National Engineering Design Challenge (NEDC), a year-long program and competition also leading to rankings at the local, state, and national levels. In the NEDC, you concentrate on problem-solving and team-building exercises as you consider real challenges from the world of engineering. For both the TEAMS and NEDC programs, your group needs a teacher to serve as your coach, so speak to your math and science teachers and ask them to contact JETS for detailed information.

JETS, in conjunction with the U.S. Army Research Office, also offers The Uninitiates' Introduction to Engineering Program (UNITE), which helps minority high school students prepare for college through summer classes. The classes introduce students to an educational experience that parallels that of a freshmen student in a university engineering program. Learning methods include academic classes, hands-on activities, and team-based learning. Participating schools include Colorado State University, Florida International University, New Mexico MESA, the University of Delaware, and the University of Detroit-Mercy.

Junior Engineering Technical Society (JETS)

1420 King Street, Suite 405
Alexandria, VA 22314-2794
703-548-5387
jetsinfo@jets.org
http://www.jets.org

Junior Science and Humanities Symposium (JSHS)

Conference

The Junior Science and Humanities Symposium encourages high school students (grades 9 through 12) who are gifted in engineering, mathematics, and the sciences to develop their analytical and creative skills. There are nearly 50 symposia held at locations all around the United States—including Georgetown University, the University of Toledo, and Seattle Pacific University—so that each year some 10,000 students are able to participate.

Funded by the U.S. Army Research Office since its inception in 1958 (and by the U.S. Army, Navy, and Air Force since 1995), the JSHS has little to do with the military and everything to do with research. At each individual symposium, researchers and educators from various universities and laboratories meet with the high school students (and some of their teachers) to study new scientific findings, pursue their own interests in the lab, and discuss and debate relevant issues. Participants learn how scientific and engineering research can be used to benefit humanity, and they are strongly encouraged to pursue such research in college and as a career. To provide further encouragement, one attendee at each symposium will win a scholarship of about $3,000 and the chance to present his or her own research at the national Junior Science and Humanities Symposium. Finalists from each regional JSHS win all-expense-paid trips to the national symposium, where the top research students can win additional scholarships worth up to $16,000 and trips to the prestigious London International Youth Sciences Forum. For information about the symposium in your region and on eligibility requirements, contact the national Junior Science and Humanities Symposium.

Junior Science and Humanities Symposium (JSHS)

Academy of Applied Science
24 Warren Street
Concord, NH 03301
603-228-4520
phampton@aas-world.org
http://www.jshs.org

Leonardo da Vinci Competition

Competition

The Leonardo da Vinci Competition is a written test on engineering-oriented problems covering such topics as physics, chemistry, calculus, algebra, and geometry. It is available to Canadian high school students in their senior year. If you like science and math and want to determine if you have an aptitude for engineering, this test is for you. Prizes include a $3,000 scholarship for each of the top 15 candidates who apply and are accepted for a full-time first-year engineering program at the University of Toronto the September following the competition. In addition, the first place winner is awarded $1,000, second place winner receives $600, third place $500, fourth place $400, and fifth through tenth place winners are awarded $250 each.

The Leonardo da Vinci test is sent out to Canadian high schools and administered in April. The cost to take the test is $7 per student, and a teacher must volunteer to coordinate and administer the exam. To see if your school is on the mailing list, you can check the da Vinci Web site. Your teacher can add your school to the mailing list right at the site. For more information, contact the Leonardo da Vinci Competition.

Leonardo da Vinci Competition Office
University of Toronto
Faculty of Applied Science and
   Engineering
35 St. George Street, Room 157
Toronto, ON Canada M5S 1A4

416-978- 3872
davinci@ecf.utoronto.ca
http://www.ecf.toronto.edu/apsc/
   davinci

The Making of an Engineer

College Course/Summer Study

The University of Denver invites sophomores, juniors, and seniors to apply for its Making of an Engineer course, which runs for three weeks in June. As a part of the university's larger Early Experience Program, the course encourages students already interested in science and technology to consider putting those interests to work in an engineering career. All participants attend lectures and laboratory sessions providing an introduction to the tools and concepts common to most areas of engineering; there are also group outings to engineering laboratories and industrial plants. Each student also concentrates on one particular topic, such as optics and lasers or bioengineering, and meets one on one with a university professor to complete a project on that topic. The tuition cost for the Making of an Engineer course is around $115, which includes field trips and supplies. Students can choose to reside on the University of Denver campus and pay an additional fee of about $1,050 for room, board, and social activities. Scholarships are available to needy students to cover residential and/or travel costs. Interested students must submit a completed application (with essay), official high school transcript, standardized test results (PACT/ACT/PSAT/SAT), a letter of recommendation from a counselor or teacher, and a minimum GPA of 3.0/3.5 or a "B" average. All materials should be submitted by the deadline, usually in April, to the Early Experience Program coordinator who can also provide application forms and further information about the Making of an Engineer course.

The Making of an Engineer
University of Denver
Early Experience Program
Office of Academic Youth Programs
1981 South University Boulevard
Denver, CO 80208
303-871-2663
http://www.du.edu/education/ces/
   moe.html

Mentoring and Enrichment Seminar in Engineering Training
College Course/Summer Study

The Cullen College of Engineering at the University of Houston offers the Mentoring and Enrichment Seminar in Engineering Training (MESET) for rising seniors for three weeks in June. Students planning a career in engineering who have demonstrated scientific and mathematical aptitude are eligible for this residential program. All participants attend short, formal courses in such subjects as computers, physics, problem solving, and engineering design. There are also a number of field trips to industrial facilities on the Gulf Coast and tours of Cullen College's own facilities. On evenings and weekends, students can enjoy social events including games and picnics and also attend lectures by guest speakers. There are no tuition or room and board fees for MESET, but participants must cover their own travel costs, weekend meals, and incidental expenses. A few transportation scholarships are available for cases of extreme hardship. To apply, students must submit an application as well as a high school transcript and letter of recommendation from their guidance counselor by a deadline that is usually in early April. For an application or more information about the program, contact the director of MESET.

Mentoring and Enrichment Seminar in Engineering Training
University of Houston
Houston, TX 77204-4790
713-743-4222
http://www.egr.uh.edu/news/
   ?e=camps

Minority Introduction to Engineering (ITE) at Tuskegee University
College Course/Summer Study

The College of Engineering, Architecture and Physical Sciences at Tuskegee University invites minority students who are rising juniors or seniors to apply to the Minority Introduction to Engineering (ITE). Minority ITE is a two-week summer program (check with Tuskegee University for more specific dates) that allows students to fully experience campus life, from living in the dormitories to studying with current staff and students. As a participant, you spend time exploring engineering and other math and science careers and attending laboratory demonstrations by engineering faculty. There is no cost for this program except for transportation to and from Tuskegee University and a $50 application fee and enrollment fee upon acceptance to the program. For further details and application information, contact the Assistant to the Dean for Student Development and Special Programs.

Minority Introduction to Engineering (MITE)

Assistant to the Dean for Student
    Development and Special
    Programs
Tuskegee University
Tuskegee, AL 36088
334-727-8946 or 334-727-8355
http://tuskegee.edu/global/story.
    asp?s=1172515

National Association of Precollege Directors

College Course/Summer Study, Field Experience

The National Association of Precollege Directors (NAPD) is a nonprofit group trying to increase the number of ethnically underrepresented students (Latino/ Hispanic American, African-American, Native American) who pursue college degrees in engineering, mathematics, and technology. Its programs—collaborations between high schools, universities, and corporations—include in-school math instruction to ensure that students are on a college-entrance track; science and technology projects conducted with professors or engineers; students shadowing professionals throughout a day at work; and intensive summer programs on college campuses. To get a sense of the incredible variety of participants and projects, contact the NAPD for more information.

National Association of Precollege Directors

The Johns Hopkins University
Applied Physics Laboratory
Johns Hopkins Road
Laurel, MD 20723-6099

National Society of Black Engineers

Membership

The National Society of Black Engineers (NSBE) welcomes young people as members and as participants in its Pre-College Initiative (PCI) program. The PCI program links professional NSBE members with students to encourage their interests in math and science. PCI student in grades 7 through 12 are eligible to become NSBE junior members. Membership dues are only $5 per year, for which you can join or start a local chapter and participate in such things as "camping conferences" and college admissions and financial aid workshops. The National Society of Black Engineers urges you to call or e-mail them if you want to make the NSBE part of your career preparation.

National Society of Black Engineers

1454 Duke Street
Alexandria, VA 22314
703-549-2207
info@nsbe.org
http://www.nsbe.org

Operation Catapult
College Course/Summer Study

Operation Catapult is a summer program operated by the Rose-Hulman Institute of Technology. Founded in 1874 under a different name, Rose-Hulman is today one of the country's best undergraduate colleges in science and engineering. It is a relatively small facility with a teaching (not research) faculty and is extremely selective in admitting students. Rose-Hulman's Operation Catapult is equally selective, usually extending invitations only to high school juniors who have finished in the highest percentiles on such standardized tests as the PSAT. Participants must also have completed three years of high school math and one of chemistry or physics.

There are two sessions each summer—generally the last three weeks of June and of July—with some 95 students participating in each session. Working in groups of two to four, participants try to solve a "real-world" problem in engineering or another scientific field. They are assisted by Rose-Hulman's faculty and upperclassmen and make use of the institute's facilities. Throughout Operation Catapult, students also go on field trips, witness demonstrations, and hear lectures. The program is a chance to live, work, and play on a college campus as well as to meet other students from around the country. Costs total about $1,900. Operation Catapult is obviously not for everyone interested in engineering, but if you meet the academic requirements, it's a unique and challenging opportunity that merits serious consideration. Eligible students should receive an invitation from Rose-Hulman Institute of Technology; if you believe you are qualified but have not been invited, ask your guidance counselor or a teacher for direction.

Operation Catapult
Attn: Associate Director of
    Admissions
Rose-Hulman Institute of
    Technology
5500 Wabash Avenue
Terre Haute, IN 47803
800-248-7448
lisa.norton@rose-hulman.edu
http://www.rose-hulman.edu/catapult

Preface and MITE at Purdue University
College Courses/Summer Study

Purdue University offers two programs for minority high school students in conjunction with its Minority Engineering Program. The first program, Preface (Pre-Freshman and Cooperative Education), is for rising juniors and seniors who show promise in math and science. Preface runs for one week in July, during which participants explore possible engineering careers, meet professional engineers and engineering students, and work on study skills and career and life planning. There are also tours, hands-on activities, and a group project. Participants live on the Purdue campus. Tuition, room, and board costs are fully funded by Purdue's industrial partners, so Preface students are responsible only for the costs of transportation, incidentals, and an administration fee. Applications are due roughly one month before the program begins, but should be sent in earlier because of the popularity of this program.

Purdue University's second program is MITE (Multiethnic Introduction to Engineering), which runs for two weeks in mid-July. Rising seniors with a strong academic background take part in computer sessions, laboratory experiences, engineering design projects, and lectures by faculty members and engineering professionals. Participants live on campus and have access to a wide range of recreational events and facilities. Like Preface, MITE is fully funded, so students pay just for travel to and from Purdue, incidentals, and an administration fee. There is no formal admissions deadline, but students should apply as soon as the forms become available in May because eligible applicants are accepted on a first come, first served basis. For more information about both programs and details about application procedures, contact the Minority Engineering Program.

Purdue University Minority Engineering Program

Engineering Administration
    Building (ENAD), Room 222
400 Centennial Mall Drive
West Lafayette, IN 47907-2016
765 494-3974
mep@ecn.purdue.edu
https://engineering.purdue.edu/
    MEP/pre_college/mite

STEP at Purdue University
Camp

Purdue University's Department of Engineering Education offers the Seminar for Top Engineering Prospects (STEP), which allows high school students entering their senior year in high school the chance to explore various engineering disciplines and careers. Students will participate in tours, demonstrations, classroom experiences, projects, and discussions with engineering faculty members. Applicants must have completed three years of high school mathematics and one year of chemistry or physics. Sessions last one week and are typically held in July. The registration fee is about $495, which covers room, board, and tuition. Need-based scholarships are available.

Purdue University

Department of Engineering
    Education
West Lafayette, IN 47907
step@ecn.purdue.edu
https://engineering.purdue.
    edu/ENE/SpecialPrograms/
    ProspectiveStudents/step

Science Is Fun! Camp
Camp

The Center for Chemical Education at Miami University of Ohio sponsors a series of Terrific Science Camps each summer. Area ninth-graders are welcome to attend the Science Is Fun! Camp. It lasts three hours every day for one week during the month of July. As a participant, you explore the fascinating world of science, including chemistry and engineering. The cost for this commuter camp is only about $75, and free tuition is available to students truly in need of financial aid. Admission is made on a first come, first served basis, so apply well before the deadline in late April. For an application form and more information on this year's camp, contact Terrific Science Programs.

Terrific Science Programs
Attn: Kitty Blattner
200 Levey Hall
Miami University Middletown
Middletown, OH 45052
513-727-3318
http://www.units.muohio.edu/
    continuingeducation/summer/
    youth_programs/youth.htmlx

Science Olympiad
Competition

The Science Olympiad is a national competition based in schools. School teams feed into regional and state tournaments, and the winners at the state level go on to the national competition. Some schools have many teams, all of which compete in their state Science Olympiad. Only one team per school, however, is allowed to represent its state at the national contest, and each state gets a slot. There are four divisions of Science Olympiad: Division A1 and A2 for younger students, Division B for grades six through nine, and Division C for grades 9 through 12. There is no national competition for Division A.

A school team membership fee must be submitted with a completed membership form 30 days before your regional or state tournament. The fee entitles your school to a copy of the *Science Olympiad Coaches and Rules Manual* plus the eligibility to have up to 15 students at the first level of your state or regional contest. Fees vary from state to state. The National Science Olympiad is held at a different site every year, and your school team is fully responsible for transportation, lodging, and food.

Specific rules have been developed for each event and must be read carefully. There are numerous events in each division. You and your teammates can choose the events you want to enter and prepare yourselves accordingly. Winners receive medals, trophies, and some scholarships.

For a list of all Science Olympiad state directors and a membership form, go to the Science Olympiad Web site. You can also write or call the national office for information.

Science Olympiad
2 Trans Am Plaza Drive, Suite 415
Oakbrook Terrace, IL 60181
630-792-1251
http://www.soinc.org

Secondary Student Training Program (SSTP) Research Participation
College Course/Summer Study

The University of Iowa invites those who have completed grade 10 or 11 to apply to its Secondary Student Training Program (SSTP). The program allows students to explore a particular area of science, such as engineering, while experiencing the career field of scientific research. Participants work with university faculty in one of the many laboratories on campus, studying and conducting research projects for approximately 40 hours per week. At the end of the program, which usually runs from late June to early August, students present their projects to a formal gathering of faculty, staff, and fellow SSTP participants. Throughout the program students also take part in various seminars on career choices and the scientific profession, and a variety of recreational activities designed especially for SSTP participants. Students live in the University of Iowa dormitories and use many of the facilities on campus. The admissions process is highly competitive and is based on an essay, transcript, and recommendations. Those who complete the program have the option of receiving college credit from the University of Iowa. Applications are due by mid-March, and applicants will be notified of the decisions by mid-May. Tuition fees, room, and board generally total around $2,000; spending money and transportation to and from the university are not included. Financial aid is available. For an application form, financial aid information, and to discuss possible research projects, contact the Secondary Student Training Program.

Summer Programs
Opportunity at Iowa
University of Iowa
224 Jessup Hall
Iowa City, IA 52242-1316
800-553-4692, ext. 5-3876
william-swain@uiowa.edu
http://www.uiowa.edu/~provost/oi/sstp

Shadow Day
Field Experience
The Society of Women Engineers at the University of Michigan hosts a Shadow Day experience. During the school year, high school girls can take part in a Shadow Day. Participants shadow a female engineering student at the University of Michigan for the whole day or even overnight. The itinerary usually includes a tour of the College of Engineering and a typical day of classes. The cost is only $12, which covers meals. If you are interested in a Shadow Day, contact the High School Relations Chair.

Shadow Day
Society of Women Engineers
University of Michigan
1226 EECS Building
1301 Beal Avenue
Ann Arbor, MI 48109
734-763-5027
dannelly@umich.edu
http://www.engin.umich.edu/soc/swe

Society of Women Engineers High School Conference
Conference
The Society of Women Engineers (SWE) at Texas A&M University welcomes female and male high school students at all grade levels to its annual High School Conference. Each March, conference participants spend a weekend on the Texas A&M campus learning about the many engineering disciplines and seeing what the university has to offer. Students attend typical classes, participate in a design competition, attend a seminar on each engineering discipline, attend an informal banquet, tour the campus, and tour the departments of engineering that most interest them and learn more about those disciplines. The registration fee

is $25. For more information about the conference, including specific dates and times, contact SWE's High School Conference Chairwomen.

The Society of Women Engineers at Texas A&M University is in the process of planning a summer camp for young women who are rising juniors and seniors in high school. Contact SWE for the latest information.

Texas A&M University

Society of Women Engineers High
    School Conference
Dwight Look College of Engineering
204 Zachary Engineering Center
College Station, TX 77843-3127
979-862-2314
katy@msc.tamu.edu
http://www.tamu.edu/swe/
    Committees/high_school.htm

Student Introduction to Engineering at North Carolina State University

College Course/Summer Study

The Student Introduction to Engineering (SITE) is a summer program sponsored by the College of Engineering at North Carolina State University. Open to rising juniors and seniors from all backgrounds, SITE offers high school students a realistic look at the professional lives of engineers and the preparation needed to pursue such a career via 11 programs. Programs include aerospace engineering, autonomous robotics, biological engineering, chemical engineering, civil engineering/construction management, computer science, materials science and engineering,

mechatronics, textiles (including textile engineering), wolfpack motorsports, and a Young Investigators Program in nuclear technology

As a participant, you spend one week living on the NCSU campus and participating in discussions and demonstrations in its lecture halls and laboratories. You also meet with engineering students and practicing engineers to learn what you can expect in the years to come. North Carolina State University provides information on college admissions and financial aid to all the students in the SITE program. The cost of participation is about $550 (note: the Young Investigators in Nuclear Technology programs costs about $950), which includes room, board, tuition, gymnasium access, and insurance coverage. Some financial assistance is available. The same material is covered in two different SITE sessions, both of which run in June or July. To apply, select the session you want and submit the application form by early April. Applicants are judged on the basis of scholastic performance, interest in math and science, teacher recommendations, and standardized test scores. Underrepresented minorities (Hispanic American, African-American, and Native American) and women are strongly encouraged to apply. For more information and a copy of the application form, contact the SITE coordinator.

Student Introduction to Engineering (SITE) at North Carolina State University

College of Engineering
Campus Box 7904
Raleigh, NC 27695-7904

919-515-9669
http://www.engr.ncsu.edu/
summerprograms

Summer College for High School Students at Syracuse University

College Course/Summer Study

The Syracuse University Summer College for High School Students features an Engineering and Computer Science Program for those who have just completed their sophomore, junior, or senior year. The Summer College runs for six weeks and offers a residential option so participants can experience campus life while still in high school. The Engineering and Computer Science Program has several aims: to introduce you to the many specialties within the engineering profession; to help you match your aptitudes with possible careers; and to prepare you for college, both academically and socially. Participants take two courses: everyone takes the Survey of Engineering Problems course, as well as a liberal arts and sciences course of their choice to complement it. All students take part in a number of engineering-related field trips and group design projects, the results of which are presented at the end of the course. Syracuse University awards college credit for completion of the two courses. Admission is competitive and is based on recommendations, test scores, and transcripts. The total cost of the residential program is about $5,300; the commuter option costs about $3,800. Some scholarships are available. The application deadline is in mid-May, or mid-April for those seeking financial aid. For further information, contact the Summer College.

Syracuse University Summer College for High School Students
111 Waverly Avenue, Suite 240
Syracuse, NY 13244-2320
315-443-5297
sumcoll@syr.edu
http://summercollege.syr.edu

Summer High School Engineering Institute

College Course/Summer Study

Since 1963, the College of Engineering at Michigan State University (MSU) has offered the High School Engineering Institute to rising juniors and seniors each summer. Taking place in July, the program gives students with strong interests in math and science the chance to explore engineering as a career. Participants live on campus and participate in hands-on activities, discussions, and laboratories with MSU faculty members and graduate assistants. During the course of the institute, you are exposed to eight engineering disciplines offered at the university, including biosystems, civil, electrical, and mechanical. There are also opportunities to experience the social life on campus, enjoy the recreational facilities, and learn more about the entire college admissions process. Admittance to the program is subject to considerations of academic performance, class rank, and the recommendation of a teacher or counselor. Applications must be submitted in May (check the Web site for an exact date) along with a $100 deposit (to be refunded if you are not accepted into the institute). Costs of the program total around $450, from which the deposit is deducted. A limited amount of financial aid is available to those students otherwise unable to afford the program. Contact the High School Engineering Institute for the latest information and an application.

Summer High School Engineering Institute
College of Engineering
Michigan State University
East Lansing, MI 48824-1226
517-355-6616, ext. 1
radforda@egr.msu.edu
http://www.egr.msu.edu/egr/
    programs/bachelors/hsei.php

Summer Institute in Science and Engineering
College Course/Summer Study

The Summer Institute in Science and Engineering for High School Juniors is held on the Alfred University campus for one week at the end of July. By "juniors," the university means both rising juniors and those who have just completed their junior year (i.e., rising seniors). Participants live in campus dormitories and participate in 7 hands-on labs they have selected from a choice of about 25; past lab topics have included ceramic manufacturing, genetic engineering, and cryptography. Students must apply for the Summer Institute by the beginning of June, submitting an application form, transcript, and two letters of recommendation from high school teachers. The total cost for tuition and room and board is approximately $495 (which includes a $75 deposit), and some financial aid is available. Participants who submit a paper on a given topic before the first day of the institute will be in competition for a four-year scholarship to Alfred University, the winner to be decided based on the quality of the writing. Contact the director of the Summer Institute for more information.

Summer Institute in Science and Engineering
New York State College of Ceramics
    at Alfred University
Office of Continuing Education
2 Pine Street
Alfred, NY 14802-1296
607-871-2425
wightman@alfred.edu
http://www.alfred.edu/summer/html/
    scienceandengineering.html

University of Wisconsin-Stout TCEA High Mileage Vehicle
Competition

This engineering competition to research, develop, and design a single-person, fuel-efficient vehicle out of a Briggs & Stratton engine takes place every spring. Facilitated by University of Wisconsin-Stout students of the Technology Collegiate Education Association (TCEA), the contest has been running since 1991 and draws from high schools all over Wisconsin. However, any school is eligible to sponsor a team, which usually consists of about five people. To enter, all you have to do is transport your car to the competition site. The competition is held over a Friday and Saturday. Cars roll in on Friday and go through qualifying tests for safety, durability, and weight and stoppage requirements. On Saturday, the competition begins at a nearby industrial park. Winners receive trophies in four categories: stock class, modified class, teamwork, and design. The sponsoring school usually helps teams with the cost of transportation and lodging, and many teams solicit the help of businesses and corporations in their town. The entry fee is about $30. To receive information about the competition, contact the Communications, Education, and Training Department at the University of Wisconsin-Stout.

University of Wisconsin-Stout TCEA High Mileage Vehicle
Menomonie, WI 54751
715-232-1122
http://www.teca.uwstout.edu/hmv.htm

Visit in Engineering Week (VIEW) Summer Program
College Course/Summer Study
The Pennsylvania State University (Penn State) invites rising freshman, sophomores, and juniors to apply to its Visit in Engineering Week (VIEW) residential summer program. Participants must be academically talented, motivated, and genuinely interested in engineering. Members of an underrepresented minority group are especially encouraged to apply. There are three weeklong VIEW sessions each summer for current juniors; freshmen and sophomores are invited to participate in a three-day program. Each session provides experiences in design, modeling and implementation, communications, group dynamics, and project management. Participants explore many different areas within the field of engineering and also sample college life as an engineering student. All fees, including tuition and room and board, are underwritten by corporate sponsors, so VIEW is free to all students. You must submit an application form, transcript, and essay by the end of April to the program director, who is also available to answer your questions.

Visit in Engineering Week (VIEW) Summer Program
The Pennsylvania State University
Multicultural Engineering Programs
208 Hammond Building
University Park, PA 16802
800-848-9223
http://www.engr.psu.edu/mep/VIEW.htm

Women in Engineering Program at Purdue University
Camp/Field Experience
Purdue's Women in Engineering Program (WIEP) offers two precollege camps for female high school students who are interested in learning more about engineering. The LEAP Summer Camp is for girls entering 7th through 9th grades. Campers may view engineering laboratories on campus, design a Web page, design and program a robot, and reassemble a computer from its parts. The five-day camp is usually held in June or July.

EDGE Summer Camp (Exciting Discoveries for Girls in Engineering) is offered to girls entering their sophomore and junior years of high school. Campers will tour engineering laboratories and a production facility, build their own electronics device, and program an experiment using Lego Investigator, among other activities. The six-day camp is typically held in June.

The WIEP also sponsors a Preview Day for female high school juniors who are interested in learning more about Purdue University and its engineering programs. Attendees receive a tour of the college's engineering facilities and get to meet engineering students and educators. Information about the following engineering disciplines is available: aeronautical and astronautical, agricultural and biological, biomedical, chemical, civil, construction, electrical and computer, industrial, materials, mechanical, and nuclear. The Preview Day is typically held in April. Contact the WIEP for more information on program costs.

Women In Engineering Program
Purdue University
Civil Engineering Building,
   Room G167
550 Stadium Mall Drive
West Lafayette, IN 47907-2051
765-494-3889
puwie@ecn.purdue.edu or cgss@
   ecn.purdue.edu
https://engineering.purdue.edu/WIEP

Women in the Sciences and Engineering (WISE) Week
Camp
The Pennsylvania State University (Penn State) offers a Women in the Sciences and Engineering (WISE) Week program in June for female rising juniors and seniors. Participants are academically talented with strong math and science skills, headed for college, and considering their career path. Students apply to one WISE option, either Sciences or Engineering. Competition is considerable as only 36 young women are accepted into each option. Once in the Engineering option, participants take part in eight engineering and two science workshops while completing a week-long engineering design project. During WISE Week you also meet female role models in academic and industrial engineering and learn about educational opportunities at Penn State. Accommodation is in a campus residence hall with collegiate women as your supervisors. The cost of the program is about $350, which covers everything except transportation to and from Penn State's University Park campus; a limited number of need-based scholarships are available. A completed application form, one letter of recommendation, an essay, any recent standardized test scores, and a current high school transcript must be submitted by the beginning of April. Members of minority groups and students with physical disabilities are strongly encouraged to apply. For further information about WISE Week and the application process, contact the program.

Women in the Sciences and Engineering (WISE) Week
The Pennsylvania State University
111G Kern Building
University Park, PA 16802
814-865-3342

nap2@psu.edu
http://www.equity.psu.edu/wise/
    wisecamp.asp

Women's Technology Program
Summer Study

This residential summer program, sponsored by the Massachusetts Institute of Technology's Department of Electrical Engineering and Computer Science, seeks to introduce high school girls to electrical engineering and computer science. Students who have completed the 11th grade are eligible to participate in the four-week program, which includes classes in computer science, electrical engineering, and mathematics taught by women Ph.D. candidates, guest speakers and lab tours, hands-on experiments, and team-based projects. Forty participants are selected each year. Students are expected to be able to handle college-level material, but they do not have to have prior experience in computer programming, physics, or engineering. The cost of the program is approximately $2,000 which includes books, lab materials, food, and housing. Transportation to and from MIT is not covered. Financial aid is available.

Massachusetts Institute of Technology
Women's Technology Program
Attn: Director
MIT Room 38-491
77 Massachusetts Avenue
Cambridge, MA 02139
617-253-5580
wtp@mit.edu
http://wtp.mit.edu

Worldwide Youth in Science and Engineering (WYSE)
College Course/Summer Study

The College of Engineering at the University of Illinois, Champaign-Urbana, sponsors a Worldwide Youth in Science and Engineering (WYSE) program twice each summer. Rising high school juniors or seniors are eligible for the program, which is subtitled: "Exploring Your Options . . . Tomorrow's Careers in Science and Engineering." The weeklong program features visits to each department within the College of Engineering, where faculty, graduates, and undergraduates conduct presentations, discussions, and hands-on activities concerning their particular area. Participants can make personal appointments with faculty members in engineering and nonengineering fields alike. Students live and eat on campus. Participants are selected according to the following factors: GPA, class ranking, curriculum, PSAT/SAT/ACT scores, letters of recommendation, and a personal essay. Applications are due at the beginning of May and applying earlier is encouraged. The all-inclusive fee for the program is about $600; some financial aid is available for women and minority students. For more information about the WYSE program and an application, contact the program director.

Worldwide Youth in Science and Engineering (WYSE)
Attn: Director
Worldwide Youth in Science and Engineering
400 Engineering Hall, MC-268

1308 West Green Street
Urbana, IL 61801
800-843-5410
wyse@uiuc.edu
http://www.engr.uiuc.edu/wyse

Young Scholars Program: Engineering
College Course/Summer Study

The University of Maryland sponsors the Young Scholars Program for motivated juniors and seniors. Participants in the three-week program spend July exploring the field of engineering and taking a college-level course. College credit is awarded to students who satisfactorily complete the course. Participants live in the residence halls at the University of Maryland and take their meals on campus or in selected College Park restaurants. To apply, you must submit an application form, an essay, two letters of recommendations, a current transcript, and an application fee of $50 by mid-May. Admissions decisions are based primarily on the recommendations, a GPA of 3.0 or better, and overall academic ability. For further details (including information on cost of tuition) and an application form, visit the Web site below or contact the Summer Sessions and Special Programs staff.

Summer Sessions and Special Programs
Mitchell Building, 1st Floor
University of Maryland
College Park, MD 20742
877-989-7762
http://www.summer.umd.edu/youngscholars

In addition to the aforementioned programs, visit the following Web sites for searchable databases of even more opportunities:

American Society for Engineering Education
http://www.engineeringk12.org/educators/making_engineers_cool/search.cfm

Engineers Make it Real
http://www.engineerinyou.com

Society of Women Engineers
http://www.swe.org/stellent/idcplg?IdcService=SS_GET_PAGE&nodeId=89&ssSourceNodeId=5

Read a Book

When it comes to finding out about engineering, don't overlook a book. (You're reading one now, after all.) What follows is a short, annotated list of books and periodicals related to engineering. The books range from biographies of well-known engineers, to books about what it's like to be an engineer, to professional volumes on specific topics. Don't be afraid to check out the professional journals, either. The technical stuff may be way above your head right now, but if you take the time to become familiar with one or two, you're bound to pick up some of what is important to this profession.

This list includes recent materials as well as old favorites. Always check for the latest editions. And if you find an author or series you like, ask your librarian to help you find more.

❑ BOOKS

Anderson, John David, Jr. *A History of Aerodynamics: And Its Impact on Flying Machines.* New York: Cambridge University Press, 1997. A historical treatment of the development of aerodynamics, stretching as far back as Aristotle and ending with modern day advancements.

Aviation Week Group. *The Aviation & Aerospace Almanac 2002.* New York: McGraw Hill-Professional, 2001. Filled to the brim with interesting information and facts about space engineering, science, mathematics, transportation, and general aviation.

Baine, Celeste. *High Tech Hot Shots: Careers in Sports Engineering.* Alexandria, Va.: National Society of Professional Engineers, 2004. A great guide to atypical engineering options for those who may have sports on the brain more than academics, this book covers sports engineering opportunities in extreme sports, such as skateboarding, as well as more traditional sports like swimming and golf.

———. *Is There an Engineer Inside You?: A Comprehensive Guide to Career Decisions in Engineering.* Belmont, Calif.: Professional Publications, 2004. Provides detailed descriptions of the engineering profession, an overview of the different areas in which to specialize, and information on education and professional societies.

———. *The Fantastical Engineer: A Thrillseeker's Guide to Careers in Theme Park Engineering.* Ruston, La.: Bonamy Publishing, 2000. An engaging book that shows the reader how engineers are responsible for theme parks, roller coasters, zoos, and other fun recreation options while providing career guidance information for this fun field of engineering.

Brandt, Daniel A. *Metallurgy Fundamentals.* South Holland, Ill.: Goodheart-Willcox Co., 1999. Engaging overview of metallurgy theory and practice.

Bucciarelli, Louis L. *Designing Engineers: Inside Technology.* Cambridge, Mass.: MIT Press, 1996. An engineer and educator answers the questions of how the products we use every day—products of engineering design—came to be the way they are, from conceptualization to production.

Bulger, Ruth Ellen, Elizabeth Meyer Bobby, and Harvey V. Fineberg. *Society's Choices: Social and Ethical Decision Making in Biomedicine.* Washington, D.C.: National Academies Press, 1995. Presents a fascinating set of perspectives on ethical issues in biomedicine and biomedical engineering, incorporating the recommendations of various interest groups.

Chaikin, Andrew, and Smithsonian Institute. *Air and Space: The National Air and Space Museum Story of Flight.* New York: Bulfinch Press, 2000. Drawing on the peerless collection of the National Air and Space Museum, this magnificent book captures the daring innovations and adventures that became a part of humanity's conquest of the skies.

Chen, Wai-Fa, and J.Y. Richard Liew, eds. *The Civil Engineering Handbook.* 2d ed. Boca Raton, Fla.: CRC Press, 2002. This indispensable, award-winning reference provides information on almost every aspect of civil engineering.

Cheshier, Stephen R. *Studying Engineering Technology: A Blueprint for Success.* Burbank, Calif.: Discovery Press, 1998. Comprehensive guide that spells out what engineering students will need to learn and offers suggestions as to how they can go about doing so.

Chiles, James R. *Inviting Disaster: Lessons from the Edge of Technology.* New York: HarperBusiness, 2002. A detailed look at more than 50 technological disasters, the events leading up to them, and what we can learn from them.

Clark, David E., Diane C. Folz, and Thomas D. McGee, eds. *An Introduction to Ceramic Engineering Design.* Westerville, Ohio: American Ceramic Society, 2002. This book reviews the fundamental elements of the ceramic engineering design process and uses case histories, illustrations, and examples to complement the text.

Dubbel, Heinrich, W. Beitz, and K. H. Kuttner. *Handbook of Mechanical Engineering.* New York: Springer Verlag, 1994. An excellent manual to mechanical engineering, technology, and the industrial arts.

Fenichell, Stephen. *Plastic: The Making of a Synthetic Century.* New York: HarperColllins, 1997. An expert and entertaining look at plastic in the 20th century, including its social history and cultural legacy.

Ferrari, Mario, Ralph Hempel, and Guilio Ferrari. *Building and Programming LEGO Mindstorm Robots Kit.*

Cambridge, Mass.: Syngress Publishing, 2002. An instruction book for how to design and build exotic robots, as well as how to program them.

Floyd, Thomas L. *Electronics Fundamentals: Circuits, Devices, and Applications.* 6th ed. Upper Saddle River, N.J.: Prentice Hall, 2003. An extensive examination of basic electrical and electronic concepts that focuses on fundamental principles and their applications.

Gurstelle, William. *Building Bots: Designing and Building Warrior Robots.* Chicago: Chicago Review Press, 2002. An exciting guide to designing and building robots; includes information for enthusiasts of all ages and engineering levels.

Hambley, Allan R. *Electrical Engineering: Principles and Applications.* 3d ed. Upper Saddle River, N.J.: Prentice Hall, 2004. User-friendly text providing a solid foundation in the basics of circuits, electronics (radio and digital), and electromechanics.

Hawkins, Lori, and Betsy Dowling. *100 Jobs in Technology.* New York: Mac-Millan, 1996. Among the many careers and jobs listed in this comprehensive book are CD-ROM producer, environmental engineer, physicist, Internet access provider, and biotechnology researcher.

Hibbeler, Russell C. *Engineering Mechanics: Dynamics.* 10th ed. Upper Saddle River, N.J.: Prentice Hall, 2003. The latest edition of a highly respected and well-known text for courses in engineering mechanics. Accessibly focused on fundamental principles instead of "cookbook" problem solving.

Iovine, John. *Robots, Androids, and Animatrons: 12 Incredible Projects You Can Build.* 2d ed. New York: McGraw-Hill/TAB Electronics, 2001. This guide provides an introduction to such concepts as robotics, motion control, sensors, and neural intelligence, and gives the reader 12 impressive projects to try on their own.

James, Peter, and Nick Thorpe. *Ancient Inventions.* New York: Ballantine Books, 1995. A fascinating look at inventions from prior to 1492 and how they reflected upon society at the time.

Jarvis, Adrian. *The Liverpool Dock Engineers.* Stroud, U.K.: Sutton, 1997. First book to be written specifically on dock engineers and their work; discusses in great detail the development of the field and its working methods.

Kletz, Trevor. *What Went Wrong?: Case Histories of Process Plant Disasters.* 4th ed. New York: Gulf Professional Publishing, 1998. An insightful examination of various case histories that reveals the causes and aftermaths of various plant disasters, providing insight into how such catastrophes can be avoided.

Kreith, Frank, and D. Yogi Goswami, eds. *The CRC Handbook of Mechanical Engineering.* Boca Raton, Fla.: CRC Press, 2004. A reference book that covers all the basics about mechanical engineering, written for the professional engineer.

Landels, John G. *Engineering in the Ancient World.* Rev. ed. Berkeley, Calif.:

University of California Press, 2000. An overview of the technological advances of the ancient Greeks and Romans.

Lewis, Grace Ross. *1,001 Chemicals in Everyday Products.* 2d ed. Hoboken, N.J.: John Wiley & Sons, 1998. Informative and user-friendly guidebook covering a wide range of chemicals in common household products, from food, cosmetics, and cleaning products to gardening and care products.

Lewis, Tom. *Divided Highways: Building the Interstate Highways, Transforming American Life.* New York: Penguin Books, 1999. An informative and lively account of our greatest public works project—a rich brew of energy, greed, and dreams.

Lindeburg, Michael R. *101 Solved Civil Engineering Problems.* 4th ed. Belmont, Calif.: Professional Publications, 2001. A preparation guide for the civil PE exam, this book presents different civil engineering problems—with detailed solutions—for prospective test takers to work through.

Lokensgard, Erik. *Industrial Plastics: Theory and Application.* 4th ed. Stamford, Conn.: Thomson Delmar Learning, 2003. An informative and readable technical account of plastics and plastics engineering.

Maples, Wallace. *Opportunities in Aerospace Careers.* 3d ed. New York: McGraw-Hill, 2002. Offers excellent vocational advice to the young reader about various fields within aerospace, especially aeronautical engineering.

McComb, Gordon. *Robot Builder's Sourcebook: Over 2,500 Sources for Robotic Parts.* New York: McGraw-Hill/TAB Electronics, 2002. A great way to tend to an interest in robotics, this book provides the robot/engineering enthusiast not only with places to find robotic parts, but also contains information on robot building and the related technology involved.

McGraw-Hill. *Dictionary of Engineering.* 2d ed. New York: McGraw-Hill Professional, 2003. This comprehensive reference covers all of the terms and concepts used in the primary fields of engineering.

Meikle, Jeffrey L. *American Plastic: A Cultural History.* Piscataway, N.J.: Rutgers University Press, 1997. An illustrated and detailed exploration of America's love-hate relationship with plastic, from Bakelite radios and nylon stockings to Tupperware and Disney World.

Miller, Rex, and Mark R. Miller. *Electronics the Easy Way.* 4th ed. Hauppauge, N.Y.: Barron's Educational Series, 2002. A useful and easy-to-read guide for anyone interested in electronics.

Milne, R.J.W., ed. *Structural Engineering: History and Development.* New York: Brunner-Routledge, 1998. A basic overview of the field of structural engineering.

National Geographic Society. *The Builders: Marvels of Engineering.* Washington, D.C.: National Geographic Books, 1998. This beautifully illustrated book recounts the stories of some of the most outstanding engineering marvels—past and present—in the world, and those responsible for creating them.

Peterson's Guides. *Peterson's Graduate Programs in Engineering & Applied Sciences 2005.* Lawrenceville, N.J.: Peterson's, 2004. Lists more than 4,000 programs, from bioengineering and computer science to mechanical and electrical engineering. Absolutely indispensable.

Petroski, Henry. *Engineers of Dreams: Great Bridge Builders and the Spanning of America.* New York: Vintage Books, 1996. A great writer and historian reveals the science, the politics, the egotism, and the magic of America's great bridges, recounting the fascinating stories of the men and women who built them.

———. *The Evolution of Useful Things.* New York: Vintage, 1994. Written from both an engineering and historical standpoint, this book traces the development of some of the most common and useful items we rely on today.

———. *Invention by Design: How Engineers Get From Thought to Thing.* Cambridge, Mass.: Harvard University Press, 1998. A collection of case studies that detail through words, photographs, and illustrations how various engineers created important new gadgets or structures.

———. *Remaking the World.* New York: Vintage, 1998. In this engaging collection of previously published vignettes, Petroski examines the lives of engineers, their methods, and notable feats of engineering.

Pool, Robert. *Beyond Engineering: How Society Shapes Technology.* New York: Oxford University Press, 1999. Written in such a way that even nonengineers can enjoy it, this book uses interesting anecdotes to show how society and engineering affect each other.

Salvendy, Gavriel, ed. *Handbook of Industrial Engineering.* 3d ed. Hoboken, N.J.: John Wiley-Interscience, 2001. This comprehensive book presents the concepts and applications of industrial engineering, along with many tables, graphs, formulas, and hundreds of step-by-step descriptions of problem-solving techniques.

Scarl, Donald. *How to Solve Problems: For Success in Freshman Physics, Engineering, and Beyond.* 6th ed. Glen Cove, N.Y.: Dosoris Press, 2003. Just what it sounds like—a guide for students, giving them the tools they need to tackle any problem.

Scarre, Chris, ed. *The Seventy Wonders of the Ancient World: The Great Monuments and How They Were Built.* New York: Thames & Hudson, 1999. A beautifully illustrated collection of stories about some of the most impressive structures dating back to ancient times.

Seifer, Marc J. *Wizard: The Life and Times of Nikola Tesla: Biography of a Genius.* New York: Citadel Press, 1998. An excellent and comprehensive biography of one of the most influential and enigmatic electrical engineers of our century.

Sparke, Penny. *The Plastics Age: From Bakelite to Beanbags and Beyond.* New

York: The Overlook Press, 1994. A history of plastics products from the 19th century to the present, in 15 essays and 150 color and black-and-white photographs. Explores such topics as industrial design and commercial art, perceptions of plastic, and pop culture.

Strong, A. Brent. *Plastics: Materials and Processing.* 2d ed. Upper Saddle River, N.J.: Prentice Hall, 1999. Introduces plastic to a wide range of readers who either need to gain, refresh, or improve their knowledge of plastic materials and processing.

Tobin, James. *Great Projects: The Epic Story of Building America: From the Taming of the Mississippi to the Invention of the Internet.* New York: The Free Press, 2001. Using engaging writing and illustrated with photographs, this book describes eight of the most important engineering projects in the United States.

Vogel, Steven, and Kathryn K. Davis. *Cat's Paws and Catapults: Mechanical Worlds of Nature and People.* New York: W. W. Norton & Company, 2000. Describes the parallels between biology and mechanics from an engineering perspective; and provides successful, and not-so-successful, engineering examples that have resulted from attempts to copy nature's designs.

Wachtman, John B., ed. *Ceramic Innovations of the 20th Century.* Westerville, Ohio: American Ceramic Society, 1999. Describes more than 100 of the greatest breakthroughs in ceramics during the last century.

Walesh, Stuart G. *Engineering Your Future: The Non-Technical Side of Professional Practice in Engineering and Other Technical Fields.* 2d ed. Reston, Va.: American Society of Civil Engineers, 2000. Written for engineering and technical students as well as entry-level engineers, this book offers practical advice in such nontechnical areas as interpersonal communication and organization skills.

Webster, L. F. *The Wiley Dictionary of Civil Engineering and Construction.* Hoboken, N.J.: John Wiley and Sons, 1997. Contains more than 30,000 definitions of engineering terms from the areas of construction, forestry, surface mining, and public works.

White, John H. *The American Railroad Freight Car: From the Wood-Car Era to the Coming of Steel.* Baltimore: Johns Hopkins University Press, 1995. A history of the American freight car, discussing the various types of specialized cars used to handle America's growing freight traffic, and examining the technological developments that influenced freight-car design.

White, Richard M., and Roger Doering. *Electrical Engineering Uncovered.* 2d ed. Upper Saddle River, N.J.: Prentice Hall, 2001. Perfect undergraduate introduction to electrical engineering that also gives a good sense of what professional engineers do.

Willis, Carol, and Donald Freidman, eds. *Building the Empire State.* New York: W. W. Norton & Company, 1998. By using documentation found in a notebook from the 1930s, which detailed the many facets of the construction process, this book provides a different perspective of the building of the Empire State Building.

Wood, Robert B., and Kenneth R. Edwards. *Opportunities in Electrical Trades.* VGM Career Horizons. New York: NTC Publishing Group, 1997. Offers sound vocational guidance for aspiring electrical engineers, with a focus on emerging careers.

❏ PERIODICALS

Aerospace America. Published monthly by the American Institute of Aeronautics and Astronautics, 1801 Alexander Bell Drive, Suite 500, Reston, VA 20191-4344, 800-639-2422, custserv@aiaa.org. Features articles about advancements in aerospace engineering and job listings. Read sample issues at http://www.aiaa.org/aerospace.

Aerospace Engineering. Published 10 times annually by the Society of Automotive Engineers, 400 Commonwealth Drive, Warrendale, PA 15096-0001, 724-776-4970, CustomerService@sae.org, http://www.sae.org/aeromag. A detailed and nicely produced survey of breakthroughs in the aerospace trade, published by a premier organization in automotive and aerospace engineering.

AIAA Student Journal Online. Published by the American Institute of Aeronautics and Astronautics (AIAA), 1801 Alexander Bell Drive, Suite 500, Reston, VA 20191-4344, 800-639-AIAA, http://www.aiaa.org. Offers information to students about scholarship and design competitions, activities of AIAA student-member groups, and papers written by AIAA student-members.

American Society of Highway Engineers Scanner Newsletter. Updated daily by the American Society of Highway Engineers at http://www.highwayengineers.org/scanner.html. Extensive coverage of developments—state, federal, or otherwise—in highway transportation. Offers an excellent sense of the complexity of public projects.

AMM On-line. Updated twice daily by the American Metal Market, 800-947-9553, custserv@espcomp.com, http://www.amm.com. A colorful and thorough news network for metallurgists, offering top stories about the metals trade all over the world.

Annals of Biomedical Engineering (The Journal of the Biomedical Engineering Society). Published monthly by Kluwer Academic Publishers, 101 Philip Drive, Assinippi Park, Norwell, MA 02061, 781-871-6600, kluweronline@wkap.com, http://www.kluweronline.com/issn/0090-6964. Interdisciplinary, international journal collecting original articles in major fields of bioengineering and biomedical engineering.

ASEE PRISM. Published monthly by the American Society for Engineering Education, 1818 N Street, NW, Suite 600, Washington, DC 20036-2479, 202-331-3500, prism@asee.org. Offers information on trends in engineering education and employment. Read sample articles at http://www.prism-magazine.org.

ChemMatters. Quarterly magazine for high school chemistry students published by the American Chemical Society, 1155 Sixteenth Street, Room O-900, Washington, DC 20036, 800-227-5558. Shows examples of chemistry at work in our everyday lives. A teacher's guide is also available. Read sample issues at http://www.chemistry.org.

Chemical & Engineering News. Published weekly by the American Chemical Society, PO Box 182977, Columbus, OH 43218-2977, 800-333-9511, service@acs.org, http://pubs.acs.org/cen. Offers coverage of the scientific, educational, technical, business, and governmental aspects of chemistry.

Chemical Engineering. Published monthly by Access Intelligence, 110 William Street, New York, NY 10038, 212-621-4900, http://www.che.com. Offers indispensable and entertaining coverage of the industry, including up-to-date articles on new products and the companies that make them, the job field, safety measures, and technological innovations.

Chemical Week. Published weekly by Access Intelligence, 110 William Street, New York, NY 10038, 212-621-4900, http://www.chemweek.com. A fun and lively magazine about the diverse chemical industry, offering news and in-depth coverage of the theory, practice, and business of chemicals.

Civil Engineering. Published monthly by the American Society of Civil Engineers, 1801 Alexander Bell Drive, Reston, VA 20191, 703-295-6210, http://www.asce.org/cemagazine. Covers innovations in civil engineering around the world.

Converting Magazine. Published monthly by Reed Business Information, 8878 Barrons Boulevard, Highlands Ranch, CO 80129-2345, 800-446-6551, subsmail@reedbusiness.com. Official publication for manufacturers involved in converting paper, paperboard, film, and foil into packaging and other products.

Crossroads: The International ACM Student Magazine. Published quarterly by the Association for Computing Machinery, 1515 Broadway, New York, NY 10036, 800-342-6626, crossroads@acm.org. Student-written publication that covers computer-related topics. Features educational and career articles, opinion columns, and reviews of books, software, and conferences. Read it online at http://www.acm.org/crossroads.

EETimes On-line. Updated daily at http://www.eet.com. An excellent guide to the semiconductors, systems, software, design, and technology industries that offers day-to-day news, career advice, product analysis, features, and columns.

Electronic Products: The Engineer's Magazine of Product Technology. Published monthly by Hearst Business Communications Inc., 50 Charles Lindbergh Boulevard, Suite 100, Uniondale, NY

11553, http://electronicproducts.com. Details both the latest developments in electronics and unusual or new applications of products or technologies.

Engineers. Published quarterly by the American Association of Engineering Societies, 1828 L Street, NW, Suite 906, Washington, DC 20036, 202-296-2237, http://www.aaes.org. Reports on engineering surveys conducted by the organization.

Environmental Engineer. Published quarterly by the American Academy of Environmental Engineers, 130 Holiday Court, Suite 100, Annapolis, MD 21401, http://www.aaee.net/newlook/magazine.htm. Professional journal that offers articles on well-known environmental engineers, the history of the field, and advances in environmental engineering practice.

Industrial Engineer. Published monthly by the Institute of Industrial Engineers, 3577 Parkway Lane, Suite 200, Norcross, GA 30092, 800-494-0460, http://www.iienet.org/magazine. Offers industrial engineers and managers tips and advice on increasing efficiency and boosting productivity.

Industrial Management. Published bimonthly by the Institute of Industrial Engineers' Society for Engineering & Management Systems, 3577 Parkway Lane, Suite 200, Norcross, GA 30092, 800-494-0460, http://www.iienet.org. Offers advice to aspiring and working engineers in management; topics covered include worker motivation and work culture, strategic planning, quality manage-ment systems, and management performance and techniques.

International Journal of Applied Ceramic Technology. Published bimonthly by Blackwell Publishing (350 Main Street, Malden, MA 02148-5020, 800-835-6770, subscrip@bos.blackwellpublishing.com, http://www.blackwellpublishing.com/journal.asp?ref=1546-542X&site=1) on behalf of the American Ceramic Society. Professional journal that publishes applied research on the commercialization of engineered ceramics, products, and processes.

International Journal of Industrial Engineering. Published quarterly by the School of Industrial Engineering, University of Cincinnati, Cincinnati, OH 45221-0116, amital@uceng.uc.edu, http://www.ijienet.org. With an emphasis on engineering design, covers consumer product design, engineering economy and cost estimation, information systems, materials handling, and much more.

ITE Journal. Published monthly by the Institute of Transportation Engineers, 1099 14th Street, NW, Suite 300 West, Washington, DC 20005-3438, 202-289-0222, http://www.ite.org/ite-journal/index.asp. Presents research in transportation planning, geometric design, traffic operations, goods movement, signs and markings, parking, safety, ride sharing, and mass transit.

Journal of Clinical Engineering. Published quarterly by Lippincott Williams & Wilkins, PO Box 1620, Hagerstown, MD 21741, 800-638-3030, http://www.lww.com. Focuses on the needs of hospital-based clinical engineers, educators, researchers, and other professionals engaged with the development and applications of medical technology.

Journal of Engineering Education. Published quarterly by the American Society for Engineering Education, PO Box 96675, Washington, DC 20090-6675, http://www.asee.org/about/publications/jee. A scholarly journal that provides information on the status of engineering education, including current trends and innovations.

Journal of Manufacturing Science and Engineering. Published monthly by the American Society of Mechanical Engineers, 22 Law Drive, PO Box 2900, Fairfield, NJ 07007-2900, 800-843-2763, infocentral@asme.org, http://www.asme.org/pubs/journals/nmorder.html. Articles on computer-integrated manufacturing, design for manufacturing, girding and abrasive machining, inspection and quality control, robotics, and a lot more.

Journal of Technology Education. Published twice annually by the *Journal of Technology Education,* Department of Industry and Technology, Millersville University, PO Box 1002, Millersville, PA 17551-0302, http://scholar.lib.vt.edu/ejournals/JTE. Provides a forum for scholarly discussion of technology education research, philosophy, theory, and practice. Includes book reviews, articles, and interviews.

Journal of the American Ceramic Society. Published monthly by Blackwell Publishing (350 Main Street, Malden, MA 02148-5020, 800-835-6770, subscrip@bos.blackwellpublishing.com, http://www.blackwellpublishing.com/jace) on behalf of the American Ceramic Society. Professional journal that publishes original research on the science of ceramics and ceramic-based composites.

Journal of the Air & Waste Management Association (AWMA). Published monthly by the AWMA, One Gateway Center, Third Floor, Pittsburgh, PA 15222, 412-232-3444, subscriptions@awma.org, http://www.awma.org/journal. Offers articles on developments in environmental engineering.

looking.forward. Published quarterly by the IEEE Computer Society, 1730 Massachusetts Avenue, NW, Washington, DC 20036-1992. Student-written e-zine that focuses on developments in the computer industry. Issues are available at http://www.computer.org/students/looking.

Mechanical Engineering. Published monthly by the American Society of Mechanical Engineers, Three Park Avenue, New York, NY 10016-5990, 800-THE-ASME, http://www.memagazine.org. Covers aerospace, computers in engineering, design engineering, electronic packaging, environmental control, and other issues that pertain to mechanical engineering.

Mining Engineering. Published by the Society for Mining, Metallurgy, and Exploration, PO Box 277002, 8307 Shaffer Parkway, Littleton, CO 80127-4102, 800-763-3132, http://www.smenet.org/digital_library/library_

mining.cfm. Features industry news and articles and papers related to mining and processing metallic and nonmetallic ores and coal.

Nuclear News. Published monthly by the American Nuclear Society, 555 North Kensington Avenue, LaGrange Park, IL 60526, http://www.ans.org/store/vi-130000. Covers latest developments in nuclear power and nonpower uses of nuclear science and technology, such as nuclear medicine, food irradiation, and space nuclear applications.

Optical Engineering. Published monthly by SPIE—The International Society for Optical Engineering, 1000 20th Street, Bellingham, WA 98225, 360-676-3290, spie@spie.org, http://spie.org. Provides updates on advancements in optical engineering and related technology.

Packaging Digest. Published monthly by Reed Business Information, 8878 Barrons Boulevard, Highlands Ranch, CO 80129-2345, 800-446-6551, http://www.packagingdigest.com. Thorough review of the packaging industry, specializing in food and electronics packaging.

Plastics Engineering. Published monthly by the Society of Plastics Engineers Inc., PO Box 403, Brookfield, CT 06804-0403, http://www.4spe.org/pub. Explores, through technical articles and industry news, the science and technology of plastics engineering within the context of the plastics business.

The Pre-Engineering Times. Published monthly by the Junior Engineering Technical Society, 1420 King Street, Suite 405, Alexandria, VA 22314, 703-548-5387. Offers information for students and educators on engineering disciplines, profiles of interesting engineers and engineering programs, scholarship opportunities, Web links, engineering salaries, and much more. Available for free at http://www.jets.org/publications/petimes.cfm.

SWE, Magazine of the Society of Women Engineers. Published five times annually by the Society of Women Engineers, 230 East Ohio, Suite 400, Chicago, IL 60611-3265, 312-596-5223, hq@swe.org, http://www.swe.org. Offers stories on the achievements of women engineers, career development resources, and career guidance for students.

Today's Engineer Webzine. Published online monthly by the Institute of Electrical and Electronics Engineers, 1828 L Street, NW, Suite 1202, Washington, DC 20036-5104. Discusses topics—such as professionalism, management skills, engineering performance, engineering skills and competencies, product development practices, project management issues, innovation and entrepreneurship, and business practices—that are of interest to today's engineers. Available online at http://www.todaysengineer.org.

Winds of Change. Published five times (including a College Guide) a year by American Indian Science and Engineering Society Publishing, Inc., 4450 Arapahoe Avenue, Suite 100, Boulder, CO 80303. Information on career and educational advancement for American Indians and Native Alaskans/Hawaiians.

Surf the Web

You must use the Internet to do research, to find out, to explore. The Web offers a wealth of information on engineering and often does it in a way where you can actually have fun while learning. This chapter gets you started with an annotated list of Web sites related to engineering. Try a few. Follow the links. Maybe even venture as far as asking questions in a chat room. The more you read about and interact with engineers, the better prepared you'll be when you're old enough to participate as a professional.

One caveat: you probably already know that URLs change all the time. If a Web address listed below is out of date, try searching on the site's name or other key words. Chances are, if it's still out there, you'll find it. If it's not, maybe you'll find something better!

❏ THE LIST

All Engineering Schools
http://www.allengineeringschools.com0

Visit this site for a one-stop online shop of different engineering programs, from online certificates to bachelor's degrees to doctoral programs. Search by degree program, state, or among their short list of featured programs. Each school listing includes contact information, a link to their Web site, and details about each engineering program offered. Visit the Q&A section for basic information about choosing a program, short descriptions of different specialties within engineering, and tips on applying to a school.

ASEE Engineering K12 Center
http://www.engineeringk12.org

Sponsored by the American Society for Engineering Education (ASEE), this Web site supplies exactly the information "pre-college engineers" are looking for. Go to the Students section and browse the Engineering Alphabet, featuring information on different jobs (and their largest employers) within the engineering field. In the Studying Engineering FAQs section, read about the academic background you'll need to get accepted into a good engineering institution, and the SAT or ACT scores you should shoot for.

In case you're wondering whether you'll be able to handle those engineering courses in college, you can take a science/math aptitude test online at this site. If you make it over that hurdle, there's specific information to help you pick the right engineering school and secrets on getting admitted. Then link right to the Web pages of hundreds of colleges and universities in the United States that offer strong engineering programs.

Of course, you'll need to pay for college, and this site has considerately thought of that, too. Visit the section Finding and Affording the Right School for links to the Web sites of the Department of Education and various federal loan, grant, and work-study programs.

Ask Dr. Science . . . He knows more than you do!
http://www.drscience.com

"There is a thin line between ignorance and arrogance," writes Dr. Science, "and only I have managed to erase that line." If you're a fan of his daily radio show, you now have a chance to get another dose of this sly, self-spoofing comedian-scientist online.

Click on the Question of the Day—and get ready to laugh. In other words, don't take him too seriously. One week's worth of questions involved burping, dogs e-mailing, birth control, and living entirely on Hostess products. This site is more than just a radio program typed on the screen; it offers honest-to-goodness interactivity. For instance, you can submit your own question, or visit the vault of knowledge to search by keyword for any topic that you think Dr. Science might have covered. (Let your mind run wild.)

If you like this site so much you never want to miss it, you can ask Dr. Science to send you his daily Q&A by e-mail. Real Dr. Science junkies can ask for a printed catalog of paraphernalia and bulletins.

Blobz Guide to Electric Circuits
http://www.andythelwell.com/blobz

This educational and entertaining game will teach you the basics about electric engineering, open versus closed circuits, different power supplies, and how to interpret circuit diagrams. Read the short "lesson" about the subject, try the lesson activity, then take the short quiz to see if you were really paying attention. What makes this site work is it's interactive and information is doled out in small, easy to understand bites. Get all five quizzes right to receive a bonus prize . . . not to be revealed here.

Bridge Engineering
http://www.scsolutions.com/bridge.html

Are you in awe of those stretches of bridge that seem to be held up by mere wires or planks of wood? You're not alone. In fact, there's a whole engineering community devoted to building and studying bridges. Read here about bridge "events" in places as far away as Edinburgh, Scotland, and Mumbai, India—and as close to home as Columbus, Ohio.

The site was created by SC Solutions, a California engineering firm, in order to provide a comprehensive link to all bridge-related material on the Web. Even if you think a bridge is a bridge is a bridge, this site could make you think again. There are descriptions of prestressed concrete bridges, covered bridges, wood bridges, and so on, all with societies or councils you can link to from here. Many federal and state transportation agencies are also represented by links, as are a number of universities and research institutions. If you're scouting out internship possibilities, you might look at the list of links to U.S. companies that do bridge construction.

The Exhibits section is a wonderful diversion—even for casual bridge enthusiasts. You can link to photos of a Popsicle stick bridge, the world's largest bridges, or view a video clip about the Tacoma Narrows Bridge, one of the most documented bridge failures ever.

Engineer Girl
http://www.engineergirl.org

This site, developed by the National Academy of Engineering, aims to promote engineering to all people at any age, but particularly to women and girls. Did you know that a woman named Emily Roebling supervised construction of the Brooklyn Bridge? Or that a famous Hollywood actress helped pave the way for current wireless technology? Check out the site to read other curious stories about projects created by women engineers and fun facts about the field. Under the Women Engineers section, read day-in-the-life accounts of women engineers at work, including recommendations for preparing for college and a career in the sciences.

How Stuff Works
http://www.howstuffworks.com

If you spend a lot of time wondering how stuff you use or see everyday actually works, engineering is a good fit for you. This site should also be on your short list of Web sites to explore, as it covers how "stuff," as varied and timely as tsunamis to identity theft, works. Complex concepts are carefully broken down and examined, including photos and links to

current and past news items about the subject. The Engineering section of the site covers random items, such as how zippers, bowling pin setters, and rollercoasters work. For example, did you know that it takes the combined effort of over 4,000 parts to reset your bowling pins after each roll? Things you might not even be interested in will seem captivating as the site explains how commonly used and overlooked devices work. In addition to exploring the Engineering topics, check out the Health and General Science section to read about more topics that affect everyday people, such as how alcohol, aspirin, or cholesterol works, and how it can help or hurt you.

Human-Powered Hydrofoil
http://lancet.mit.edu/decavitator

It's a bird, it's a plane . . . it's a Decavitator. A what? If you're worried that college is going to be all work and no play, check out this site for a blend of the two. The students at the Massachusetts Institute of Technology (MIT) are known for their engineering prowess, and the Decavitator, a human-powered hydrofoil, is yet another demonstration of it. This student-developed boat was funded by MIT's SeaGrant program, and in 1993 was even awarded the DuPont prize for the fastest human-powered watercraft—a title it still holds today.

Visit this site to read a description of hydrofoil basics that even a literature major could understand, and then watch videos of the Decavitator in action. If you're inspired to build one of your very own, you'll find a three-dimensional drawing and specifications, as well as a page that describes methods and materials used to manufacture the boat. And, should you really want to talk hydrofoil, you can even e-mail some of the members of the team who built it.

Imagine
http://www.jhu.edu/~gifted/imagine

Imagine is a bimonthly journal for the go-getter high school student with his or her eye on the future. Its tag line, "Opportunities and resources for academically talented youth," says it all.

If you're always searching for good academic programs, competitions, and internships, this publication can keep you well informed on what's available and when you need to apply.

Along with the current issue, selected portions of back issues can be read online. Previous issues have included articles about the USA Computing Olympiad and the ThinkQuest Competition, as well as general tips on entering academic competitions and choosing summer academic programs. For $30 a year, you can subscribe and get the printed journal delivered to your home—or for free, you can just read back issues online.

Junior Engineering Technical Society (JETS)
http://www.jets.org

This site, another great resource brought to you by the American Society for Engineering Education, offers an unbelievable amount of useful and interesting information for junior high and high school students interested in engineering. The mission of JETS is to increase college enrollment in the technology and engineering fields by providing opportunities for students to explore these careers while they're still in high school.

At the JETS home page, click on JETS Programs for a link to TEAMS (Tests of Engineering Aptitude, Mathematics, and Science) to learn about this program in which teams of students work with an engineering mentor, then participate in an open-book, open-discussion engineering problem competition. Follow the link to the National Engineering Design Challenge to find out about another program that challenges teams of students working with an advisor to design, fabricate, and demonstrate a working solution to a social need. Finally, take the self-administered National Engineering Aptitude Search to determine if your education is on the right track.

For each of these programs, you can view sample problems and their solutions. In addition, many brochures are posted online, including *Engineering is For You!* which provides descriptions of different disciplines and ways to "try on" engineering, and several different Engineering Specialty Brochures, which explain in more detail jobs in different areas of the engineering field. In addition to these online publications, JETS also offers a broad range of brochures, books, and videos for sale.

Peterson's Guide to Summer Programs for Teenagers
http://www.petersons.com/summerop

Your commitment to a brilliant academic future might waver when you visit this site. Along with some great information about academic and career-focused summer programs, you'll be tantalized by summer camps that revolve around activities that are less mentally rigorous—like white water rafting or touring Switzerland on a bicycle. Shake it off. You're here to further your education, and this site offers good tips on assessing any summer program or camp you're considering.

Finding a camp that suits your interests is easy enough at this site; just search Peterson's database of academic, travel, and camping programs. Under the Engineering section, you'll find a list of links to more than 30 summer programs, from such prestigious institutions as Carnegie Mellon, Johns Hopkins, Northwestern, and Smith—to name a few. Click on a specific program or camp for a quick overview description. In some instances you'll get a more in-depth description, along with photographs, applications, and online brochures. If you need to limit your search to your home state, that's easy enough, too. You can sift through Peterson's database by geographic region or alphabetically.

Science is Fun in the Lab of Shakhashiri

http://scifun.chem.wisc.edu

This site, created by a chemistry professor at the University of Wisconsin-Madison, offers fun and educational resources alike. Professor Bassum Z. Shakhashiri covers topics as basic as the periodic table to as wild as a home experiment that makes raisins dance. Though written for a college audience, the information at this site

is broad-based enough to appeal to high school students as well.

If you live in the Midwest, check out the Events of Interest section to learn about opportunities to meet Professor Shakhashiri or other scientists such as Nobel Laureate Ronald Hoffman or author Phillip Ball.

A Sightseer's Guide to Engineering

http://www.engineeringsights.org

The National Society of Professional Engineers and National Engineers Week developed this fun and interactive sight to explore the work of engineers nationwide. Click on the map to see projects from a particular state, such as Illinois' Sears Tower or California's Golden Gate Bridge. Lesser-known engineering marvels such as Oklahoma's Pensacola Dam or Arkansas's Museum of Bells are also featured. Even Mother Nature's impressive engineering marvels are included, such as Utah's Rainbow Bridge Natural Monument. The photos alone are worth checking out in addition to the informative listings of fun facts about the featured location, contact information, and hours of operation (when applicable).

U.S. News & World Report: America's Best Colleges 2007

http://www.usnews.com/usnews/edu/college/majors/majors_index_brief.php

Use this free online service to search schools by national ranking, location, name, or major. (The link above will allow you to search by major.) The Engineering subsection alone lists hundreds of schools that offer engineering programs, and each school link includes contact information and details about services and facilities, campus life, mission, and extracurriculars offered. Note: In order to read the full account information about each school, you must either buy the print publication or pay for the Premium Online Edition.

Yahoo: Engineering

http://dir.yahoo.com/science/
   engineering

It might seem odd to include the popular search engine Yahoo among a list of engi-neering Web sites, but it won't seem so after you've visited it. If you're hungry for more after visiting the sites listed in this appendix, pull up a chair at Yahoo's feast.

Yahoo has done a tremendous amount of legwork for you. For example, if you're interested in electrical engineering, then scan through the 990 sites currently included here. Industrial engineering posts an impressive 99 sites. Even welding engineering offers 11 sites you probably wouldn't have known to look for otherwise. In addition to sites about engineering professions, you'll also find engineering education sites, events, journals, and magazines.

Ask for Money

By the time most students get around to thinking about applying for scholarships, they have already extolled their personal and academic virtues to such lengths in essays and interviews for college applications that even their own grandmothers wouldn't recognize them. The thought of filling out yet another application form fills students with dread. And why bother? Won't the same five or six kids who have been fighting over grade point averages since the fifth grade walk away with all the really good scholarships?

The truth is, most of the scholarships available to high school and college students are offered because an organization wants to promote interest in a particular field, encourage more students to become qualified to enter it, and finally, to help those students afford an education. Certainly, having a good grade point average is a valuable asset, and many organizations that grant scholarships request that only applicants with a specified minimum grade point average apply. More often than not, however, grade point averages aren't even mentioned; the focus is on the area of interest and what a student has done to distinguish himself or herself in that area. In fact, sometimes the only requirement is that the scholarship applicant must be studying in a particular area.

❏ GUIDELINES

When applying for scholarships there are a few simple guidelines that can help ease the process considerably.

Plan Ahead

The absolute worst thing you can do is wait until the last minute. For one thing, obtaining recommendations or other supporting data in time to meet an application deadline is incredibly difficult. For another, no one does his or her best thinking or writing under the gun. So get off to a good start by reviewing scholarship applications as early as possible—months, even a year, in advance. If the current scholarship information isn't available, ask for a copy of last year's version. Once you have the scholarship information or application in hand, give it a thorough read. Try to determine how your experience or situation best fits into the scholarship, or if it even fits at all. Don't waste your time applying for a scholarship in literature if you couldn't finish *Great Expectations*.

If possible, research the award or scholarship, including past recipients and, where applicable, the person in whose name the scholarship is offered. Often, scholarships are established to memorialize an individual who majored in religious studies or who loved history, for example, but in other cases, the scholarship is to memorialize the work of an individual. In those cases, try to get a feel for the spirit of the person's work. If you have any similar interests or experiences, don't hesitate to mention these.

Talk to others who received the scholarship, or to students currently studying in the same area or field of interest in which the scholarship is offered, and try to gain insight into possible applications or work related to that field. When you're working on the essay asking why you want this scholarship, you'll have real answers—"I would benefit from receiving this scholarship because studying engineering will help me to design inexpensive but attractive and structurally sound urban housing."

Take your time writing the essays. Make sure you are answering the question or questions on the application and not merely restating facts about yourself. Don't be afraid to get creative; try to imagine what you would think of if you had to sift through hundreds of applications: What would you want to know about the candidate? What would convince you that someone was deserving of the scholarship? Work through several drafts and have someone whose advice you respect—a parent, teacher, or guidance counselor—review the essay for grammar and content.

Finally, if you know in advance which scholarships you want to apply for, there might still be time to stack the deck in your favor by getting an internship, volunteering, or working part time. Bottom line: the more you know about a scholarship and the sooner you learn it, the better.

Follow Directions

Think of it this way: many of the organizations that offer scholarships devote 99.9 percent of their time to something other than the scholarship for which you are applying. Don't make a nuisance of yourself by pestering them for information. Simply follow the directions as they are presented to you. If the scholarship application specifies that you write for further information, then write for it—don't call.

Pay close attention to whether you're applying for an award, a scholarship, a prize, or financial aid. Often these words are used interchangeably, but just as often they have different meanings. An award is usually given for something you have done: built a park or helped distribute meals to the elderly; or something you have created: a design, an essay, a short film, a screenplay, or an invention. On the other hand, a scholarship is frequently a renewable sum of money that is given to a person to help defray the costs of college. Scholarships are given to candidates who meet the necessary criteria based on essays, eligibility, grades, or sometimes all three.

Supply all the necessary documents, information, and fees, and make the deadlines. You won't win any scholarships by forgetting to include a recommendation from a teacher or failing to postmark the application by the deadline. Bottom line: get it right the first time, on time.

Apply Early

Once you have the application in hand, don't dawdle. If you've requested it far enough in advance, there shouldn't be any reason for you not to turn it in well in advance of the deadline. You never know—if it comes down to two candidates, your timeliness just might be the deciding factor. Bottom line: don't wait, don't hesitate.

Be Yourself

Don't make promises you can't keep. There are plenty of hefty scholarships available, but if they all require you to study something that you don't enjoy, you'll be miserable in college. And the side effects from switching majors after you've accepted a scholarship could be even worse. Bottom line: be yourself.

Don't Limit Yourself

There are many sources for scholarships, beginning with your guidance counselor and ending with the Internet. All of the search engines have education categories. Start there and search by keywords, such as "financial aid," "scholarship," and "award." But don't be limited to the scholarships listed in these pages.

If you know of an organization related to or involved with the field of your choice, write a letter asking if they offer scholarships. If they don't offer scholarships, don't stop there. Write them another letter, or better yet, schedule a meeting with the president or someone in the public relations office and ask them if they would be willing to sponsor a scholarship for you. Of course, you'll need to prepare yourself well for such a meeting because you're selling a priceless commodity—yourself. Don't be shy: be confident. Tell

them all about yourself, what you want to study and why, and let them know what you would be willing to do in exchange—volunteer at their favorite charity, write up reports on your progress in school, or work part time on school breaks, full time during the summer. Explain why you're a wise investment.

❏ THE LIST

Air Force ROTC
Scholarship Actions Branch
551 East Maxwell Boulevard
Maxwell AFB, AL 36112-5917
866-423-7682
http://www.afrotc.com

The Air Force ROTC provides a wide range of four-year scholarships (ranging from partial to full tuition) to high school students planning to study engineering, architecture, computer science, physics, or other majors in college. Scholarships are also available to college and enlisted students. Visit the Air Force ROTC Web site to apply.

American Chemical Society (ACS)
ACS Scholars Program
1155 16th Street, NW
Washington, DC 20036
800-227-5558, ext. 6250
http://www.chemistry.org/portal/a/c/
    s/1/acsdisplay.html?DOC=minority
    affairs%5Cscholars.html

African American, Hispanic/Latino, and American Indian students interested in pursuing undergraduate college degrees in chemical sciences and chemical technology are eligible to participate in the

ACS Scholar Programs. Graduating high school seniors and college freshmen, sophomores, and juniors are eligible to apply. Awards range from $2,500 to $3,000. Visit the ACS Web site for an application and additional details.

American Helicopter Society
Vertical Flight Foundation
217 North Washington Street
Alexandria, VA 22314-2538
703-684-6777
staff@vtol.org
http://www.vtol.org/awards.html

Ten to 15 AHS Vertical Flight Foundation Scholarships of $2,000 to $4,000 are awarded annually to college students who are studying engineering or a related field. Visit the society's Web site for scholarship details.

American Indian Science and Engineering Society (AISES)
PO Box 9828
Albuquerque, NM 87119-9828
505-765-1052
http://www.aises.org/highered/
    scholarships

The AISES offers a variety of scholarships to Native American students at the undergraduate and graduate level. Applicants must be student members. Contact the society for more information and to download applications.

American Institute of Aeronautics and Astronautics (AIAA) Foundation
1801 Alexander Bell Drive, Suite 500
Reston, VA 20191-4344

800-639-2422
http://www.aiaa.org/content.
    cfm?pageid=211

College sophomores, juniors, and seniors and graduate students interested in pursuing careers in aeronautics, astronautics, and related fields are eligible to apply for a variety of scholarships that range from $2,000 to $10,000. Contact the AIAA Foundation for more information.

American Nuclear Society
555 North Kensington Avenue
La Grange Park, IL 60526
708-352-6611
http://www.ans.org/honors

The society offers a variety of scholarships and fellowships (ranging from $2,000 to $4,000) to undergraduate (who have completed their freshman year) and graduate students pursuing study in nuclear science, nuclear engineering, or a nuclear-related field. Contact the society for a list of scholarships and to download applications.

American Public Transportation Foundation
1666 K Street, NW
Washington, DC 20006
202-496-4800
http://www.apta.com/services/
    human_resources/program_
    guidelines.cfm

The foundation awards several scholarships to upper-level undergraduate and graduate students who are pursuing study in public transportation engineering. Visit the foundation's Web site for more information.

American Radio Relay League Foundation

225 Main Street
Newington, CT 06111
860-594-0200
http://www.arrl.org/arrlf

Members of the league who are majoring in engineering, science, or related fields are eligible for a variety of scholarships. Awards range from $500 to $10,000.

American Society of Agricultural Engineers Foundation

2950 Niles Road
St. Joseph, MI 49085-9659
269-429-0300
http://www.asae.org/membership/students

Student members who are majoring in biological or agricultural engineering are eligible to apply for several different $1,000 scholarships and grants. Contact the foundation for more information.

American Society of Civil Engineers (ASCE)

Attn: Student Services
1801 Alexander Bell Drive
Reston, VA 20191-4400
http://www.asce.org

Currently enrolled college junior or senior civil engineering students are eligible to apply for several scholarships (ranging from $2,000 to $3,000) to help finance study in civil engineering. Applicants must be student members of the society. Contact the ASCE for more information.

American Society of Mechanical Engineers (ASME)

Coordinator, Educational Operations
Three Park Avenue
New York, NY 10016-5990
212-591-8131
oluwanifiset@asme.org
http://www.asme.org/Education/FinancialAid

High school seniors and undergraduate and graduate students who are interested in or currently studying mechanical engineering are eligible to apply for a variety of scholarships that range from $1,000 to $10,000. Visit the ASME Web site for further details and to complete an online application. Applicants for all scholarships must be student members of the society. The ASME also offers low-interest student loans.

American Society of Safety Engineers Foundation

Attn: Maria Rosario
1800 East Oakton Street
Des Plaines, IL 60018
847-768-3441
http://www.asse.org

Students pursuing undergraduate and graduate degrees in occupational safety and health or a closely related field are eligible for a variety of scholarships that range from $1,000 to $6,000. Applicants must be student members to be eligible for the scholarships (except for the Thompson Scholarship for Women in Safety). Visit the foundation's Web site to download an application.

ASM International Materials Education Foundation

Scholarship Program
9639 Kinsman Road
Materials Park, OH 44073-0002
http://www.asminternational.
    org/Content/NavigationMenu/
    ASMFoundation/
    UndergraduateScholarships/
    Undergraduate.htm

A variety of scholarships are available for college students who are studying or planning to study metallurgy or materials science. Must be a student member of ASM International. Scholarships range from $1,500 to full tuition. Visit the foundation's Web site for more information and to apply online. You may also contact the foundation for a list of local chapters that may award aid.

Associated General Contractors Education and Research Foundation

333 John Carlyle Street, Suite 200
Alexandria, VA 22314
703-837-5342
agcf@agc.org
http://www.agc.org/page.ww?section
    =AGC+Foundation&name=Undergr
    aduate+Scholarships

College sophomores and juniors who are majoring in construction or civil engineering are eligible for scholarships of $2,000 per year. Visit the foundation's Web site for more information and to apply online.

Automotive Hall of Fame

21400 Oakwood Boulevard
Dearborn, MI 48124
http://www.automotivehalloffame.
    org/scholarships.php

High school seniors and college students who are interested in a career in the automotive industry can apply for a variety of scholarships. The AHF awards more than $20,000 in scholarships annually. Visit its Web site for a list of scholarships and to download an application.

Collegeboard.com

http://apps.collegeboard.com/
    cbsearch_ss/welcome.jsp

This testing service (PSAT, SAT, etc.) also offers a scholarship search engine. It features scholarships (not all engineering-related) worth more than $3 billion. You can search by specific major and a variety of other criteria.

CollegeNET

http://www.collegenet.com

CollegeNET features 600,000 scholarships (not all engineering-related) worth more than $1.6 billion. You can search by keyword (such as "engineering") or by creating a personality profile of your interests.

FastWeb

http://fastweb.monster.com

FastWeb is one of the largest scholarship search engines around. It features 600,000 scholarships (not all engineering-related) worth over $1 billion. To use this resource, you will need to register (free).

Experimental Aircraft Association (EAA)
Scholarship Department
PO Box 3086
Oshkosh, WI 54903-3086
920-426-6815
scholarships@eaa.org
http://www.eaa.org/education/
   scholarships

High school seniors and undergraduates who plan to or who are currently studying aerospace engineering or another aviation-related field are eligible to apply for a variety of scholarships (ranging from $500 to $5,000). Applicants must be student members. Visit the EAA Web site for details and to download applications.

Foundation for the Carolinas
PO Box 34769
Charlotte, NC 28234
704-973-4500
infor@fftc.org
http://www.fftc.org

The foundation administers more than 70 scholarship funds that offer awards to undergraduate and graduate students pursuing study in engineering and other disciplines. Visit its Web site for a searchable list of awards.

GuaranteedScholarships.com
http://www.guaranteed-scholarships.
   com

This Web site offers lists (by college) of scholarships, grants, and financial aid (not all engineering related) that "require no interview, essay, portfolio, audition, competition, or other secondary requirement."

Illinois Career Resource Network
http://www.ilworkinfo.com/icrn.htm

Created by the Illinois Department of Employment Security, this useful site offers a great scholarship search engine, as well as detailed information on careers (including engineering). You can search for engineering scholarships based on engineering majors and keywords. This site is available to everyone, not just Illinois residents; you can get a password by simply visiting the site. The Illinois Career Information System is just one example of sites created by state departments of employment security (or departments of labor) to assist students with financial- and career-related issues. After checking out this site, visit your state's department of labor Web site to see what they offer.

Institute of Electrical and Electronics Engineers (IEEE)
1828 L Street, NW, Suite 1202
Washington, DC 20036-5104
ieeeusa@ieee.org
http://www.ieee.org

IEEE a variety of scholarships and fellowships to its student members who are pursuing education in electrical and electronic engineering and computer science. Applicants must be undergraduate or graduate students. Contact IEEE for more information.

Institute of Industrial Engineers (IIE)
3577 Parkway Lane, Suite 200
Norcross, GA 30092

800-494-0460
http://www.iienet.org/public/articles/
index.cfm?Cat=525

IIE offers a variety of scholarships to its student members who are currently majoring in industrial engineering. Scholarships range from $600 to $4,000. The organization also offers fellowships to graduate students. Nominations for these scholarships must be made by industrial engineering college department heads; visit the IIE Web site for a nomination form.

Institute of Transportation Engineers (ITE)
1099 14th Street, NW, Suite 300 West
Washington, DC 20005-3438
202-289-0222
ite_staff@ite.org
http://www.ite.org/education/
scholarships.asp

The institute awards scholarships and fellowships to graduate students who are interested in pursuing careers in transportation engineering. Contact the ITE for more information.

The Minerals, Metals & Materials Society
Student Awards Program
184 Thorn Hill Road
Warrendale, PA 15086
724-776-9000
students@tms.org
http://www.tms.org/Students/
AwardsPrograms/Scholarships.html

Undergraduate and graduate student members majoring in metallurgical engi-neering, materials science and engineering, or related fields are eligible to apply for several scholarships (ranging from $2,000 to $5,000). Visit the Society's Web site to download an application and additional details.

National Action Council for Minorities in Engineering (NACME)
440 Hamilton Avenue, Suite 302
White Plains, NY 10601-1813
914-539-4010
scholarships@nacme.org
http://www.guidemenacme.org/
guideme/parents/scholar.jsp

NACME offers information on the scholarship process for high school students interested in engineering. It encourages students to e-mail the NACME Scholarship Source with scholarship-related questions. A searchable scholarship database is available at the Web site.

National Coalition for Aviation Education
3146 Valentino Court
Oakton, VA 22124
http://www.aviationeducation.
org/html/scholarshipsandawards/
scholarshipsandawards.htm

The coalition provides a list of scholarships and awards provided by its member organizations.

National Federation of the Blind
Scholarship Committee
805 Fifth Avenue
Grinnell, IA 50112
641-236-3366
http://www.nfb.org/sch_intro.htm

Scholarships of $3,000 are available to blind high school seniors and undergraduates who are interested in or who are currently studying engineering or computer science. Write for further details. Visit the federation's Web site for an application.

National Ground Water Association

National Ground Water Research and Educational Foundation
Scholarship Coordinator
601 Dempsey Road
Westerville, OH 43081
smasters@ngwa.org
http://www.ngwa.org/ngwef/assante. cfm

High school seniors and college undergraduates are eligible to apply for scholarships from the Len Assante Scholarship Fund. Applicants may be entering any field of study. Visit the association's Web site for details and to download an application.

National Society of Black Engineers (NSBE)

1454 Duke Street
Alexandria, VA 22314
703-549-2207
scholarships@nsbe.org
http://www.nsbe.org/programs/ index.php#scholarships

High school and college student members of the NSBE are eligible to apply for a variety of scholarships that range in value from $500 to $5,000. Visit the society's Web site for a complete list.

National Society of Professional Engineers

1420 King Street
Alexandria, VA 22314-2794
703-684-2800
http://www.nspe.org/scholarships/sc-home.asp

The society offers a variety of scholarships (ranging from $1,000 to $10,000) to high school seniors and undergraduate and graduate students who are interested in pursuing careers in engineering. High school students will be most interested in learning more about the Maureen L. and Howard N. Blitman, P.E. Scholarship to Promote Diversity in Engineering ($5,000, ethnic minorities); the Auxiliary Scholarship ($1,000 a year for four years, females); and the Virginia D. Henry Memorial Scholarship ($1,000, females). Visit the society's application page, http://www.nspe.org/scholarships/sc1-appl.asp, to fill out an online application.

National Urban League (NUL)

120 Wall Street
New York, NY 10005
info@nul.org
http://www.nul.org/scholarships.html

In addition to offering the American Chemical Society Minority Scholars Programs in conjunction with the American Chemical Society, this civil rights organization offers a scholarship in association with the University of Rochester, and a detailed list of minority-focused scholarships from other organizations. Minority high school seniors and undergraduate and graduate students are eligible for these awards. Visit the NUL's Web site for more information.

Plastics Institute of America (PIA)

333 Aiken Street
Lowell, MA 01854-3686
978-934-3130
info@plasticsinstitute.org
http://www.plasticsinstitute.org/
   scholarships.php

Scholarships of $1,500 are awarded to students enrolled in certificate and two- and four-year programs in plastics technology. Visit PIA's Web site for an application and more information.

Scholarship America

One Scholarship Way
St. Peter, MN 56082
800-537-4180
http://www.scholarshipamerica.org

This organization works through its local Dollars for Scholars chapters in 41 states and the District of Columbia. In 2003, it awarded more than $29 million in scholarships to students. Visit Scholarship America's Web site for more information.

Scholarships.com

http://www.scholarships.com

Scholarships.com offers a free college scholarship search engine (although you must register to use it) and financial aid information.

Sigma Xi Scientific Research Society

PO Box 13975
3106 East NC Highway 54
Research Triangle, NC 27709
800-243-6534
giar@sigmaxi.org

http://www.sigmaxi.org/programs/
   prizes/index.shtml

The society provides grants of up to $1,000 to support student research efforts in the sciences and engineering via its Grants-in-Aid of Research Program. College undergraduates and graduate students are eligible. Visit the society's Web site for an application.

Society for Mining, Metallurgy, and Exploration

8307 Shaffer Parkway
Littleton, CO 80127
303-973-9550
http://www.smenet.org/education/
   Students/sme_scholarships.cfm

SME awards approximately 25 scholarships of up to $2,000 each to student members who are studying mining engineering, metallurgy, civil engineering, mechanical engineering, geology, or a related field. Applicants must have completed their sophomore year in college. Contact the society to obtain an application.

Society for the Advancement of Material and Process Engineering

Undergraduate Awards Program
1161 Park View Drive
Covina, CA 91724-3751
626-331-0616
http://www.sampe.org/studentp.html

College freshmen, sophomores, and juniors are eligible for scholarships (ranging from $750 to $2,000) to help finance study in engineering and engineering technology. Applicants must be student members of the society. Visit the society's Web site for an application.

Society of Automotive Engineers
Scholarship Administrator
755 West Big Beaver, Suite 1600
Troy, MI 48084
724-776-4970
scholarships@sae.org
http://students.sae.org/awdscholar

The society offers a variety of scholarships and grants to high school seniors and undergraduate and graduate students. High school students will be particularly interested in the SAE Engineering Scholarships, which range from $400 to full tuition. Visit the society's Web site for more information and to apply online.

Society of Hispanic Professional Engineers/Hispanic Scholarship Fund
5400 East Olympic Boulevard, Suite 210
Los Angeles, CA 90022
323-725-3970
http://oneshpe.shpe.org

The society partners with the Hispanic Scholarship Fund to offer scholarships to Hispanic high school seniors and undergraduate and graduate students pursuing degrees in engineering, mathematics, science, and computer science. Visit the society's Web site for an application.

Society of Manufacturing Engineers Education Foundation
PO Box 930
Dearborn, MI 48121

800-733-4763, ext. 3304
foundation@sme.org
http://www.sme.org/cgi-bin/
    smeefhtml.pl?/foundation/
    scholarships/fsfstudp.htm&&&SEF&

The foundation offers a variety of scholarships to high school seniors and undergraduate and graduate students who are interested in or currently studying manufacturing engineering, manufacturing engineering technology, or a closely related engineering field of study. Awards range from $1,000 to $20,000. Visit the foundation's Web site for details.

Society of Naval Architects and Marine Engineers (SNAME)
601 Pavonia Avenue
Jersey City, NJ 07306
800-798-2188
http://www.sname.org/scholarships_
    undergraduate.htm

College students interested in the study of naval architecture, marine engineering, ocean engineering or marine industry–related fields may apply for scholarships of up to $2,000. Applicants must be entering their junior or senior year. You can request an application by sending an e-mail to efaustino@sname.org or visit the SNAME's Web site for more information. The society also offers graduate scholarships.

Society of Petroleum Engineers International
Professional Development Coordinator
PO Box 833836
Richardson, TX 75083-3836

800-456-6853, ext. 359
sspears@spe.org
http://www.spe.org/spe/jsp/
   basic/0,2396,1104_12167_0,00.
   html

The $5,000 Archie Memorial Scholarship is available to first-year college students majoring in petroleum engineering. Visit the society's Web site for more information and to apply online. You may also contact the society for a list of local chapters that may award aid.

Society of Plastics Engineers (SPE) Foundation
14 Fairfield Drive
Brookeville, CT 06804
203-740-5447
foundation@4spe.org
http://www.4spe.org/foundation/
   scholarships.php

Scholarships of up to $4,000 are available to students who have finished one year in an engineering college or technical institute and are interested in careers in the plastics industry. Priority is given to student members of the society or to children of members. Visit the SPE Foundation's Web site for an application and further details.

Society of Satellite Professionals International (SSPI)
The New York Information
   Technology Center
55 Broad Street, 14th Floor
New York, NY 10004
212-809-5199
http://www.sspi.org

SSPI encourages high school seniors and undergraduate and graduate students interested in the field of satellite technology to apply for a variety of scholarships (ranging from $2,000 to $5,000). Contact the society for eligibility details, or look for scholarships under the Education section of the SSPI Web site.

Society of Women Engineers
230 East Ohio Street, Suite 400
Chicago, IL 60611-3265
312-596-5223
http://www.swe.org

Female high school seniors and college students who plan to or who are currently studying engineering or computer science are eligible for a variety of scholarships ranging from $1,000 to $10,000. Visit the Collegiate Programs section of the SWE Web site for details and an application.

SPIE-The International Society for Optical Engineering (ISOE)
PO Box 10
Bellingham, WA 98227-0010
360-676-3290
spie@spie.org
http://www.spie.org/
   communityServices/
   StudentsAndEducators/index.
   cfm?fuseaction=students_
   scholarships

The society offers a variety of scholarships to student members who are pursuing optical engineering majors. Visit the SPIE's Web site for more information.

TAPPI
15 Technology Parkway South
Norcross, GA 30092
770-209-7536
vedmondson@tappi.org
http://www.tappi.org

College students who are studying engineering or environmental topics and demonstrate significant interest in pursuing careers in pulp, paper, and related industries are eligible to apply for a variety of scholarships, ranging from $500 to $2,500. Visit the TAPPI Web site for details and an application.

Triangle Education Foundation (TEF)
Chairman, Scholarship & Loan
    Committee
120 South Center Street
Plainfield, IN 46168
http://www.triangle.org/tef/
    programs/scholarships

The foundation offers a variety of scholarships (ranging from $1,000 to $8,000) to undergraduate and graduate student members who are currently studying engineering and other "hard sciences." The foundation also offers loans. Contact the TEF for more information and to download applications.

United Negro College Fund (UNCF)
http://www.uncf.org/scholarships/
    index.asp

Visitors to the UNCF Web site can search for thousands of scholarships and grants, many of which are administered by the UNCF. High school seniors and undergraduate and graduate students are eligible. The search engine allows you to search by engineering major, state, scholarship title, grade level, and achievement score.

Virginia Society of Professional Engineers
5206 Markel Road, Suite 300
Richmond, VA 23230
vspe@aol.com
http://www.vspe.org

Students who are attending one of the eight engineering schools in Virginia are eligible to apply for a $1,000 scholarship. The schools are George Mason University, Old Dominion University, Hampton University, University of Virginia, Virginia Commonwealth University, Virginia Military Institute, Virginia Polytechnic Institute & State University, and Virginia State University. Contact the society for more information.

Women's Transportation Seminar
1666 K Street, NW, Suite 1100
Washington, DC 20006
202-496-4340
    wts@wtsnational.org
http://www.wtsinternational.org

This organization offers the Sharon D. Banks Memorial Scholarship of $3,000 to female undergraduate students who are interested in studying transportation engineering or related fields. Graduate scholarships are also available. Visit the seminar's Web site for an application.

Look to the Pros

The following professional organizations offer a variety of materials, from career brochures to lists of accredited schools to salary surveys. Many of them also publish journals and newsletters that you should become familiar with. A number also have annual conferences that you might be able to attend. (While you may not be able to attend a conference as a participant, it may be possible to cover one for your school or even your local paper, especially if your school has a related club.)

When contacting professional organizations, keep in mind that they all exist primarily to serve their members, be it through continuing education, professional licensure, political lobbying, or just "keeping up with the profession." While many are strongly interested in promoting their profession and passing information about it to the general public, these professional organizations are also very busy with other activities. Whether you call or write, be courteous, brief, and to the point. Know what you need and ask for it. If the organization has a Web site, check it out first: what you're looking for may be available there for downloading, or you may find a list of prices or instructions, such as sending a self-addressed, stamped envelope with your request. Finally, be aware that organizations, like people, move. To save time when writing,

first confirm the address, preferably with a quick phone call to the organization itself or a visit to its Web site.

❏ THE SOURCES

Accreditation Board for Engineering and Technology (ABET)

111 Market Place, Suite 1050
Baltimore, MD 21202-4012
410-347-7700
http://www.abet.org

Contact the ABET for a list of accredited engineering schools and programs.

Aerospace Industries Association of America

1000 Wilson Boulevard, Suite 1700
Arlington, VA 22209-3928
703-358-1000
http://www.aia-aerospace.org

Contact this association for industry news and statistics and publications with information on aerospace technologies, careers, and space.

Air Force Organization

1501 Lee Highway
Arlington, VA 22209-1198
703-247-5839
aefstaff@aef.org
http://www.afa.org

The Air Force Organization and the Aerospace Education Foundation combined forces in 2006. Contact this organization for information about scholarships, colleges, and career opportunities.

American Academy of Environmental Engineers
130 Holiday Court, Suite 100
Annapolis, MD 21401
410-266-3311
info@aaee.net
http://www.aaee.net

Contact the academy for information on certification, careers, and salaries, or to view an online version of the *Environmental Engineering Selection Guide,* which lists the names of accredited environmental engineering programs and professors who have board certification as environmental engineers.

American Association of Engineering Societies (AAES)
1620 I Street, NW, Suite 210
Washington, DC 20006
202-296-2237
http://www.aaes.org

Contact the AAES for information on salaries and their quarterly bulletin, *Engineers,* which discusses careers in engineering.

American Ceramic Society
735 Ceramic Place, Suite 100
Westerville, OH 43081
614-890-4700
info@ceramics.org
http://www.ceramics.org

Contact the society for an overview of ceramics, information on student chapters, a list of colleges and universities that offer materials engineering programs, and a list of how ceramics have played a role in the top achievements in engineering.

American Chemical Society (ACS)
1155 16th Street, NW
Washington, DC 20036
800-227-5558
help@acs.org
http://www.chemistry.org

The ACS Education Division, one of whose goals is to attract students into careers in chemistry, offers a wide range of resources and services for high school chemistry teachers and students. It publishes an award-winning quarterly magazine for high school chemistry students, *ChemMatters.* The Web site contains a wealth of material, including online Career Briefs, which are short narratives illustrating various career options available to students majoring in chemistry, a searchable database of companies offering internships and other types of work experiences in chemistry (including chemical engineering), and information on the U.S. National Chemistry Olympiad.

American Indian Science and Engineering Society
PO Box 9828
Albuquerque, NM 87119-9828
505-765-1052
http://www.aises.org

Through a variety of educational programs, this society offers financial, academic, and cultural support to American Indians and Alaska Natives from middle school through graduate school who are interested in science and engineering. It publishes *Winds of Change* five times annually to provide information on career and educational advancement for American Indians and Native Alaskans/Hawaiians.

The *Annual College Guide for American Indians*—which describes the top colleges as well as preparation and application information, emphasizing the schools with significant Native American communities and support programs—is published as a special *Winds of Change* issue annually. The organization also offers job listings and a resume database at its Web site.

American Institute of Aeronautics and Astronautics (AIAA)

1801 Alexander Bell Drive, Suite 500
Reston, VA 20191-4344
800-639-2422
http://www.aiaa.org

Contact the AIAA for information on careers and education requirements in aeronautical and astronautical engineering; accredited schools; scholarships, awards, and competitions; the *AIAA Student Journal*; and student chapters of AIAA.

American Institute of Chemical Engineers

3 Park Avenue
New York, NY 10016-5991
800-242-4363
xpress@aiche.org
http://www.aiche.org

Contact the institute for information on careers in chemical engineering, accredited programs, awards, and student chapters.

American Society for Engineering Education (ASEE)

1818 N Street, NW, Suite 600
Washington, DC 20036-2479
202-331-3500
http://www.asee.org and http://www.engineeringk12.org/students/default.htm

ASEE's precollege Web site is a guide for high school students and others interested in engineering and engineering technology careers. Here you can learn about the different engineering and engineering technology fields, interesting people who got their start as engineers, what engineers actually do, and how to get (and pay for) an engineering education. One of its most useful publications is *Engineering: Go For It*, which is available for a small fee.

American Society of Certified Engineering Technicians

PO Box 1348
Flowery Branch, GA 30542
770-967-9173
General_Manager@ascet.org
http://www.ascet.org

Contact the society for information on training and certification.

American Society of Civil Engineers (ASCE)

1801 Alexander Bell Drive
Reston, VA 20191-4400
800-548-2723
http://www.asce.org

Contact the ASCE for information on civil engineering careers, certification, educational programs, contests and competitions, and scholarships. The Kids & Careers section of its Web site should be especially useful to readers of this book.

American Society of Mechanical Engineers
Three Park Avenue
New York, NY 10016-5990
800-843-2763
infocentral@asme.org
http://www.asme.org

This organization offers information on mechanical engineering and mechanical engineering technology, student membership, internships, and contests and competitions. Visit the Student Center of its Web site for these and other useful resources.

ASM International
9639 Kinsman Road
Materials Park, OH 44073-0002
800-336-5152
cust-srv@asminternational.org
http://www.asm-intl.org

Contact this organization for information on material engineering careers, scholarships, educational programs, and job listings.

The Biomedical Engineering Network
http://www.bmenet.org

Visit this Web site for information on educational programs, job listings, grants, and links to other biomedical engineering sites.

Biomedical Engineering Society (BES)
8401 Corporate Drive, Suite 225
Landover, MD 20785-2224
301-459-1999
info@bmes.org
http://www.bmes.org

Contact the BES for a copy of *Planning a Career in Biomedical Engineering*, which outlines typical duties, the specialty areas, employment opportunities, and career preparation.

Electronic Industries Alliance
2500 Wilson Boulevard
Arlington, VA 22201-3834
703-907-7500
http://www.eia.org

Contact the alliance for information on the electronics industry.

Electronics Technicians Association International
5 Depot Street
Greencastle, IN 46135
800-288-3824
eta@eta-i.org
http://www.eta-sda.com

This organization offers information on certification and student membership.

Environmental Careers Organization (ECO)
30 Winter Street
Boston, MA 02108
617-426-4375
http://www.eco.org

The ECO offers information on environmental internships and careers.

Institute of Electrical and Electronics Engineers (IEEE)

1828 L Street, NW, Suite 1202
Washington, DC 20036-5104
ieeeusa@ieee.org
http://www.ieee.org

Contact the IEEE for information on careers in electrical and electronic engineering. Their Web site has a Precollege page full of information for high school students.

Institute of Industrial Engineers

3577 Parkway Lane, Suite 200
Norcross, GA 30092
800-494-0460
http://www.iienet.org

Visit the Student Center of the institute's Web site for comprehensive information on industrial engineering careers, accredited programs, scholarships, and student membership.

Institute of Transportation Engineers (ITE)

1099 14th Street, NW, Suite 300 West
Washington, DC 20005-3438
202-289-0222
ite_staff@ite.org
http://www.ite.org

Contact the ITE for information on student chapters and careers in traffic and transportation engineering.

International Society of Certified Electronics Technicians

3608 Pershing Avenue
Fort Worth, TX 76107-4527
817-921-9101

info@iscet.org
http://www.iscet.org

Contact the society for information on certification and student membership.

Junior Engineering Technical Society (JETS)

1420 King Street, Suite 405
Alexandria, VA 22314
703-548-5387
jetsinfo@jets.org
http://www.jets.org

Contact the JETS for information on starting a local student chapter in your high school and for details on high school programs that provide opportunities to learn about engineering technology. JET's Guidance Brochures and Brochures for Most Engineering Specialties (both suitable for middle and high school students) may be reviewed at the Web site. Titles include *Engineering and You, Engineering Is For You, Engineering Technologists and Technicians, Biological Engineering, Electrical Engineering, Environmental Engineering, Mechanical Engineering,* and *Safety Engineering.*

The Minerals, Metals & Materials Society

184 Thorn Hill Road
Warrendale, PA 15086-7514
800-759-4867
tmsgeneral@tms.org
http://www.tms.org

The society offers information on ceramics, materials, and metallurgical engineering programs, careers, scholarships, and student chapters. Its online Career

Resource Center provides an overview of materials science engineering, a self-test to determine your aptitude for the career, and profiles of workers in the field.

National Action Council for Minorities in Engineering (NACME)
440 Hamilton Avenue, Suite 302
White Plains, NY 10601-1813
914-539-4010
http://www.nacme.org

Contact NACME for information on scholarships and career options.

National Coalition for Aviation Education
3146 Valentino Court
Oakton, VA 22124
http://www.aviationeducation.org

Contact the coalition for information on aviation camps, scholarships, and careers (including books, videos, and CD-ROMs).

National Council of Examiners for Engineering and Surveying (NCEES)
PO Box 1686
Clemson, SC 29633-1686
800-250-3196
http://www.engineeringlicense.com
and http://www.ncees.org

Visit the NCEES Web site for information on licensing for engineers and to read profiles of licensed engineers.

National Engineers Week Foundation
1420 King Street
Alexandria, VA 22314

703-684-2852
eweek@nspe.org
http://www.eweek.org

Contact this organization for information on National Engineers Week Programs, which are held in many locations throughout the United States. For additional resources, check out Meet the Engineers, Discover Engineering, and The Creative Engineer at the organization's Web site.

National Institute for Certification in Engineering Technologies
1420 King Street
Alexandria, VA 22314-2794
888-476-4238
http://www.nicet.org

This organization offers information on certification for engineering technicians and technologists.

National Society of Black Engineers (NSBE)
1454 Duke Street
Alexandria, VA 22314
703-549-2207
info@nsbe.org
http://www.nsbe.org

Contact the NSBE for information on careers in engineering, educational programs, scholarships, activities for high school students, and student membership.

National Society of Professional Engineers (NSPE)
1420 King Street
Alexandria, VA 22314-2794
703-684-2800
http://www.nspe.org/students

Contact the NSPE for information on careers in engineering and on student memberships. Visit the Student Information page of its Web site for a variety of information of interest to high school students considering engineering.

National Solid Wastes Management Association
4301 Connecticut Avenue, NW,
  Suite 300
Washington, DC 20008-2304
202-244-4700
membership@envasns.org
http://www.nswma.org

This organization offers information about the private waste services industry. Visit its Web site for answers to frequently asked questions about hazardous waste, nonhazardous waste, municipal solid waste, source reduction, recycling, waste combustion, landfills, and the solid waste industry.

Plastics Institute of America
333 Aiken Street
Lowell, MA 01854-3686
978-934-3130
info@plasticsinstitute.org
http://pia.caeds.eng.uml.edu

Contact the institute for information about the plastics industry, scholarships, seminars, and training.

Society of Hispanic Professional Engineers (SHPE)
5400 East Olympic Boulevard,
  Suite 210
Los Angeles, CA 90022
323-725-3970
http://www.shpe.org

Contact the SHPE for information on their competitions and educational programs for engineering students and for information on careers in engineering.

Society for Mining, Metallurgy, and Exploration
PO Box 277002
8307 Shaffer Parkway
Littleton, CO 80127-4102
800-763-3132
sme@smenet.org
http://www.smenet.org

This organization offers information on mining engineering, education, accredited schools, and student membership.

Society of Manufacturing Engineers (SME)
One SME Drive, PO Box 930
Dearborn, MI 48121
800-733-4763
http://www.sme.org

Contact SME for information on certification and scholarships.

Society of Plastics Engineers
14 Fairfield Drive
Brookfield, CT 06804-0403
203-775-0471
info@4spe.org
http://www.4spe.org

Contact SPE for information on careers in plastics engineering and scholarships.

Society of the Plastics Industry
1801 K Street, NW, Suite 600
Washington, DC 20006
202-974-5200
http://www.socplas.org

Contact the society for statistics on the plastics industry and information on careers, college programs, and certification.

Society of Women Engineers (SWE)
230 East Ohio Street, Suite 400
Chicago, IL 60611-3265
312-596-5223
hq@swe.org
http://www.swe.org

Contact the SWE for information on scholarships, student membership, and mentor programs. The society also offers research and statistics about the status of women in engineering.

Student Conservation Association (SCA)
689 River Road
PO Box 550
Charlestown, NH 03603-0550
603-543-1700
http://www.sca-inc.org

Contact the SCA for information about internships for high school students.

The Whitaker Foundation: Biomedical Engineering Curriculum Database
1700 North Moore Street, #2200
Arlington, VA 22209
http://www.whitaker.org/academic

Contact the foundation for information on biomedical engineering careers, educational programs, and earnings.

Index

Entries and page numbers in bold indicate major treatment of a topic.